OVERCOMING OBSTACLES IN CBT

Craig Chigwedere, Yvonne Tone,
Brian Fitzmaurice & Michael McDonough

OVERCOMING
OBSTACLES
IN CBT

Los Angeles | London | New Delhi
Singapore | Washington DC

SAGE Publications Ltd
1 Oliver's Yard
55 City Road
London EC1Y 1SP

SAGE Publications Inc.
2455 Teller Road
Thousand Oaks, California 91320

SAGE Publications India Pvt Ltd
B 1/I 1 Mohan Cooperative Industrial Area
Mathura Road
New Delhi 110 044

SAGE Publications Asia-Pacific Pte Ltd
3 Church Street
#10-04 Samsung Hub
Singapore 049483

Library of Congress Control Number: 2011929698

British Library Cataloguing in Publication data

A catalogue record for this book is available from the British Library

ISBN 978-1-84920-615-0
ISBN 978-1-84920-616-7 (pbk)

Typeset by C&M Digitals (P) Ltd, Chennai, India
Printed by MPG Books Group, Bodmin, Cornwall
Printed on paper from sustainable resources

To Petronella Chigwedere from all of us

CONTENTS

LIST OF FIGURES

LIST OF TABLES

ABOUT THE AUTHORS

Craig Chigwedere is a cognitive behavioural psychotherapist, clinical lecturer and director of the Foundation Course in CBT at St Patrick's University Hospital and Trinity College Dublin. He has many years of experience as a CBT clinician, trainer and supervisor. He trained in CBT at Maudsley Hospital and Institute of Psychiatry, London. His main area of clinical interest is in the field of medically unexplained disorders, where he has been involved in treatment of, and research into, non-epileptic seizures. He has taught and presented at workshops and conferences internationally, as well as being involved in the authoring of peer-reviewed publications in CBT. He is currently involved in research into the utility of self-practice and self-reflection in CBT training.

Yvonne Tone is an experienced cognitive therapist at the Student Counselling Service, Trinity College Dublin. In addition to clinical work, she co-ordinates group therapy development and training. A registered psychiatric and general nurse, she gained valuable mental health experience as Senior Cognitive Behavioural Psychotherapist at St Patrick's University Hospital over many years. She completed her MSc in CBT at Trinity in 1999 and devised and facilitated two five-day foundation-level training courses in CBT for nurses in 2005/2006. She was an active committee member, developing the CBT Diploma/Master's course at Trinity College, where she is an honorary lecturer and supervisor. She is a member of BABCP and NABCT and is accredited as a trainer, supervisor and therapist.

Dr Brian Fitzmaurice is the Postgraduate Course Director for the Postgraduate Diploma and MSc in Cognitive Psychotherapy at Trinity College Dublin and also Clinical Senior Lecturer in the School of Medicine. He is a Consultant Psychiatrist and Psychiatric Tutor in Wicklow Mental Health Services. He has special interests in the integration of CBT into community mental health services, early intervention services, medical education and the use of e-learning in healthcare. He has researched, received grants and published papers in these fields. He is a founding director of a campus company (www.etu.ie) that uses personalised e-learning to teach communication skills.

Dr Michael McDonough is a full-time consultant psychiatrist and BABCP accredited CBT therapist at St Patrick's University Hospital. He is director of the hospital's anxiety disorders service and psychotherapy tutor on the Trinity College Dublin psychiatric training programme. He is honorary clinical lecturer at the Department of Psychiatry, TCD and supervises, examines and teaches on the department's postgraduate CBT courses. He trained in CBT at the Maudsley Hospital and Institute of Psychiatry, London. He has researched and published on a wide range of mental health topics including CBT, anxiety disorders, pharmaco-therapy, medical education and addictions.

ACKNOWLEDGEMENTS

We would like to thank many colleagues, family and friends from whom we have received support, advice and encouragement in the writing of this book. It is not possible to thank everyone by name; however, we would primarily wish to offer our thanks to:

- our partners Jô, Sean, Alison and Alice and our families for the patience, tolerance, love and support during the writing process;
- our colleagues for their support, stimulating discussions and assistance in the inception and development of this project, the layout of the manuscript, and review and reading of chapters, in particular Colette Kearns, Patricia Maher, Mary McGoldrick, Maria McMorrow, Melissa Hayde and Deirdre Flynn;
- our patients, students and supervisees, from whom we have drawn the inspiration for the vignettes and many of the ideas for the obstacles and hypotheses presented in this book;
- the editorial team at SAGE, in particular Suzanna Trefgarne, Alice Oven and Kate Wharton, and their reviewers, for their support and guidance.

1

INTRODUCTION

CRAIG CHIGWEDERE, YVONNE TONE, BRIAN FITZMAURICE AND MICHAEL MCDONOUGH

Standard cognitive behavioural therapy (CBT) texts are generally organised around specific disorders with the emphasis on commonalities within those disorders. This is effective when the presenting problem 'fits' neatly into the model and when the patient engages well with therapy and the therapist. This is not always the case. Practising clinicians, trainees and teachers are aware that therapeutic work frequently becomes derailed or stuck at various stages of the process. The likelihood of successfully achieving therapy outcomes is then impeded, causing frustration, distress and confusion for both therapists and those seeking help. Obstacles to progress often connect to recurrent patterns and themes, general and specific, which are embedded in the therapy process.

Therapy is about overcoming difficulties. Therapists and supervisors are therefore routinely challenged to understand and negotiate a wide range of therapeutic obstacles. Cognitive behavioural (psycho)therapy is an established psychotherapeutic modality, with an unrivalled empirical evidence base. It continues to be driven by theorists, researchers and clinicians with a desire to work through evidence-based treatments with clients. Whilst acknowledging the evidence base of CBT and its undoubted importance there is much to be gained from sharing tales from the therapy room.

THE ART OF CBT

The less researchable principles of CBT practice are often omitted in the dissemination of CBT literature. CBT is viewed by some as a simple set of tools, used to superficially tinker with the client's problem. This is often put forward as a criticism of CBT. As professionals, we are all aware of the dangerous potential of insufficiently trained and supervised individuals who having read a CBT manual believe themselves to be knowledgeable and competent enough to apply it in therapy with clients. In contrast novice therapists may believe themselves to be ineffective, when the protocols and techniques that are outlined in a book do not yield an expected outcome. The unseen intricacies that gel CBT into an effective therapy are not often readily apparent. The therapeutic journey is paved with obstacles. The established protocols prepare the therapist for impasses along the way but many arise unexpectedly. Negotiating these obstacles is a central challenge for supervision and therapy. It is therefore of great importance that clinical experience from the frontline offers a valuable contribution to the ongoing evolution of CBT. Highlighting obstacles in therapy by sharing enriching therapeutic experiences arising through the application of empirical techniques offers an important additional learning opportunity for both novice and experienced therapists.

CBT is both a science and an art. The science is appropriately and clearly detailed in scientific journals and books and this will continue. The art of CBT is the experience and richness of knowledge that engagement in therapy offers to both client and therapist. These experiences are passed on from generation to generation, are remodelled to suit the new carrier of the torch and rarely remain the same. They are shared often as clinical anecdotes in supervision or with like-minded colleagues.

Thankfully, emerging literature detailing process factors, much of which is informed by clinical experience, is growing. The writings of Leahy (2003; Gilbert and Leahy, 2007), Safran and Segal (1990) and others highlight the growing recognition of the importance of the therapeutic relationship within CBT. No more can CBT be accused of being too mechanistic, lacking humanity or of being a kind of 'brutalism' (Clarke, 1999). The complexity of its application – *the art of CBT* – is now being recognised. Work also abounds on the development of the 'self of the CBT therapist'. This work concerns itself with exploring how therapists can increase their self-knowledge and reflective qualities (Bennett-Levy, 2006; Bennett-Levy and Thwaites, 2007).

THE AIM OF THIS BOOK

The main aim of this text is to share information and experience with illustrated case examples, bridging the gap between theory and clinical practice. These clinical experiences are utilised to illustrate the complexities of practising CBT with clients. It goes further by suggesting how to overcome therapeutic obstacles encountered in everyday clinical practice.

This book is written for the novice therapist starting out in CBT as well as the more experienced CBT practitioner. It may also be of interest to counsellors or therapists with a level of skill and knowledge of working within a CBT framework. It is intended as a resource for practitioners, to assist in those moments of reflection on therapy experiences with clients, when feeling lost, or confused. The book offers the clinician an opportunity to keep abreast of research around the subject matter of each chapter, in a practical and clinically relevant way. While including relevant references to the literature, its primary focus is on our experiences from clinical and supervision practice. The text is intended to be rich in information of what emerges at the coal-face of clinical practice, with illustrative case vignettes. While not exhaustive, we have attempted to give an account of the experiential aspects of working through 'stuck points' with clients. We have reflected on how this feels for both therapist and client and suggested ways forward. Learning exercises related to each topic are also included.

BOOK OUTLINE

Each chapter offers a list of clear learning objectives. To increase accessibility for the reader, the structure of the chapters are somewhat similar. Each chapter is, however, unique and, though primarily the work of one author, every chapter is a reflection of the differing experiences of the four authors, who all contributed thoughts and ideas, especially in the editing process. The book can be read as a whole or each chapter can be utilised as a resource relating to a specific problem area. Some terms, such as patient and therapist, formulation and conceptualisation, therapeutic relationship and therapeutic alliance are used interchangeably. To minimise offence or discrimination, when referring to individuals in the third person, the gender-neutral term 'they' is used as much as possible but, depending on context, the gender specific he or she are also used.

The book is divided into three sections. Part 1, 'The Process of Therapy' (Chapters 2–5), reflects on how obstacles can present and affect the attainment of therapeutic goals impeding progress. The first important stage in the therapeutic journey is to engage the client and develop the therapeutic relationship. This, and its related obstacles, is the focus of Chapter 2. Chapter 3 elaborates on the importance of assessment, clear problem focus, model selection and formulation. This is crucial as, without a clearly identified and formulated problem, therapy is likely to stall at the first hurdle. It helpfully explores the importance of using disorder-specific models and adjusting and sequencing interventions to suit the client. Alongside the development of the therapeutic alliance, assessment, problem focus and model selection, recognising the appropriate timing of interventions is important. Chapter 4 considers the obstacles that can present as a result of poorly paced and timed interventions. Sequencing and timing problems can contribute to therapeutic impasse and failure. Timing of interventions, the developing therapeutic relationship, problem focus and conceptualisation generally revolve around the client and therapist. The client does not, however, exist as an island. Therapists and clients have lives outside the therapeutic relationship, which reciprocally influence the therapeutic process. Chapter 5 explores obstacles relating to these 'extra-therapeutic relationships' which can impact on therapy progress.

Part 2, 'Psychopathology-related Obstacles' (Chapters 6–10), though not exhaustive, considers some important clinical themes. These overlapping themes are not limited to any one specific disorder. Chapter 6 considers the issue of perfectionism in both therapist and client and how it can present obstacles to progress and goal attainment. Perfectionism can present as an issue in its own right. It can also present as an underlying complicating factor with other conditions. Working clinically with experiential intolerance is the focus of Chapter 7. This is not a topic that is routinely taught on training courses but, like perfectionism, it can create challenges in therapeutic practice. Chapter 8 explores the experience of guilt and shame and how these present in therapy. Guilt and shame can present as separate entities or be associated with a range of conditions. Their emergence can have wide-reaching effects and present frequently enough in therapy to merit discussion. Chapter 9 gives the reader a unique insight into experiences of intrusions into awareness, rumination and agitation. This chapter defines and outlines the differing types of intrusions related to different diagnoses, in such a way that might not be taught on most CBT courses. In keeping with the ethos of the book, it shares the authors' clinical experiences as learning opportunities for the reader. Chapter 10 concludes this section by considering some of the different ways physical symptoms can create obstacles to therapeutic work and suggests ways of managing this. Throughout the text, efforts are made to consider the presenting obstacles in a thematic way, avoiding a laundry-list approach. Hypotheses based on the clinical vignettes are presented and explored, which can be referred to by the reader as a guide to decision making in treatment.

Part 3, 'Therapeutic Context', concerns itself with the context of therapy. Chapter 11 explores the theme of supervision and the challenges of nurturing the skills of new therapists within services. Organisations play a pivotal role in the provision of CBT, both for the client, the therapist and the developing therapeutic services. Chapter 12 explores this organisational perspective, covering two major themes: (1) the ways in which organisations can impede the development of the therapist; and (2) the ways in which they can create therapeutic obstacles in work with clients. The structure of this chapter elaborates on the development of the therapist, from qualification to experienced practitioner to service developer.

SUMMARY

In compiling this book, the authors draw from many years of experience working clinically with clients, supervision of trainees and involvement in CBT training and teaching. We attempt to lead by example in sharing our experience of 'what really happens' when therapist and client meet. Our hope is that this book will both inform and stimulate the interests of other clinicians in writing up their own enriching experiences of client work. This could be encouraged through single-case reports or as a reflection on 'what works and when'-type scenarios. Such sharing of experience is a rich source of learning for all therapists. The writing of this text has been an enjoyable and therapeutically educational experience for us. We hope it will be equally stimulating and educational for the reader, providing an integrative approach to managing obstacles in therapeutic practice.

REFERENCES

Bennet-Levy, J. (2006) 'Therapist skills: a cognitive model of their acquisition and refinement', *Behavioural and Cognitive Psychotherapy*, 34: 57–78.

Bennett-Levy, J and Thwaites, R. (2007) 'Self and self-reflection in the therapeutic relationship: a conceptual map and practical strategies for the training, supervision and self supervision of interpersonal skills', in P. Gilbert and R.L. Leahy (eds) *The Therapeutic Relationship in the Cognitive-Behavioural Psychotherapies*. London: Routledge. pp. 255–81.

Clarke, L. (1999) 'Nursing in search of a science: the rise and rise of the new nurse brutalism', *Mental Health Care*, 2: 270–2.

Gilbert, P. and Leahy, R (eds) (2007) *The Therapeutic Relationship in the Cognitive Behavioural Psychotherapies*. London: Routledge.

Leahy R.L. (2003) *Roadblocks in Cognitive Behavioural Therapy Transforming Challenges into Opportunities*. New York: Guilford Press.

Safran, J.D. and Segal, Z.V. (1990) *Interpersonal Processes in Cognitive Therapy*. New York: Basic Books.

Part 1
THE PROCESS OF THERAPY

2

THE COLLABORATIVE THERAPEUTIC ALLIANCE

YVONNE TONE

LEARNING OBJECTIVES

After reading this chapter, the reader should:

- understand what commonly impacts on the therapeutic alliance;
- understand how to engage effectively with reticent or wary clients;
- know how to negotiate common obstacles that arise in the therapeutic relationship.

INTRODUCTION

The relationship between client and therapist (the 'therapeutic relationship') is central to the healing process. While historically focusing more on the maintenance cycles of disorders, cognitive therapy literature has recently been more attentive to the therapeutic relationship (e.g. Safran and Segal, 1990; Wright and Davies, 1994; Waddington, 2002; Gilbert and Leahy, 2007). The therapeutic relationship has been defined as 'the personal qualities of the patient, personal qualities of the therapist, and the interaction between them' (Wright and Davies, 1994: 27). The aim of this chapter is to explore common ways this complex interaction can break down under the pressure of CBT work. The focus will be primarily on short-term CBT therapy, with some reference to schema-focused therapy and its associated limited reparenting techniques. Four illustrative cases will explore common themes and obstacles associated with engagement and rupture in therapy.

KEY INGREDIENTS OF THE THERAPEUTIC RELATIONSHIP IN CBT

A good relationship between therapist and client underpins all aspects of therapeutic work. The importance of the therapeutic relationship in CBT is now informed by a very broad set of theories and concepts, including attachment.

Attachment and Alliance

The main tenet of attachment theory is that human beings have an instinct towards the nurturance of stable relationships with attachment figures. Early attachment experiences are known to influence relationships formed in later life (Bowlby, 1973) and have been incorporated into CBT theories (e.g. Beck et al., 1979; Young et al., 2003). Early in the development of psychotherapy, Freud referred to the importance of the therapeutic relationship in his reference to 'positive transference' (Freud, 1940). Clients may regress to an earlier stage of development during therapy. This activates schemas, which can exert a powerful influence on the therapeutic relationship, requiring significant therapist skill in their recognition and management.

   The therapy relationship can helpfully act to disconfirm dysfunctional beliefs about the self and others, formed in early life through caregivers (Safran and Segal, 1990). Exploring the client's interpersonal belief system and relational style can be important, as clients with an under-developed relational style do less well in CBT (Hardy et al., 2001).

Transference and Counter-transference

The concepts of transference and counter-transference, usually associated with the psychodynamic approach, have been examined in CBT practice (e.g. Leahy, 2001). Leahy posits that 'transference and counter-transference exist, no matter how objective or technique driven you are as a therapist' (Leahy, 2001: 5). Transference not only occurs in therapy but in all relationships. It can be positive or negative and relates to feelings from past interactions, which transfer into current relationships. Therapists who manage this issue well tend to form better alliances with clients than those who do not (Ligiero and Gelso, 2002). To build successful transference, therapists are encouraged to use self-insight, conceptualisation, empathy and anxiety-management skills with clients. Leahy's view supports the proliferation of therapist personal development methods in CBT. Self-practice and self-reflection (SP/SR), for example, has been shown to impact on therapist perceptual skills and self-awareness (Bennett-Levy et al., 2003). Therapists need to be comfortable dealing with feelings evoked through transference and counter-transference in themselves and their clients.

Attuning to the Client

Attunement is a perceptual skill, mediated via emotion-involving thoughts, physical and behavioural experiences. In therapy, 'normal interaction moves from positive to negative to positive, so that good interactions can be described as a process of rupture and repair' (McCluskey, 2005: 48). Caregiving and care-seeking in therapy is an interactive process of great complexity. When the needs of the caregiver and care-seeker are met, there is satisfaction and relief on both sides (McCluskey, 2005). The ability of therapists to connect with the client and empathically tune into their emotional experience is therefore important. Four key components of therapeutic empathy are emphasised in CBT:

- genuine warmth
- accurate empathic attitude/stance
- attunement
- communication and knowledge (Thwaites and Bennett-Levy, 2007)

The quality of attunement is aided by non-judgemental acceptance of the client and the ability to establish trust and rapport.

THE WORKING ALLIANCE

Bordin's (1994) model of the therapeutic relationship identifies important factors common to successful therapeutic intervention. Three main areas are emphasised within the working alliance.

1   *the bond*: this relates to the complex network of interpersonal communication and attachments that occur between therapist and client. Strengthening this bond is facilitated by mutual respect, trust, acceptance and confidence in the process.
2   *the goals*: these centre on the mutually agreed aims of therapy and the desired outcome.
3   *the tasks*: This task-focused work needs to be relevant and make sense to the client and therapist. Tasks may be alliance focused or relate to effecting change for the client.

CBT is an open collaborative approach that explicitly orientates the client to the goals and tasks of therapy. It also highlights the bond through the importance of working together in a mutually respectful, non-judgemental manner. Socialisation to elements of the CBT model has been shown to be central to the therapeutic alliance in CBT (Daniels and Wearden, 2011). The socialisation stage within CBT, establishing the collaborative alliance, mirrors Bordin's concept of 'The Bond'. Therefore, inadequate socialisation to the CBT model can create obstacles to effective therapy.

UTILISING FORMULATION

CBT practitioners view case conceptualisation as an essential part of the treatment process (Kuyken et al., 2008; Grant et al., 2008). Formulation helps the therapist and client hypothesise the development and maintenance of the client's problem. It also informs on interpersonal processes in the therapeutic relationship. Conceptualisation evolves as therapy progresses, informing treatment planning and therapeutic goals and tasks. Kuyken (2006) suggests that therapists should aim for evidence based 'good enough' conceptualisations, based on the following guide:

- Develop a provisional case conceptualisation.
- Hold alternative conceptualisations in mind.
- Test the conceptualisation through behavioural experiments.
- Test out hypotheses with the client, through the client's network, supervision and standardised assessments.
- Be sensitive to the impact of issues, which may impair judgement (e.g. task complexity, time pressure).
- Be guided by manualised protocols and best practice through CBT theory and research.
- Justify and adjust conceptualisation through case-discussion and supervision. (Kuyken, 2006)

Case formulation can translate theory into practice and a simple diagrammatic representation of the client's experience can be powerful in enabling an individual to feel deeply understood, validating their distress and/or emotional experience.

DEVELOPING THE COLLABORATIVE THERAPEUTIC ALLIANCE

The CBT therapist needs to have the ability to engage clients, be knowledgeable and be skilled in cognitive and behavioural conceptualisations to guide clients towards therapeutic change and self-discovery. The main focus of therapy is around helping clients understand how beliefs and attitudes influence feelings and behaviour. Utilisation of the alliance as an agent of change is central to CBT. Clear explanations of therapeutic aims and reading materials can aid socialisation. Therapeutic tasks, such as exposure and behavioural experiments, are likely to be more effective if there is a strong collaborative alliance between therapist and client (Bennett-Levy et al., 2004). A client is unlikely to agree to undertake a distressing exposure or behavioural experiment task in the absence of a good bond with the therapist. The alliance is influenced by the relationship history of both client and therapist, their bond and agreement on the tasks and goals of treatment. Developing a therapeutic alliance is complex and is subject to change from session to session over time.

COMPONENTS OF THE COLLABORATIVE THERAPEUTIC ALLIANCE

Due to the complexity of the collaborative therapeutic alliance and the multiple influences upon it, the following skills are essential to its development:

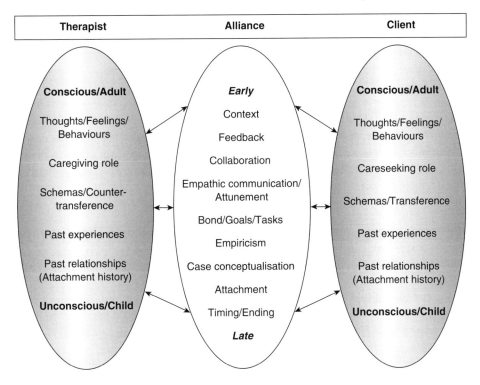

Figure 2.1 Collaborative therapeutic alliance structure

- effective interpersonal skills
- empathic, curious exploration of the client's problem
- eliciting and clarifying the client's distressing thoughts
- encouragement of emotional expression in a safe context
- integrating new information through formulation
- competence in working with disorder specific models
- recognising, managing and repairing potential ruptures as they arise
- awareness of client and therapists belief as self

Engaging and developing a collaborative therapeutic alliance with a client is the first and most important hurdle in therapy.

Figure 2.1 represents diagrammatically the inputs to a collaborative therapeutic alliance and how conscious and unconscious aspects of the therapist's and client's interpersonal and intrapersonal experiences can dynamically influence the alliance.

CORE BELIEFS AND SCHEMAS

The cognitive model suggests that early experiences may lead to the development of faulty belief systems, creating a rigid view of situations thereby causing distress. These strong value systems and attitudes evolve during childhood and adolescence, and become more rigidly elaborated on during adulthood (Beck et al., 1979). While cognitive therapists begin by understanding the client's frame of reference, therapy involves asking for evidence supporting their particular beliefs and helping clients develop alternative perspectives. These core beliefs, also known as schemas, affect the client's inter- and intra-personal worlds and are also evident in how clients engage with a therapist.

Schemas exert a powerful maintenance effect, because they determine what is attended to, noticed and remembered in experience. Someone with a self-schema 'I am a failure' will focus on their personal defects, be self-critical and less likely to notice or attend to successes (Beck et al., 1990). It is important to teach clients how schemas and core beliefs can affect their interpersonal interactions and can play themselves out through the therapeutic relationship.

THE CASE OF EVA: THE DISTRESSED, EVASIVE CLIENT

Eva is a 35-year-old married woman and mother of three. The oldest of three children (1 brother, 1 sister), she grew up in an emotionally abusive family environment where her father drank heavily and her mother suffered from depression. She recalls her mother as kind and caring and her father as critical and having high expectations that she felt she could never meet, even when she did well in school.

After school she worked for years as a shop assistant and recently decided to return to full-time education 'to better myself.' She has insight into this decision as being motivated in part by trying to prove herself 'a success' to her parents to gain their approval. She experiences a sense of isolation in her relationships, and is especially distant with her family of origin. She harbours anger towards her father about his drinking, for favouring her younger brother and for causing her to feel 'not good enough'.

She was referred by her GP with symptoms of intense anxiety, low mood, and persistent feelings of anger and irritability. She describes feelings of worthlessness and a personal sense of failure. She realises her low mood is connected to emotional abuse she suffered as a child, but dismisses this, saying 'there is nothing I can do about that'. Her problems are impacting on her relationship with her husband and children.

It is difficult to engage Eva in therapy as she is uneasy and reluctant to talk about her problems. She presents as distressed with poor eye contact. She is guarded and states that seeking psychological help means 'I am weak'. Answering questions about her personal life is difficult.

Identifying the Problem

Therapy with Eva is at a crossroads. The therapist endeavours to engage her but she is evasive, defensive and seems distrustful. Through the assessment process, gathering information through questioning is challenging. Eva's unease increases, she states 'I've had enough' and asks to leave. The therapist offers her a further appointment, which she reluctantly accepts. The therapist, after discussing the case at supervision, deemed it necessary to discuss with Eva what she was looking for from therapy. Eva arrives for her next appointment expressing dissatisfaction with the last session. The therapist explores this with Eva, who is hesitant and defensive. She states that she dislikes 'all the questions'. It seems memories of criticism in childhood and schemas of being a failure are activated, leading to her possibly leaving and never returning. What needs to be considered here?

- Eva's story illustrates the importance of careful engagement before utilising CBT interventions. An understanding of the complex interplay of influences on the therapeutic relationship is crucial to avert early disengagement by susceptible clients.
- With Eva, her ability to move through childhood emotional development towards autonomy and individuation was compromised due to a poor relationship and emotional abuse from her father. This was impairing her ability as an adult to trust and be open in relationships, including the therapeutic relationship.
- The assessment process activated core beliefs of her being 'a failure'. As they became evident, they impacted greatly on her functioning in sessions. Whilst belief questionnaires such as the Dysfunctional Attitude Scale (Weissman and Beck, 1978) or the Young Schema Questionnaire (Young and Brown, 1990) are sometimes helpful in early identification or confirmation of suspected schema patterns, the use of more scales or questionnaires might have been experienced as invalidating of Eva's distress in the session or insensitive to her current needs.

OBSTACLES RELATED TO THE THERAPEUTIC RELATIONSHIP

Eva's case is an illustrative example of how a variety of obstacles can arise early in the therapeutic relationship. Figure 2.2 illustrates how her experience might be represented within the CBT specific five areas model (Williams, 2003). It is evident that there are multiple challenges to successfully developing a good collaborative therapeutic alliance with a client like Eva. How the therapist and client feel, establishing rapport, fostering trust, choosing useful therapeutic options, and activation of client and therapist relational schemas all need management.

OBSTACLES RELATED TO CLIENT MISTRUST AND POOR EMOTIONAL EXPRESSION

Eva is evasive, displays overt signs of anxiety and is reticent in answering questions. She experiences the collaborative questioning style of therapy as challenging and exposing. This is a defining moment in developing a therapeutic alliance to enable therapy to progress. Being cognisant that Eva brings with her a belief system, where fear of negative judgement features strongly, the therapist employs core relational skills of empathy, validation and unconditional positive regard (Rogers, 1965).

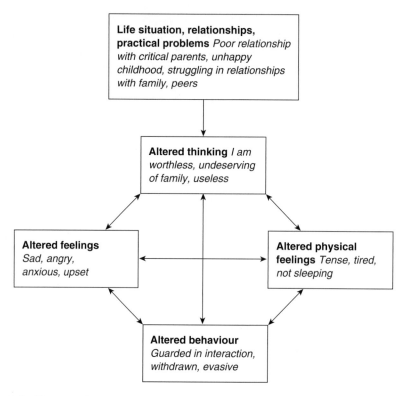

Figure 2.2   The case of Eva: five areas assessment

Source: Williams, C. (2003) *Overcoming Anxiety. A five areas approach*. London. Reproduced by permission of Hodder Education.

Therapists need to take time to empathically 'tune-in' to the client's emotions and fears in addition to socialising the client to the cognitive model. Whilst the diagrammatic representation of the collaborative therapeutic alliance in Figure 2.1 visually sequences feedback, collaboration and goals typically preceding attachment/transference issues, in Eva's case, these potential obstacles to the alliance needed to be sensitively managed early in the assessment process.

With Eva it was important to explain the aim of 'questioning' was to enable new understandings to emerge through collaboration, rather than to challenge her in a critical way. The therapist's awareness of the client's past relational theme, in this instance, is a key component to building a successful alliance. The therapist empathised by saying: 'I notice your unease and hesitancy when I ask questions. Is there anything that would help make this process a little easier?' With Eva, the therapist's empathic responsiveness and attunement, helped reduce her unease about engaging in therapy. Eva then took more of a lead in session and the therapist asked fewer questions, allowing information emerge with minimal prompting.

A tentative hypothesis was then offered by the therapist to Eva, identifying possible activation of 'failure' schemas, that might be connected to her past experience. This made sense to Eva and resonated with 'inexplicable' past experiences of feeling as if she was a failure. This was crucial in activating Eva's curiosity to better understand her experiences.

The early consideration of attachment and formulation in this case averted the high risk of premature disengagement or 'rupture' of the emerging collaborative therapeutic alliance. Survival and enhancement of this collaborative therapeutic alliance can ultimately promote positive schema change as trust and rapport are developed. The therapeutic alliance provided powerful evidence 'disconfirming' or challenging the strong beliefs Eva held about interpersonal relationships (e.g. no-one can help me).

SCHEMA-RELATED THERAPEUTIC OBSTACLES

Eva's challenging childhood influenced the struggle experienced in developing and strengthening the therapeutic alliance. Difficulties forming trusting relationships, due to lack of positive affirmation in her early years, impacted on Eva's ability to engage with her family and also in therapy. The therapist hypothesised that activated schemas about failure, mistrust and emotional inhibition contributed to her distress. Utilisation of Socratic questioning was triggering Eva's failure and mistrust schemas, as she feared she was not engaging well in therapy. Despite her dislike of questioning, which created the initial obstacle, therapy moved to exploration of more balanced alternative schemas. A primary objective in therapy is to identify schemas and explore how they interfere with therapy. In Eva's case, her responses to the therapist's interventions were consistent with her schemas. She was extremely self-critical and lacked understanding of how her past life connected to her here and now experience of believing herself to be 'worthless and weak'. The cognitive model reminds us that early experiences influence the development of faulty belief systems creating distress. These belief systems exert effects on how clients interact in the world and interpersonally at a relational level. Although developed in the context of early attachment, they can continue to influence interpersonal relationships throughout life. Once the activated beliefs of client and therapist are recognised and explored, the therapeutic relationship and alliance is more likely to strengthen. Exploration of more challenging complex issues and their effects on the relationship can then progress. Transference and counter-transference experiences between client and therapist may also need management. In Eva's case, therapy moved from identification and exploration of interpersonal schemas to their modification (Young, 1990). This is illustrated in the following dialogue:

Eva:	I can't put words on what I feel. I'm such a failure, nothing but scum.
Therapist:	What do you have in mind when you say someone is a failure or nothing but scum?
Eva:	When I say scum, I suppose that would describe someone despicable, who would want to wilfully hurt others, so maybe I'm not that bad …

(Continued)

(Continued)

Therapist:	I'm struck by the strong self-critical language you use about yourself. Whose words are these?
Eva:	[*pauses*] I never got anything right at home, Dad called me 'good for nothing' and I'm hurting my husband and kids by not being a success.
Therapist:	What is a successful person?
Eva:	Someone who doesn't need help to manage her life, can do things herself, rears their family and does good by them.
Therapist:	I recall, your husband supports your decision to go back to education and describes you as a great person and a good mother. You also passed the first set of exams. Does this count as success?
Eva:	There is some truth in what you say. I am somewhat successful but keep thinking I'm a failure.
Therapist:	It sounds like when you were growing up a lot of attention was paid to things you didn't get on well with. You seem to have dismissed anything you did well, and viewed the criticism of your dad as a truth, rather than just his view ... does that sound familiar?
Eva:	Yeah ... maybe I got some things right ... like my mum used to say, I was great with my hands and I did manage to complete exams ... maybe I'm not a complete failure.

Working in this way helped Eva understand how early maladaptive schemas had informed her present coping mechanisms. Evolving a schema-focused case conceptualisation helps clients to understand self-defeating life patterns, early developmental processes and coping styles, which impact on current problems and treatment (Young et al., 2003).

DEVELOPING A WORKING ALLIANCE

The working alliance focuses on the bond between the therapist and client. Therapists need to be tuned in to the client's changing needs as they arise and be flexible in response. As outlined in Bordin's model, developing the therapeutic relationship, collaboratively setting therapeutic goals and their achievement is important. Collaborating and agreeing with Eva, the direction, exploration and pacing of therapy sessions was important. If therapy advanced too quickly there was a risk she would feel threatened and disengage (see Chapter 4). Goals evolved around challenging her negative view of herself and being able to engage more with her children. Other goals emerged around improving her confidence interacting with peers and being more open in expressing her feelings, particularly with her husband.

COLLABORATING ON THERAPEUTIC OPTIONS

Developing a range of therapeutic options to improve client engagement and instilling hope is also important. Language supporting a shared decision-making process fosters engagement; for example:

- 'It might be useful to discuss how I work as a therapist. My aim is that we can work together and collaborate on how therapy might be useful. With this in mind, I may check with you that what we are working on is helpful. How does that sound to you?'
- 'It is important that you let me know if what we are doing is not helpful. This enables us to make adjustments, allowing us to work productively at your pace.'
- 'Can we discuss what you would like to get from therapy? How would you like things to be? What aspect of the problem would be helpful to work on?'

In Eva's case, this helped her to share her sense of irritation and unease with the therapist's questioning style. Adjustments were then made accordingly on how sessions were conducted.

UNDERSTANDING RUPTURES WITHIN THE COLLABORATIVE THERAPEUTIC ALLIANCE

In CBT, the relationship is based on collaborative empiricism. Even experienced therapists will often encounter alliance difficulties, incomplete conceptualisation maps or dissatisfaction about the session. These 'stuck points' can be used as an opportunity to refine the client's conceptualisation. Central to this process is the 'ongoing negotiation' (Safran and Muran, 2000) that occurs between the therapist and client around goals and tasks. Ruptures within session may relate to how one negotiates one's needs against the needs of another, or it may relate to a breach of the clients ability to relate. Safran and Segal (1990) note that, 'If the therapist is able to empathise with the patient's experience accurately during an alliance rupture and convey understanding of this experience to the patient, the patient may feel understood and find it easier to explore what is going on in the interaction' (p. 160).

Rupture offers an opportunity to explore problematic patterns of interpersonal behaviour, possibly related to past experiences, that can be enacted within therapy. When a rupture arises the therapist should suspend the use of cognitive techniques and focus on the impasse in an open and genuine way. Identifying and resolving minor ruptures as they arise is imperative. This reduces the emergence of more serious obstacles later in therapy. Hazards and hints might include:

- Clients feeling misunderstood due to a lack of 'therapeutic empathy' (Burns, 1990).
  - *Hint*: Taking a disarming role and changing the focus from the content of the client's criticism to one of interpersonal process may prove helpful.

- Clients withdrawing or demonstrating negative feelings indirectly. In this instance the client might break eye contact or refuse to answer questions. The therapist is left wondering what has contributed to this sudden disengagement, which needs to be acknowledged.

  - *Hint*: Exploring interpersonal fears, expectations and internal criticisms, which hamper the client's ability to express their inner needs assertively are likely to promote re-engagement. Eva's therapist explored the experience and difficulty she had in her childhood expressing feelings or asserting herself.

- Clients might engage in confrontation ruptures, not expressing their underlying needs and become demanding or blaming towards the therapist.

  - *Hint*: The therapist in this instance needs to be non-defensive, open and empathic. Exploring the fears that impede the client's expression of their underlying needs might identify feelings of vulnerability, which may help resolve this rupture.

With Eva it was important that she felt more at ease in therapy, to facilitate exploration of her relationship with her father, which had impacted on her confidence and self-worth, activating schemas of her being 'a failure'.

Generally empathic responding, such as paraphrasing and reflecting back to the client what has been said, taking a disarming role, the use of gentle enquiry and changing the focus from the content of the client's criticism to one of interpersonal process can be helpful in resolving ruptures.

THE VALUE OF REFLECTIVE PRACTICE

Therapists need to reflect on their own psychological process and its impact on therapy. There is an increased awareness of the similarity between self and client experience in therapy using SP/SR. Therapists in training learn much about how clients feel, through observing and reflecting on their own subjective experience (Bennett-Levy et al., 2001). The importance of therapist perceptual skills such as empathy in CBT practice has been highlighted in recent years (Thwaites and Bennett-Levy, 2007). The Declarative-Procedural-Reflective (DPR) information processing model (Bennett-Levy, 2006) suggests that therapists' ability to reflect and to learn perceptual skills, which are important in alliance building, is central to clinical practice, professional and personal development. With Eva, it was helpful to reflect on aspects of the above model, outlined in Figure 2.3.

Understanding what creates obstacles to engagement can be complex. Clients' verbal and non-verbal behaviour can evoke both cognitive and 'felt' responses from the therapist. Eye contact or lack of it, changes in posture and silences when painful issues are discussed can indicate activation of underlying schemas, which impact on the ability of the client to engage. Clarifying with the client what they hope to gain through therapy and conveying a sense of being understood is important. Reflective questions are useful, for example:

- Is there something that does not make sense to me working with this client? (What issues came up in session, which if not understood and explored might create an obstacle to therapy?)

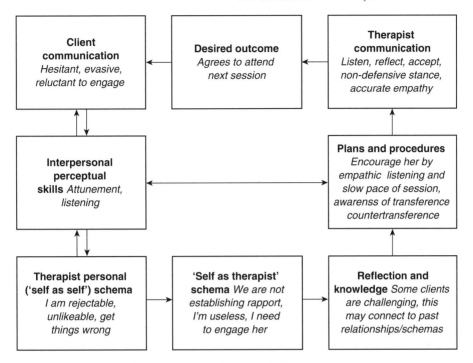

Figure 2.3   Therapist reflection on relational issues with Eva

Adapted from: Bennett-Levy, J. (2006) 'Therapist skills: A cognitive model of their acquisition and refinement', *Behavioural and Cognitive Therapy*, 34: 57–78.

- How best can I attend to this client? (E.g. by evolving and sharing hypotheses, highlighting important life events and eliciting feedback on the progress and process of therapy)
- How much of myself do I bring to the therapy room? (What beliefs and schemas have been activated in me?)

The ability to reflect on how we form relationships – including the therapeutic relationship – and how it relates to early social learning experiences is important. Therapists are encouraged to develop reflective skills to help separate the effects of their past from the interactions with their clients.

OBSTACLES RELATED TO ACTIVATION OF THERAPIST BELIEFS ('I MUST BE A GOOD THERAPIST AND GET THIS CLIENT CURED')

The therapist's sense of competence and self-esteem may be influenced by their ability to work well with clients. Therapists can feel defensive and irritated if problems arise. They can feel discouraged when clients struggle and they fail to make sense of the client's experience. Therapists can often experience self-doubt, and question themselves. In Eva's case, beliefs might be activated within the therapist around competence. The therapist might be concerned that limited training around psychodynamic issues would compromise her ability to work effectively with Eva. Sharpening our awareness of the differing beliefs we hold of 'self-as-therapist' and 'private self', and being cognisant of their impact on therapy was important. With Eva a range of therapist cognitions were activated:

- 'I'm not engaging with her well in therapy.'
- 'I'm not sure this is working. I'm not good enough.'
- 'What if she thinks I'm useless?'
- 'If the client doesn't want to talk, we may as well finish up.'
- 'What if she cancels the next session?'

Therapist cognitions are based on assumptions. Such assumptions might trigger therapist behaviours, termed 'defensive responses', against the rising feelings of inadequacy. While the therapist's assumptions are activated, so too are the client's. In the case of Eva, while her therapist was feeling useless, she may have thought:

- 'I'm really pleased I've been able to talk about my painful childhood experiences. My therapist is being very patient and attentive.'
- 'If I can't answer the therapist's questions she will think I'm stupid, weak and I'm being difficult, just like my parents did.'

Therapists need to be aware of this process in order to reduce the danger of reacting on the basis of their own underlying beliefs being activated. This might result in an ill-informed judgement of how the therapeutic engagement or intervention is going, creating a further obstacle in therapy.

THE CASE OF EVELYN: THE RELUCTANT TO ENGAGE EATING-DISORDER CLIENT

18-year-old Evelyn has been referred by her university health centre GP with a two-year history of anorexia nervosa. She appears pale, emaciated and tired, with mottled skin due to feeling the cold. She wears layers of clothes and is restless and uneasy about the appointment. She looks withdrawn and is reticent in session, denying there is a problem. She says her parents overreact and are constantly 'on my case'. She believes that others, including her family, peers and tutors, are unnecessarily concerned for her. They are not allowing her attend the gym, where she worked out for one hour daily.

The GP weighed her and is concerned her BMI, at 16, is too low. 'I suppose you will want to weigh me too,' she says in a challenging, defensive way. She is only attending therapy because her academic tutor directed her to do so. She is reluctant to engage and answers most questions by shrugging her shoulders, saying 'I don't know.' She admits frustration at feeling tired, which is interfering with her college course. She may have to repeat the year. She has become increasingly socially isolated.

Identifying Evelyn's Problem

It was clear during this initial session that Evelyn was ambivalent about attending therapy. She was feeling increasingly isolated, identifying herself as 'causing trouble' and displeasing everyone. She was resistant to gaining weight or eating. The therapist was concerned about her low BMI and explained to Evelyn that restricting food in this way was detrimental to her health and she would be encouraging her to gradually increase her dietary intake. This would be important in enabling her to engage psychologically in therapy. Evelyn became upset and defensive, expressing the opinion that the therapist would be 'someone else on my case'. She became monosyllabic and distant. It was challenging to engage her in session. Her therapist needed to address the evident emotional distance and her limited motivation to engage in therapy. In addition, exploring if her family's beliefs were stifling progress was important, before moving to address activated underlying schemas.

OBSTACLES RELATED TO EMOTIONAL DISTANCE

Some clients have difficulty expressing their needs and naming emotions. This was the case with Evelyn. Despite the strength shown in being able to control their weight and shape with tenacity, the eating-distressed client can appear fragile, fearful and emotionally distant. Understandably, fear and emotional distance presents obstacles to engagement and the treatment process, which can make the establishment of a therapeutic alliance challenging. The eating disorder, characterised by extreme preoccupation about shape, weight and a pursuit of thinness, is often accompanied by low self-esteem, feelings of worthlessness, anxiety and perfectionism. Generally, such clients do not share the view of others about their need to change (Treasure and Schmidt, 2001). Engaging Evelyn in a dialogue around the social context of her experience, how the expression of her feelings has become hampered by the overt 'symptom' expression of her illness and evolving an understanding of her 'social story' was useful (see Chapter 4).

COLLABORATION AND MOTIVATIONAL INTERVIEWING

With Evelyn the therapist's initial focus was on establishing a collaborative therapeutic alliance. In cases such as this, the use of specific change methods or goal setting may need to be put on hold until the therapeutic alliance has been strengthened. In Evelyn's case, she agreed to attend for an initial three sessions. The therapist hypothesised that Evelyn might not collaborate in therapy unless she experienced a sense of trust, safety and control. It was therefore, important that therapists:

- Establish a therapeutic relationship with the patient as an equal collaborator.
- Are cognisant of the patient's motivation to change: The 'stages of change model' (Prochaska et al., 1992) was helpful in assessing Evelyn's ambivalence about therapy.
- Recognise patients' unique requirements so as to engage in change: The therapist hypothesised that Evelyn needed a sense of power over any change process around

her ability to make changes. Utilising techniques of motivational interviewing approach was useful here (Prochaska and Di Clemente, 2005). Useful questions were:

- – 'What does it mean for you to be out of control?'
- – 'What for you is the biggest challenge about changing your eating habits?'
- – 'Aside from restricting food what other ways could you manage your emotional distress?'

- Minimise blaming: Acceptance and non-judgementality, making certain not to appear blaming of the client or engage in 'fault finding', was important.
- Maximise the use of interventions that make therapist an ally: The therapist fostered a relationship with Evelyn in which she was seen as non-threatening and, with time, as an ally.

OBSTACLES RELATED TO SIGNIFICANT OTHERS

Aware of the conflict at home, the therapist, with Evelyn's consent, met with her parents, who were worried and invested in 'getting her to eat more'. They described her as a perfectly happy young girl, who 'never gave an ounce of trouble'. They were unaware of any triggers to Evelyn restricting her food. They expressed frustration at how the illness had caused conflict within their home 'changing everything'. Engaging significant others in this case was crucial due to these interpersonal influences. The involvement of others in therapy needs to be approached with care as it can raise further obstacles, which can impact on the therapeutic relationship (see Chapter 5). The therapist was conscious of Evelyn's perception that her parents, GP and dietician were frustrated with her lack of progress. She therefore used the session to reduce Evelyn's sense of alienation by not focusing immediately on increasing her nutritional intake. She included a systemic approach, involving the parents in a co-therapy role (see Chapter 5), so that all were supporting Evelyn towards acknowledging she had a problem and that together they wanted to help and support her. This enabled the alliance between therapist and client to strengthen as Evelyn felt the therapist was 'on her side'. Interventions, such as increasing the families understanding of the complex nature of the eating disorder, the encouragement of emotional expression, and discussion of the physical and psychological impact of anorexia, were then an important initial treatment focus.

WORKING ON ENGAGEMENT BEFORE TRIGGERING SCHEMAS

Engaging Evelyn was the first obstacle to overcome. An initial contract was agreed as follows:

Therapist:	As you are struggling right now, it might be useful for us to meet, so I can work with you around your eating distress.
Evelyn:	What would we have to do? Would you be asking me to eat, like my parents?

Therapist:	I thought we might focus on the preoccupation you have about your shape and weight and how that upsets you. What is the most challenging aspect of this for you?
Evelyn:	I am scared of putting on weight, feeling awful and not in control.
Therapist:	You do sound frightened about any change in weight, but it sounds like your pursuit of this ideal body image and being in control has its down sides. It seems to cut you off you from people you care about and has affected your self-confidence.
Evelyn:	I do feel very lonely and hate myself sometimes. I could do with some support right now, I feel quite alone … . No-one understands really what this is like for me.
Therapist:	We can approach this in stages. Initially this would involve a weekly meeting. The main thing I want to emphasise is that this eating problem is 'not your fault'. It is most probably your best way of coping right now. Perhaps together we can work out other ways for you to manage it.
Evelyn:	It is nice to hear that I feel so guilty and ashamed about all the worry I cause everyone. I do feel it is my fault and I am a horrible person. Maybe we could meet a few times or so.

It took several sessions to establish a working alliance with Evelyn. Her initial reluctance to attend implied she was not invested in change. The establishment of a working alliance was fostered by agreeing the objectives of treatment and involving her parents as significant others in the treatment plan. Challenging unhelpful cognitions, behaviours related to body image and increasing dietary intake were then identified as therapeutic goals.

As engagement progressed the emergence of schemas became apparent. Evelyn felt a particular bond with her mother who, as a busy solicitor, had little time to spend with her. Evelyn was reluctant to verbalise this. The assumption was that, 'If I express my needs, I will be seen as a burden and be rejected.' Evelyn was artistic and creative, her older sister, who was close to Mum, was academic and studied law. Her core beliefs centred around acceptability: 'I am not good enough' and 'others are more acceptable and rejecting'. She held 'defectiveness' and 'rejection' schemas (Young, et al., 2003). These became evident early in the development of the therapeutic relationship. Evelyn's reluctance to express her needs and emotions and an expressed sense that there was no point in trying were coupled with a fear she would be rejected by the therapist if the therapist found out what she was 'really like'. This illustrates the notion of schemas being expressed within the therapeutic relationship, creating opportunities to challenge them.

The therapist needed to establish a strong and trusting relationship before undertaking specific interventions. Though triggering of interpersonal schemas is necessary for their modification, the initial relationship needed to be one in which schema activation was minimised. Inappropriate triggering of interpersonal schemas too early in therapy may have been too challenging, creating a risk of disengagement. The timing of the commencement of change focused interventions is crucial and therapists need to be explicit about motivating the client towards change to be successful in engagement and treatment. The general practice of working with eating-disorder clients involves self monitoring, stimulus-control techniques, affect-control and emotion-regulation strategies in addition to working with self-esteem and improving the client's ability to identify and express their needs.

These clients are challenging to engage, often drop out of treatment and theoretical understandings of this complex group needs ongoing refinement. Therapists need to be open and flexible in integrating techniques from different theoretical models and sequencing these interventions in collaboration with their client for best success. They need also to be prepared to work clinically over a longer period of time with this client group.

For a comprehensive exploration of eating disorders the reader is referred to *Cognitive Behaviour Therapy and Eating Disorders* (Fairburn, 2008). In addition, eloquent behavioural and cognitive models are available when working with eating disorders (Shafran and De Silva, 2003; Waller and Kennerley, 2003).

THE CASE OF JANE: THE DISSATISFIED CLIENT

Jane is a 28-year-old post-graduate university student. She is an only child from an academically and professionally successful family. She is an accomplished student – excelling throughout years in private school in both her studies and extensive extra-curricular activities. Her mother is active in charity work, and encouraged her in volunteering from an early age.

Jane self-referred with a four-week history of panic attacks. These attacks emerged immediately after spending the summer volunteering in an overseas orphanage, which was poorly staffed and populated with disturbed and often aggressive children. She highlighted a specific occasion, when an older resident locked her in a room with a distressed child for 40 minutes before she was rescued. She recalled being tearful and shaky with her heart racing, as she tried to reassure the child. Following this, she believed she was 'a failure', and questioned her competence, self-control and ability to cope. She experienced sleep disturbance, concentration difficulties and loss of confidence in her work. Her goal for therapy was to stop the panic attacks and return overseas for more volunteer work.

IDENTIFYING THE PROBLEM

Jane clearly had a clear goal she wished to achieve from therapy. 'I want to stop the panic attacks and get back to my volunteer work.' On the basis of assessment, the therapist hypothesised that Jane was managing more than she could cope with, felt under threat because of this and she shared this initial hypothesis with Jane early in session. Jane became defensive and dismissive of this initial formulation and voiced ambivalence about attending a further session, on the basis of her believing her 'needs were not met' creating a rupture in the alliance.

EXPLORING SOLUTIONS

First impressions are important and are guided by information derived through assessment, evolving maintenance and treatment hypotheses. The accuracy of these initial hypotheses should be collaboratively shared with the client. In this case, the therapist hypothesised Jane might be expecting too much of herself personally and did not possess the resources she needed to help her cope with current demands. Both therapist and client bring with them to therapy previous experiences, beliefs and expectations. Disagreements and misunderstandings can occur within a therapeutic encounter as in all other relationships. Therapist and client need to agree on what Bordin (1994) describes as the goals and tasks of therapy and establish a therapeutic bond to facilitate such work.

SHARING FORMULATION

The therapist shared her initial hypothesis with Jane and explored practical solutions for accessing help and support for her work in the orphanage. The process of agreeing an initial conceptualisation can go wrong, becoming an obstacle to progress. Jane was irritated and expressed disappointment about the session. She stated she knew all the practical solutions, which was not what she needed from therapy. The therapist's understanding of the conceptualisation differed from Jane's understanding creating an obstacle to progress. Not having established a strong enough bond at this early stage of therapy may also have been a factor. Early session information gathering, establishing a stronger alliance and later session sharing of formulation, may have improved the engagement process in this instance (Tryon, 2002).

Conceptualisation is best evolved in a collaborative way, so that it is idiosyncratically and carefully derived from the client specific information. The language used by therapists should be jargon free and easy to understand, with regular summarising, clarifying and eliciting feedback. The timing of interventions is also important. Ill timed interventions can trigger patients' schemas, create discomfort and become obstacles to progress (see Chapter 4: Pacing Timing and Endings). Jane's therapist hypothesised that sharing the initial conceptualisation too soon may have made Jane feel 'less competent and less in control'. Obstacles related to narcissistic fragility (i.e. the client who feels wounded because their vulnerability is exposed too soon before the relationship is strong enough) can arise in therapy and contribute to therapeutic rupture. Therapist capacity to be flexible, non-blaming and accepting of errors in judgement and to recover from such mistakes is important. Therapists need to be able to recognise when they experience a relational struggle with their client. They need also to be aware of their own beliefs and their role in contributing to such a relational struggle. Being open and honest about how we feel as therapists faced with a dissatisfied client facilitates an opportunity to discuss the impasse. This is preferable to becoming defensive and critical of the client. Being mindful of reciprocal feedback mechanisms is also useful.

(Continued)

(Continued)

UTISILING FEEDBACK

Feedback and summarising, is an important part of how clients and therapists ascertain the subjective experience of therapy and of each other. Positive feedback can be affirming and facilitative of behavioural change for clients and can strengthen the therapeutic relationship (Claiborn, Goodyear and Horner, 2001). Negative feedback can impact on therapy and affect the therapeutic relationship, either with the same or future therapists.

The therapist's own sense of therapeutic omnipotence can feel challenged by therapy going wrong. Therapists need to be open to accepting negative feedback, though challenging, as constructive learning. Developing skills in effectively eliciting and giving feedback within session is essential. Summarising and chunking information at regular intervals and emphasising significant themes can help synthesise new material, highlighting areas that need further clarification. Summarising at the beginning and end of a session is important and can be done in the following way:

- 'Could you tell me some of the more important things we discussed today?'
- 'Just to summarise at the beginning of the session we talked about ... and towards the end of the session we explored ... . In what way has this been helpful?'
- 'What was the most/least helpful thing about our session today?' (James et al., 2001)

In Jane's case, the therapist acknowledged her disappointment and took time to clarify what would have been more useful. She reinforced the importance of feedback in assuring that Jane's needs were met so that any difficulties were acknowledged and worked through satisfactorily. Jane agreed to attend for a further appointment. This simple use of reciprocal feedback helped to avert a potential rupture in the relationship.

SUMMARISING COMMON OBSTACLES

Within the process of CBT, obstacles may arise related to aspects of its practice (see Table 2.1). How the therapeutic relationship navigates its way through setting boundaries, treatment options and therapeutic ruptures is complex. Acknowledging what is happening within the relationship may involve discomfort for both the client and therapist but can be validating, contributing towards better therapeutic alliances and outcome.

CONSIDERATIONS IN NON-FACE-TO-FACE THERAPEUTIC RELATIONSHIPS

Psychotherapy practitioners and service providers have been investigating the potential use of technology such as the internet, mobile-phone applications and software programmes to deliver psychological intervention (Cook and Doyle, 2002; Prado

Table 2.1 Summarising common obstacles

Obstacle	Reflective questions
Collaboration	Have the client and I been collaborative? Are we functioning as a team? Is it an alliance issue? Does it relate to diagnosis or treatment planning?
Client feedback	Do I regularly elicit feedback? Do I check in with the client when I notice a change in affect? Did a therapeutic technique contribute to the obstacle? Was it an aspect of one session or several?
Client's view of therapy	How does the client view therapy? How do they view me as a therapist? Does my client view me as competent, collaborative and caring?
Therapist's reactions	Is it a process issue? How do I feel towards the client? Do I care about them? Does my caring come across to the client? What negative thoughts do I experience about this client or myself? How could I evaluate and respond to these thoughts? Do I feel competent to work with this client?

Source: adapted from Beck, J.S. (1995) *Cognitive Therapy Basics and Beyond*. New York: Guilford. pp. 304–5.

and Meyer, 2004). The NICE guidelines recommend greater access to CBT (NICE, 2009). Computerised packages of online self-help therapy, such as 'Beating the Blues', 'Mood Gym' and 'Living Life to the Full', are available and have been evaluated with varying results (Proudfoot et al., 2003). Many services offer asynchronous and synchronous online counselling/therapy, chat rooms and discussion boards (Richards et al., 2009). Clients may be attracted to the anonymity of an online therapeutic relationship, which can be convenient for clients fitting therapy more readily into their daily routine. Such anonymity presents its own alliance challenges. Obstacles may come up for clients in engaging in therapy online or therapists may be sceptical about the ability to form a therapeutic relationship online in the absence of non-verbal cues. Alternatively, forming an alliance may be quicker, as the awkwardness and barriers present in face-to-face contact are removed. For a comprehensive review of this subject, the reader is referred to *The Use of Technology in Mental Health Application, Ethics and Practice* (Anthony et al., 2010).

THE TENTATIVE EMAIL-COUNSELLING CLIENT REQUEST

Dear Counsellor. I'm not sure if you can help, maybe I'm being over-dramatic, my mum thinks I am. I've been having these mood swings for the past year. I feel good most of the time but for long periods I feel I've no energy, my concentration goes and I get really frustrated with myself. I've tried talking to my parents but they tell me I'll be fine. I just feel they don't understand. Everyone else in the family seems ok. I seem to be the troublesome one. Lately I've been comfort eating, sometimes I vomit afterwards and my weight has gone up, which is really depressing for me. It's hard to tell my friends, because they are all busy and so confident and I feel like I'm moaning. I seem to be the only one fed up, on my own and not happy. I don't even have interest in shopping or going out, I used to love buying clothes and looked forward to nights out. I feel self-conscious now about how I look and know no-one would be interested in having a relationship with me. I'm not a bad case, so don't need to go for counselling but just feel stuck. Any advice would be great.

This client seems to be presenting with intermittent low mood, possible bulimia and issues around self-esteem.

OBSTACLES AROUND LACK OF INFORMATION/HISTORY

Picking up on themes in the absence of a full history is an important first step in engaging this client. Thus, an obstacle to the establishment of the usual therapeutic relationship is encountered at the first stage of therapy. In responding, the therapist could commend the client for getting in touch in the first place. They could reinforce that writing down what she is experiencing is a first step in seeking help. Empathising with her distress and summarising the main areas of difficulty is useful. The language used in online therapy is important. The therapist is encouraged to mirror the client's language, reducing the likelihood of alienation to strengthen the alliance. Therapist language should not be too direct but tentative and questioning, encouraging greater explanation and engagement. This helps to build a collaborative hypothesis, developing the online therapeutic alliance. This is similar to Socratic questioning in face-to-face therapy. An example, as illustrated by the therapist's response to the above client, might be to write:

> As you describe these low mood spells, I'm struck by your sadness and notice how difficult this seems to be for you. You say, 'I seem to be the troublesome one' and 'no-one would be interested in having a relationship with me'. The sense I get is that this leaves you with quite a negative view of yourself. If this is so, it might explain why you feel so 'fed up, on your own and unhappy'.

Note how the therapist does not make direct and conclusive statements but, instead, mostly refers to the felt 'sense' from reading the correspondence. This reduces the likelihood of the client feeling judged or therapist–client misunderstanding. It is important not to presume too much, so ending with a question such as, 'Does this seem to fit with your experience?' allows the client to confirm or otherwise this tentative hypothesis. Engaging with this client may involve online counselling within a CBT framework, addressing low mood, self-esteem and bulimia or referral to an online self-help programme such as 'Beating the Blues' or 'Living Life to the Full'. If issues emerge, of a more serious nature as sessions continue, the offer of a face-to-face session can be made, clarifying the importance of this with the client, who may believe they are 'not bad enough'.

OBSTACLES TO ENGAGING THE ONLINE CLIENT

Engaging clients online is a skill in its own right. Murphy et al. (2008) provide useful tips for engaging clients and avoiding obstacles in online therapy. Therapists may find it useful to:

- Begin with a greeting and set the scene to help socialise the client.
- Use the clients name at intervals, personalising the encounter.

- Identify emerging themes that may become the focus for therapeutic work.
- When highlighting a contradiction or suggesting an alternative way of being to the client, end with a question. It is important to give the client an opportunity to agree or disagree, argue or explore and take an active role in therapy.
- Provide the client with the opportunity to interact with the therapist, through the use of language, reflective questioning and feedback.
- Engage the client's thinking rather than their transference. The client may well understand what the words mean but there is no guarantee they will know what *you* as a therapist means. Try to be explicit in clarifying *your* meaning. This will help minimise the risk of subtext in your work.
- Have an explanatory framework or model that helps the client understand their experience and check with them how this feels.
- Summarise essential points. Ask the client to reflect on the content of the session and ask them to highlight themes or ideas you may have missed.
- Encourage the client to answer thoughtfully, read, review, save and return. The client can then return to this work at intervals to help consolidate.
- When ending sessions, include a goodbye or sign-off message. Each session needs to feel complete. In face-to-face work therapists summarise and elicit feedback towards the end of a session. This is no less important in online work. (Murphy et al., 2008)

Both therapists and clients need clarity, boundaries and safety when engaging in an online therapeutic relationship. Therapists should receive training on how to work with clients online due to the different presenting challenges and obstacles. It is important that online clients are registered users who can be identified and contacted in the event of suicidal or at-risk behaviours. This should be made explicit to clients when the counsellor reviews and responds to online therapy submissions. It is worth mentioning that reading, exploring and responding to an email therapy submission, more often than not, takes as much time as a one-to-one session. Therapist energy resources need to be considered as tiredness and fatigue can impact on typing quality, content and other factors on which the online therapeutic relationship is reliant. Obstacles can also arise in online therapeutic work and supervision and close monitoring of online client work is recommended.

SUMMARY

A therapeutic alliance emerges through a complex interplay of the combined collaborative skills of client, therapist and potentially supervisor. Alliances are formed in both face-to-face sessions and online therapy. The alliance can alter at any given moment depending on circumstances and may change as therapy progresses. Ruptures in the alliance can challenge the therapist's sense of competence and effectiveness. Therapists need to be aware of the transactional and vulnerable nature of the alliance and be attentive to interpersonal process. Viewing obstacles and ruptures as an opportunity to think on our feet and respond in a timely and insightful way is important. Watching the moment-to-moment interaction within the therapeutic relationship and reflecting on what impacts on it is a necessary and worthwhile part of therapeutic process.

LEARNING ACTIVITY

THE CASE OF ANNA: THE SHY AND SELF-CONSCIOUS CLIENT

20 year-old Anna presents with a four-year history of extreme self-consciousness in social interactions. She is a third-year university student and has been avoiding class due to being asked to read and present, which is a formal part of her training course. She states she feels nauseous before class, experiences facial flushing, and feels hot and sweaty, which increases her fears that other classmates think she 'is weird'. She coped over the past two years by doing group projects and avoiding taking the lead in presentations. She is the eldest of three siblings and describes her father as autocratic and critical. He expected a lot from his children and would regularly argue with them at dinner, having strong views on all matters. She never felt heard and was always made to feel 'stupid'. In session she sits with her head bowed and is reticent about engaging or talking about her problems.

Take a moment to reflect on Anna's case:

- What areas need to be considered in engaging this client?
- What obstacles to therapy might emerge?
- What CBT model would be helpful?

FURTHER READING

Beck, J.S. (2005) *Cognitive Therapy for Challenging Problems: What To Do When the Basics Don't Work*. New York: Guilford Press.
Gilbert, P. and Leahy, R. (eds) (2007) *The Therapeutic Relationship in the Cognitive Behavioural Psychotherapies*. London: Routledge.
Leahy, R.L. (2003) *Roadblocks in Cognitive Behavioural Therapy: Transforming Challenges into Opportunities for Change*. New York: Guilford Press.
Safran, D. and Segal, Z.V. (1990) *Interpersonal Processes in Cognitive Therapy*. New York: Basic Books.

REFERENCES

Anthony, K., Mere Nagel, D. and Goss, S. (2010) *The Use of Technology in Mental Health Applications Ethics and Practice*. Springfield, IL: Charles C Thomas Publications.
Beck, J. (1995) *Cognitive Therapy Basics and Beyond*. Guilford Press: New York.
Beck, A.T., Rush, A., Shaw, B. and Emery, G. (1979) *Cognitive Therapy of Depression*. New York: Guilford Press.
Beck, A.T., Freeman, A., Pretzer, J., Davis, D.D., Fleming, B., Ottavani, R., Beck, J., Simon, K.M., Padesky, C., Meyer, J. and Trexer, L. (1990) *Cognitive Therapy of Personality Disorders*. New York: Guilford Press.
Bennett-Levy, J. (2006) 'Therapist skills: a cognitive model of their acquisition and refinement', *Behavioural and Cognitive Psychotherapy*, 34: 57–78.

Bennett-Levy, J., Lee, N., Travers, K., Pohlman, S. and Hamernik, E. (2003) 'Cognitive therapy from the inside: enhancing therapist skills through practising what we preach', *Behavioural and Cognitive Psychotherapy*, 31: 143–58.

Bennett-Levy, J., Butler, G., Fennell, M., Hackman, A., Mueller, M. and Westbrook, D. (eds) (2004) *Oxford Guide to Behavioural Experiments in Cognitive Therapy*. Oxford: Oxford University Press.

Bennett-Levy, J., Turner, F., Beaty, T., Smith, M., Paterson, B. and Farmer, S. (2001) 'The value of self practice of cognitive therapy techniques and self reflection in the training of cognitive therapists', *Behavioural and Cognitive Psychotherapy*, 29: 203–20.

Bordin, E.S. (1994) 'Theory and research in the therapeutic working alliance: new directions', in O. Horvath and L.S. Greenberg (eds), *The Working Alliance*. New York: Wiley.

Bowlby, E. (1973) *Attachment and Loss* (2nd vol.). *Separation, Anxiety and Anger*. New York: Basic Books.

Burns, D.D. (1990) *The Feeling Good Handbook*. New York: Plume.

Claiborn, C.D., Goodyear, R.K. and Horner, P.A. (2001) 'Feedback', *Psychotherapy: Theory, Research, Practice, Training*, 38: 401–5.

Cook, J.E. and Doyle, C. (2002) 'Working alliance in online therapy as compared to face to face therapy: preliminary results', *Cyberpsychology and Behaviour*, 5 (2): 95–105.

Daniels, J. and Wearden, A. (2011) 'Socialization to the model: the active component in the therapeutic alliance', *Behavioural and Cognitive Psychotherapy*, 39: 221–7.

Fairburn, C. (2008) *Cognitive Therapy and Eating Disorders*. New York: Guilford Press.

Freud, S. (1940) 'The dynamics of transference', in J. Strachey (ed.), *The Standard Edition of the Complete Works of Sigmund Freud Vol. 12*. London: McMillan. pp. 122–44.

Gilbert, P. and Leahy, R. (eds) (2007) *The Therapeutic Relationship in the Cognitive Behavioural Psychotherapies*. London: Routledge.

Grant, A., Townend, M., Mills, J. and Cockx, A. (2008) *Assessment and Formulation in Cognitive Behavioural Therapy*. London: SAGE.

Hardy, G.E., Cahill, J., Shapiro, D.A., Barkham, M., Rees, A. and MacAskill, N. (2001) 'Client interpersonal and cognitive style as predictors of response to time limited cognitive therapy for depression', *Journal of Consulting and Clinical Psychology*, 68: 841–5.

James, I.A., Blackburn, I.M., Reichelt, F.K., Garland, A. and Milne, D.L. (2001) *Manual of the Revised Cognitive Therapy Scale*. Northumberland: Tyne and Wear NHS Trust.

Kuyken, W. (2006) 'Evidence based case formulation is the emperor clothed?', in N. Tarrier (ed.), *Case Formulation in Cognitive Behaviour Therapy: The Treatment of Challenging and Complex Cases*. London: Routledge.

Kuyken, W., Padesky, C.A. and Dudley, R. (2008) *Collaborative Case Conceptualisation*. New York: Guilford Press.

Leahy R. (2001) *Overcoming Resistance in Cognitive Therapy*. New York: Guilford Press.

Ligiero, D.P. and Gelso, C.J. (2002) 'Countertransferance, attachment and the working alliance:the therapist's contribution', *Psychotherapy, Research, Practice and Training*, 39: 3–11

Linehan, M.M. (1993) *Skills Training Manual for Treating Borderline Personality Disorder*. New York: Guilford Press.

McCluskey, U. (2005) *To Be Met as a Person: The Dynamics of Attachment in Professional Encounters*. London: Karnac.

Murphy, L.J., MacFadden, R.J. and Mitchel, D.L. (2008) 'Cybercounselling online: the development of a university based training programme for e-mail counselling', *Journal of Technology in Human Services*, 26: 447–69.

NICE (2009) National Institute for Health and Clinical Excellence. www.nice.org.uk.

Prado, S. and Meyer, S.B. (2004) 'Evaluation of the working alliance of asynchronous therapy via the internet', University Sao Paolo. www.psico.net/arquivos/.

Prochaska, J.O. and Di Clememte, C.C. (2005) 'The transtheoretical approach', in J.C. Norcross and M.R. Goldfired (eds) *Handbook of Psychotherapy Integration*. New York: Oxford University Press. pp. 147–71.

Prochaska, J.O., Di Clemente, C.C. and Norcross, J.C. (1992) 'In search of how people change: applications to addictive behaviour', *American Psychologist*, 47 (9): 1102–14.

Proudfoot, J., Goldberg, D., Mann, A., Everitt, B., Marks, I. and Gray, J.A. (2003) 'Computerised, interactive, multimedia, cognitive behavioural therapy for anxiety and depression in clinical practice', *Psychological Medicine*, 33: 217–27.

Richards, D., Timulak, L., Tone, Y., Rashleigh, C., Naughton, A., Flynn, D. and McLoughlin, O. (2009) 'The experience of implementing, recruiting and screening for an online treatment for depression in a naturalistic setting', *Counselling Psychology Review*, 24 (2).

Rogers, C.R. (1965) *Client Centred Therapy: Its Current Practice, Implications and Theory*. Boston: Houghton-Mifflin.

Safran, J.D. and Muran, J.C. (2000) *Negotiating the Therapeutic Alliance: A Relational Treatment Guide*. New York: Guilford Press.

Safran, J.D. and Segal, Z.V. (1990) *Interpersonal Processes in Cognitive Therapy*. New York: Basic Books.

Shafran, R. and De Silva, P. (2003) 'Cognitive behavioural models', in J. Treasure, U. Schmidt and E.Van Furth (eds), *Handbook of Eating Disorders*. Chichester: John Wiley & Sons.

Thwaites, R. and Bennett-Levy J. (2007) 'Conceptualizing empathy in cognitive therapy making the implicit explicit', *Behavioural and Cognitive Psychotherapy*, 35: 591–12.

Treasure, J., and Schmidt, U. (2001) 'Ready willing and able to change: motivational aspects of the assessment and treatment of eating disorders', *European Eating Disorders Reviews*, 9: 1–15.

Tryon, G.S. (2002) 'Engagement in counselling', in G.S.Tryon (ed.) *Counselling Based on Process Research Applying What We Know*. Boston: Allyn Bacon. pp. 1–26.

Waddington, L. (2002) 'The therapy relationship in cognitive therapy: a review', *Behavioural and Cognitive Psychotherapy*, 30: 179–91.

Waller, G. and Kennerley, H. (2003) 'Cognitive behavioural treatments', in J. Treasure, U. Schmidt and E. Van Furth (eds), *Handbook of Eating Disorders* (2nd edn). Chichester: John Wiley & Sons.

Weissman, A.N. and Beck, A.T. (1978) 'Development and validation of the dysfunctional attitude scale', paper presented at meeting of the Association of Advancement of Behaviour Therapy. Toronto, ON, March 27–31.

Williams, C. (2003) *Overcoming Anxiety: A Five Areas Approach*. London: Hodder Arnold.

Wright, J. and Davies, D. (1994) 'The therapeutic relationship in cognitive-behaviour therapy: patient perceptions and therapist response', *Cognitive and Behavioural Practice*, 1: 25–45.

Young, J.E. (1990) *Cognitive Therapy for Personality Disorders: A Schema Focussed Approach*. Sarasota, FL: Professional Resource Exchange Inc.

Young, J.E. and Brown, G. (1990) 'Young Schema Questionnaire', in J.E. Young (ed.), *Cognitive Therapy for Personality Disorders: A Schema Focussed Approach*. Sarasota, FL: Professional Resource Press.

Young, J.E., Kosko, J.S. and Weishaar, M. (2003) *Schema Therapy: A Practitioners Guide*. New York: Guilford.

3

ASSESSMENT, PROBLEM FOCUS AND MODEL SELECTION

MICHAEL MCDONOUGH

LEARNING OBJECTIVES

After reading this chapter the reader should:

- understand the value and limitations of disorder-specific models;
- understand the value of a thorough assessment;
- know how to go about selecting an appropriate CBT model;
- know when to combine models and sequence interventions where necessary;
- understand when and why to use longitudinal case conceptualisation;
- understand the importance of shifting the focus when faced with an evolving picture.

INTRODUCTION

The practice of CBT is supported by an invaluable array of tried and tested disorder- or problem-specific approaches ('models', 'protocols' – see Table 3.1). The majority of these models enjoy a thorough empirical base in theoretical and clinical research. They have been evolved from extensive direct experience with patients and are derived from the core principles of cognitive and behavioural theory. It would be folly for any CBT practitioner to ignore such riches and much of the routine work with straightforward 'Axis I' cases will involve artfully and faithfully applying these protocols. This approach also works well where there is full co-morbidity (i.e. two distinct problems, both typical presentations) as the clinical interventions can be sequenced accordingly. It should not surprise us, however, that given the multi-faceted and complex nature of psychiatric disorders, a sizeable minority of cases presenting for treatment don't entirely 'fit' any specific model or the model/diagnosis that seemed appropriate initially turns out to be wide of the mark and a new focus is required. The complex and ever-evolving art of full or longitudinal case conceptualisation is well covered in recent texts (e.g. Kuyken et al., 2009). This chapter will be confined to exploring the common sticking points in the process of identifying the problem and selecting the optimal CBT model(s) for each client. The examples are based on real-life cases drawn from our clinical practice.

IN WHAT WAY DO CASES CONFLICT WITH THE STANDARD CBT MODELS?

From the authors' experience the common categories are:

- *The underlying problem is hidden under the presenting problem* (e.g. body dysmorphic disorder presenting as depression; low self-esteem presenting as apparent social anxiety and avoidance but without significant physical anxiety or classical safety behaviours).
- *Two or more models interact but neither is complete* (e.g. agoraphobic type avoidance but panic more linked with past trauma than catastrophic misinterpretation of physical sensations).
- *The presentation lacks key elements of the model* (e.g. depressed patient who denies negative automatic thoughts; obsessional patient apparently without exaggerated responsibility beliefs – see case of John, opposite).
- *The presentation contradicts the model* (e.g. panic patient who faints).
- *No established CBT model exists yet* (e.g. conversion disorder).
- *The presentation is* consistently *distorted by a personality or developmental disorder* (e.g. histrionic patient with health anxiety who exaggerates symptoms; obsessional patient with Asperger's syndrome where frightening thoughts are mixed with ritualised fantasies – see case of Jack, p. 46).
- *The presentation is* intermittently *distorted by a fluctuating factor* (e.g. low self-esteem that lifts during hypomanic phases in bipolar disorder; binge benzodiazepine misuse causing wildly fluctuating panic symptoms without apparent linkage to cognitive events).

The 'Forced Fit'

In some of the above examples the case will ultimately fit the model with socialisation and guided discovery (e.g. a depressed patient may need time to access cognitions). Gaps in the cognitive picture can be a useful cue to negotiable barriers such as shame or guilt (see Chapter 8), difficulty accessing frightening cognitions (see Chapter 9) or an underdeveloped capacity to reflect psychologically. As ever, paradoxes, if explored can lead to a deeper understanding. Many cases, however, will require some form of re-formulation or re-conceptualisation if the work is not to become badly stuck. Persisting regardless along the same tack is fraught with dangers for both therapist and client.

THE CASE OF JOHN AND JANE'S HIDDEN COGNITIONS – THE 'PROCRUSTEAN DILEMMA'

Jane has completed a year-long foundation course and has commenced a post-graduate diploma in CBT. She has taken on her first client, John, a physics under-graduate who suffers with obsessive-compulsive disorder (OCD) marked by excessive hand washing and contamination fears. Jane prepares diligently and studies the OCD model of Salkovskis (1985) and works from Wells's text on anxiety disorders (1997). In the first session she attempts to formulate the case and explores for responsibility beliefs and meta-cognitions in keeping with her chosen CBT model. She becomes frustrated when these prove difficult to elicit. She repeatedly returns to the same questions and the session becomes derailed:

Jane: In trying to complete a full picture of what's going on, John, it might be important to understand what being contaminated means to you. What bad things might happen if you are contaminated? What does it bring to mind?

John: Every body asks me this and I just don't know. I know it's silly. It's not a bug or disease thing. It just feels horrible and I can't bear it.

Jane: OK. Let me ask this another way. In cognitive therapy we place great importance on how we perceive things. How we make sense of them. Clearly, feeling contaminated means something very powerful for you. What might that be?

John: That might be true but I can't help you there. It's just a feeling ... as far as I can tell.

Jane: I understand. It isn't always easy to be aware of what's going on in our minds. But let's spend a little more time on this as it is an important part of the treatment ...

Despite Jane's best efforts her frustration is apparent to the client who, already apprehensive about what treatment may involve, becomes reluctant to re-attend. Difficulty getting the cognitive model of OCD to fit is causing a strain in the therapeutic relationship.

Understandably, anxious thoughts are activated for Jane about not being competent or cut out for this work. She wonders if CBT is overly intellectual bearing no

(Continued)

(Continued)

relation to real-life cases. With her supervisor, she problem solves the impasse and decides to gently re-engage the client using, initially, a more behavioural rationale; exposure and response prevention (ERP: Meyer, 1966) – a model, which is less reliant on appraisal cognitions.

Jane: John, I was reflecting on our last session and I am aware that I pressed you on what feeling contaminated means to you. How did that feel? I thought afterwards that it might have been a little frustrating for you.

John: Yes. I'm glad you brought that up. I did feel like we were getting stuck and a bit like I wasn't being helpful. I felt bad and a bit annoyed afterwards.

Jane: Well. I am sorry about that … . How about giving things another go but this time using a different approach that is more based on working with the feelings and actions in OCD rather then the thoughts and meanings so much? We can look at those elements later or as they emerge.

John: Sounds good to me.

Jane: And let's agree to continue to be as open as we have been just now. To raise any concerns with each other as we go …

As planned, after gaining momentum through several sessions using the ERP approach, they attempt to re-formulate the problem cognitively. Here an important belief emerges for John: 'If I am contaminated I can't study effectively', which was challenged in several key behavioural experiments.

Later still a conditional belief emerges, 'If I reveal the full extent of my OCD I will look stupid' which prompts a longitudinal formulation. This belief connects with painful childhood experiences for John where he was ridiculed by his peers. It became apparent that this rule was active early in the sessions and was behind his difficulty accessing and disclosing the cognitive elements of his OCD.

In this example, Jane's eagerness to complete the formulation in line with the model led to a temporary breakdown in the therapeutic relationship as exaggerated responsibility beliefs were not present in this case and what cognitive elements were there took time to emerge. Ironically, in the early sessions, both Jane and John had similar beliefs activated about appearing 'stupid', which prevented effective collaboration and strained the therapeutic relationship. The interpersonal nature of therapy means that therapists' own issues can be activated by therapy and can – if they are not resolved or at least identified – interfere with the therapy (see Chapter 2). It was necessary in supervision for Jane to identify the 'hot' cognitions that therapy had activated in her. She then needed to decide if they were interfering with the therapeutic process and if she should work on them. In John's case, after the therapy reverted to a cognitive model an important meta-belief emerged through guided discovery, which became a central focus of change. By persisting with ERP this opportunity would have been lost. An alternative approach might have been to leave the Salkovskis cognitive formulation incomplete initially as a 'work in progress' and press on with behavioural experiments on the testable and visible elements of the maintenance cycle (such as the effect of safety behaviours and rituals on the intensity of 'contamination'). However, for Jane as it was her first case she found this a little too challenging and preferred the greater clarity of switching at least initially to a model that was a better fit. Later still, Jane further personalised the therapy using a longitudinal case conceptualisation which enriched and strengthened the work. Her original approach had been to try to fit the patient to the model. This led to frustration and created an obstacle to progress.

Kuyken et al. (2009) have termed this the 'Procrustean dilemma' after the mythical Greek character who stretched or hacked pieces off his guests, so that they would fit his bed. Although Jane's intentions were far more laudable, teachers and supervisors need to be aware of the pressures on therapists, particularly trainees to adhere to models that may not always fit.

ASSESSMENT

Many problems later in therapy could have been averted if the assessment was more complete. Leading practitioners agree on the importance of a good bio-psycho-social/diagnostic assessment yet practices vary from an initial cursory history review to a detailed semi-structured interview (Kuyken et al., 2009: 133–5). Assessment is an ongoing process and any initial 'snapshot', no matter how detailed, will have limitations, particularly in a fluctuating or evolving picture. However, for the kind of atypical cases relevant to this text (which comprise at least a sizeable minority of all cases) a detailed and thoughtful assessment is essential. This is because:

- Co-morbid or primary personality/Axis II/schema disorders can be difficult to identify and require a longitudinal review of life history and childhood experience and a historical sense of interpersonal style. They are the commonest reason for CBT work breaking down. Such cases usually require a full longitudinal case conceptualisation to complement the disorder specific model.
- The main presenting problem may not be the underlying problem. Several problems/ diagnoses may present together. These need to be prioritised and if possible ranked as primary or secondary considerations.
- Even when diagnostic criteria (e.g. ICD, DSM) are met, the CBT model may not fit. Highlighting this early enables adaptation or may prompt allocation of the patient to a more experienced therapist.
- There may be more pressing issues that require attention before CBT starts (e.g. family conflict, child welfare issues, alcohol detoxification, risk).
- Hidden co-morbidity should be considered (e.g. suggestions of childhood sexual abuse or other suppressed trauma).
- Family members if present at assessment can provide invaluable collateral information (see Chapter 5).
- A comprehensive family history can raise awareness of a tendency towards bipolar affective disorder or psychosis.
- The patient's track record of achievement and resilience can be recorded for use in therapy.
- Patients expect and value a thorough assessment. It builds trust and credibility.

THE IMPORTANCE OF AN ACCURATE IDENTIFICATION OF THE PROBLEM

THE CASE OF MARY – WHAT'S CAUSING WHAT?

Mary presents with a six-week history of panic and agoraphobic avoidance of leaving home. She fears a heart attack and misinterprets panic-induced chest pains as angina. Her father and uncle have died of heart disease over the past year. She had a coronary angiogram recently, which was normal. The initial assessment by the psychiatric registrar diagnosed agoraphobia/panic and recommended CBT. The therapist meets Mary and is satisfied that the presentation is in keeping with panic by collaboratively completing the Clark (1986) panic model. Over subsequent sessions Mary returns without having completed any of the agreed homework tasks. Mary complains of poor motivation and is pessimistic of success. Being at home for her is preferable to 'facing the world'. Her therapist explores this in more depth and discovers that Mary's functioning in all areas has dropped dramatically over the previous few months prior to the onset of panic. She has lost weight, is waking early but staying in bed for long spells in the day and is troubled with negative thoughts about the futility of life and her inevitable demise. Her therapist reformulates the main problem as depression and begins work using Beck's (1967) depression model.

In Mary's depressed state she went along with the CBT approach for panic even though she had reservations about it. Initially, her therapist viewed this reluctance as a standard part of the process but later listened to her disquiet and explored this further. In this case the therapist had the experience to sense that all was not right. A novice therapist may not have done so as the co-morbid but secondary panic problem appeared to fit the model nicely. More attention during assessment would have averted this risk. If depression was noticed at assessment, exploring the time-line of symptoms would have revealed depression as the primary disorder. In such cases, more often than not, panic will subside spontaneously with improvement of depression and separate panic work may not then be required. Thus, an accurate assessment and intelligent problem focus can save time and improve efficiency.

Accurate Assessment to Accurate Formulation

The assessment process needs to enable a broad initial formulation of the case (or at least best guess) bringing together key information. If it is overly detailed in any one area, it can be difficult to separate the wood from the trees or the picture becomes imbalanced. In our experience a good assessment covers all areas in a fluid way and harnesses the natural narrative of events to provide a reasonably comprehensive overview. Depending on the time available, the CBT microscope can then be focused on particular examples meriting analysis using the ABC Model (antecedents, behaviour, consequences – Kohlenberg and Tsai, 1991) and/or the Five-Part Model (a.k.a. the 'hot cross bun') (Greenberger and Padesky, 1995). Kuyken et al. (2009) provide a useful template for assessment, which has the advantage of covering biological, psychological and social aspects but other models are available (e.g. Hawton et al., 1989; Wells, 1997; Barlow, 2001).

The assessment process draws on the therapist's experience, their memory bank of previous cases, as well as their knowledge of disorders. More than almost any other aspect of the therapeutic process, curiosity and attention to detail play a key role. It is also the crucial point of engagement and relationship building with the patient. Assessments are ideally conducted jointly by an experienced and less experienced clinician, preferably with different training backgrounds. Often only a limited time is left for processing and formulating the information, planning treatment and feeding back to the patient, yet this is the most important part. Adequate time should be allowed for this as it is an excellent opportunity to engage the patient and begin socialisation to the CBT approach. Preliminary history questionnaires and rating scales can speed up the assessment, creating more time for this. Based on our experience, writing a personalised assessment report to the patient (carefully balanced with hopeful and positive information) can further aid engagement and communication (McDonough, 2008).

CHOOSING THE RIGHT MODEL

As Table 3.1 illustrates, some disorders have a leading model that has gained wider acceptance than competing models because of its elegance or superior evidence base (e.g. panic, Clark, 1986). Other disorders have several competing and overlapping models, each with differing strengths and weaknesses (e.g. generalised anxiety disorder (GAD), Wells, 1997; Borkovec and Costello, 1993; Dugas, 1998). CBT practitioners vary nationally and internationally in which models they use depending on their affiliations, geographical location (e.g. Europe versus North America) and the experience and preference of the leading therapists and researchers locally. Less complex but more efficient models tend to be learned and applied with greater ease, therefore having an advantage in the 'market place' but will not continue to be utilised if they prove inaccurate or less effective. This 'survival of the fittest' is ultimately helpful and necessary. For the novice therapist keen to put their faith in the right approach, this can become disheartening. Some therapists opt to work, regardless of the disorder, entirely from first principles and operate from the approach based on generic 'Beckian' cognitive therapy as outlined, for example, in Judith Beck's *Cognitive Therapy: Basics and Beyond* (1995). This is a shame as disorder-specific models tend to be more refined and rewarding if the time is taken to understand and utilise them. Of course all models need to be wielded with care and do not obviate the need for the core requirements of empathic engagement, alliance building and careful pacing. The following considerations are offered as guiding principles for those applying a model for the first time:

Table 3.1 Examples of disorder-specific CBT models

Problem	Leading models	Alternative models
Depression	Beck (1967)	Behavioural activation (Jacobsen et al., 1996) Compassionate mind (Gilbert, 2009) Mindfulness-based cognitive therapy for depression (Williams et al., 2006)
Bipolar disorder	Lam et al. (1999; 2003) Scott (2001)	
Panic	Clark (1986)	Barlow et al. (1989)
Obsessive compulsive disorder	Salkovskis (1985) Exposure and ritual prevention (Meyer, 1966)	Danger ideation and reduction therapy (DIRT) (Jones and Menzies,1998)
Social anxiety	Clark and Wells (1995)	Rapee and Heimberg (1997)
Health anxiety	Salkovskis (1989)	
Generalised anxiety disorder	Wells (1997) Dugas et al. (1998)	Borkovec and Costello (1993)
Post-traumatic stress disorder	Ehlers and Clark (2000)	Foa and Kozak (1986)
Specific phobias	Graded exposure (Marks, 1987) Beck et al. (1985)	Öst and Sterner (1987) (blood injury phobia)
Body dysmorphic disorder	Veale et al. (1996)	
Eating disorder	Fairburn et al. (2003)	
Low self-esteem	Fennell (2004)	
Psychosis	Fowler et al. (1995) Morrison (2002)	Kingdon and Turkington (2002)
Personality disorders	Beck et al. (2004) Schema-focused therapy (Young, 1994)	Dialectic behaviour therapy (Linehan, 1993)

- Give time to collaborate and contract with the patient on the question of which problem to focus on first.
- Consult with a colleague or peer who has experience working with this clinical problem for guidance on the leading *evidence based* model(s) (e.g. a supervisor or another clinician).
- Study this model from the original clinical text/paper giving time to socialise and reflect on it (even better, sign up to attend a workshop by the originator).
- It is important to prepare one model at a time rather than jumping from one to another without good reason. If the model doesn't seem to apply easily to the presenting issue, or if you genuinely find it hard to socialise to it, try another well established model.
- Once you have chosen a model, try it out with the patient in a collaborative, empirical way. Ensure adequate time for discussion with the patient and in supervision to iron out problems along the way. Be aware that the occasional 'wrong turn' is an important part of the journey.
- Don't abandon the model unless you have had a good go at problem-solving sticking points in supervision, preferably through review of videoed sessions.
- If, despite a faithful attempt, based on the above, things are not working out, reformulate utilising the most recent clinical information and switch to another model or approach based on an individualised case conceptualisation.

THE CASE OF CATHY – HORSES FOR COURSES

Cathy has several years experience providing individual CBT for patients with anxiety disorders in a specialist unit. She is struck by the volume of referrals for GAD and decides to run a GAD group. She is most familiar with Wells's meta-cognitive model of GAD (1997: Chapter 8) having attended a workshop by him. This model, although reasonably complex, had proven successful for Cathy and her clients, and they were able to collaboratively complete the elements of the model – positive meta-beliefs about worry, Type 1 worry, negative meta-beliefs about worry and Type 2 worry (meta-worry) and its associated cognitive, behavioural and emotional maintainers. Like most, she found the work on GAD challenging but with time could bring patients through socialisation and challenging beliefs verbally and via behavioural experiments. However, when piloting the group work, she struggles to come up with a workable way to cover all elements of the Wells model in group, without 'losing' some of the patients in its complexity. She approaches her supervisor, who helps her explore ways forward but she remains uncertain about the viability of the project. She subsequently raises her dilemma with another colleague who is familiar with Dugas's (1998) model of GAD, which has been adapted successfully for groups (Dugas et al., 2003). She studies this model and adopts it readily. Its staged approach proves considerably more applicable to the group setting (worry awareness training, coping with uncertainty, re-evaluating beliefs on the usefulness of worry, improving problem orientation/solving and processing core fears through imaginal exposure).

Therapists often work with a disorder where there are several accepted treatment models as illustrated in the case of Cathy. Cathy's experience allows her to choose a model that suits the situation. This can be a struggle for inexperienced therapists, who may either stick with the model they are comfortable with even when things aren't working out (Procrustean dilemma) or they may attempt a pick-and-mix (or 'eclectic') approach which diminishes the therapy's coherence and efficacy.

COMBINING MODELS AND SEQUENCING INTERVENTIONS

When several problem areas are active simultaneously, which is often the case, there is a danger that the patient and therapist can become demoralised or may attempt to tackle everything at once. From clinical experience, progress is best achieved by listing problems and collaboratively prioritising and sequencing interventions based on a few guiding principles:

- Prioritise treatment of the *primary or underlying problem* if this can be established (e.g. treat underlying depression first as in the case of Mary or social anxiety first if it has led to secondary depression). This is most efficient as the secondary problem often abates as the primary problem improves. Exceptions are:

  – If secondary depression is severe enough to prevent engagement or if suicide risk is high.
  – Substance misuse at a level that distorts the clinical presentation and brings it out of line with the model, e.g. alcohol or benzodiazepine dependency with intermittent withdrawal symptoms (often mimicking the primary disorder) leading to 'relief' drinking/benzodiazepine use. Here it is best to proceed to either detoxification and possibly addictions counselling, reduction of substance use to agreed 'safe' level or stabilisation by switching to a sister drug with less addictive potential (e.g. short-acting alprazolam to longer-acting clonazepam). This can be done through discussion at the multi-disciplinary team or through liaison with the patient's prescribing doctor.

• In cases of *full co-morbidity* (problems exist in their own right, neither clearly secondary to the other though they usually interact) it is necessary to be more flexible. It may make sense to work on the most disabling problem first or to tackle a more minor problem if it seems more approachable/more likely to be relieved quickly as a way of building therapeutic momentum. For example, in cases of co-morbid social anxiety and body-dysmorphic disorder (BDD) it is often preferable to work on the social anxiety elements initially, as BDD cognitions and images are more resistant to change and will in any case require therapeutic work involving social interaction.

• When the interaction of two problems is such that it is difficult to separate them out in CBT terms attempt a combined model to guide the work conceptually and to help with sequencing (see case of Leo). Depending on the model's complexity and the patient, this combined model may or may not need to be shared with the patient in keeping with the principle 'think complex act simple'.

THE CASE OF LEO'S FAINTING/PANIC ATTACKS

Leo presents with panic/agoraphobic avoidance of crowded places or confined spaces. On three occasions he has 'fainted' but recovered quite quickly (twice in a doctors' waiting area and once in a church). This is at odds with the Clark panic model (1986) where thoughts about collapse are seen as a misinterpretation of bodily sensations, usually the dizziness that comes with over-breathing. Further exploration at assessment reveals that when his panic is associated with 'gory' images of injury or illness (about one in five of his panics) the pattern differs from other episodes with more intense nausea, pale skin, sweats and sometimes fainting. He also reports avoiding gory scenes on TV/film and medical programmes.

  The problems are indentified as co-morbid panic/agoraphobia and blood injury phobia. Consideration is given to prioritising and sequencing interventions. Leo sees panic and agoraphobic avoidance as his main problem but through discussion with his therapist it becomes clear that to work effectively using the Clark panic model he will need to address his blood/injury phobia first as further fainting episodes would contradict the panic model. Therefore with his therapist he works through Öst's programme of applied tension (as a way of averting the fainting unique to blood/injury phobia) and graded exposure to gory scenes (Öst and Sterner, 1987). Soon he can encounter gory images without fainting and then proceeds successfully to standard panic/agoraphobia work. Figure 3.1 illustrates the two models at play in this case.

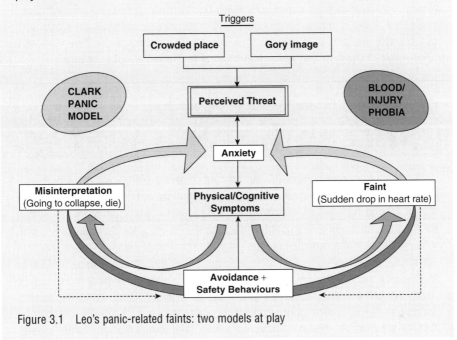

Figure 3.1   Leo's panic-related faints: two models at play

CASE CONCEPTUALISATION FROM BASIC PRINCIPLES

Not infrequently, cases require individualised case conceptualisation from basic cognitive therapy principles based on Aaron Beck's general cognitive model of emotional disorders (Beck, 1976), as detailed in leading practice texts (e.g. Judith Beck's *Cognitive Therapy: Basics and Beyond*, (1995) and the more recent *Collaborative Case Conceptualisation: Working Effectively with Clients in Cognitive-Behaviour Therapy* (Kuyken et al., 2009). In such cases no disorder specific model fully covers the complexity, historical context and uniqueness of the presentation. To avoid the pitfall of a 'Procrustean bed' situation, deriving an idiosyncratic conceptualisation is required. Beck's longitudinal approach connects early experience with core beliefs and underlying assumptions, which in turn determine – once triggered – the apparent maintenance cycle of thoughts, behaviours, feelings and emotions (Beck, 1976). The problem of course is that deriving such conceptualisations is not easy, despite the undoubted power and elegance of Beck's model. Kuyken et al. (2009) offer valuable guidance on how to address the real world challenges of case conceptualisation in a step-wise collaborative fashion and suggest additional elements (e.g. 'modes', 'strategies', and ways of incorporating strength and resilience). However, even in this approach Kuyken et al. acknowledge that the less experienced therapist may well struggle with complex cases. This results from the fact that such work requires high-level skills in collaboration, empiricism, guided discovery and Socratic questioning. It also requires knowledge of several disorder-specific models and including models of working with personality disorder (see Table 3.1). For this reason it is suggested that novice therapists gain experience with less complex cases initially, while more experienced trainees practise with only a small number of complex cases at any time. Exploring the challenges these complex cases bring is important. The case of Jack illustrates the challenges and rewards of conceptualising complex cases.

THE CASE OF JACK'S 'OBSESSIONS'

Jack has been referred with OCD but on assessment a picture emerges that suggests a more complex presentation. He was diagnosed with Asperger's syndrome at age 10 and had drifted in and out of various child and adult services without forming any substantial therapeutic attachments. He led a lonely, isolated life with little peer interaction outside his family and no vocational plan.

His OCD is assessed in CBT terms. Some of his thoughts are experienced as frightening and wrong (usually a thought that a particular person is bad or immoral) and are neutralised by grimacing or praying. Other cognitive events which had been labelled as obsessional ruminations (see Chapter 9) seem to be largely pleasurable fantasies involving imagined conversations with others, especially young women. These patterns of thinking were presented as problems and reasons why Jack had become more withdrawn and irritable. However, the OCD component seems minor and not very troubling. In fact the fantasies are more prominent and time consuming and appear to be Jack's way of coping with loneliness and loss. A careful ABC analysis (Kohlenberg and Tsai, 1991) reveals that his retreat into fantasy results in him becoming more isolated and lonely.

There are also prominent difficulties socialising – partly relating to social anxiety, partly to his difficulties with social literacy. Jack's therapist is beginning to feel swamped by the complexity of the case. Some elements are familiar (e.g. obsessions and social anxiety), whilst other elements (fantasies, Asperger's syndrome) don't seem to relate to any CBT model she is familiar with.

In discussion with her peer-supervision group his therapist realises that an individual case conceptualisation is needed, combined with very careful engagement and involvement of the multidisciplinary team. A case conceptualisation is worked out (Figure 3.2) but not shared in its entirety with Jack as it is feared that it may overwhelm him and lead to another early disengagement from services. However, it greatly helps the pacing and direction of the work.

From this formulation emphasis is given to slow and gentle engagement, building Jack's self-esteem (through challenging negative core beliefs and rigidly held, unhelpful rules), experimenting with alternatives to 'fantasies' to feel better and expanding his social network appropriately through commencing a carefully chosen rehabilitation course (with the help of an occupational therapist). Longer-term work is contracted with Jack (over 20 sessions). Specific work on obsessions and social anxiety is carried out as needed along the way using the appropriate models but care is taken not to detract from the main, schema-level focus of the therapy.

Key early experience/development

- Slow to socialise; diagnosed with Asperger's syndrome aged 10
- Bullied and teased at school for having few friends and no girlfriend
- Humiliated when tried to ask girl out
- Watched 'soaps' to feel better
- Mother protective; Jack seen as special and sensitive
- Enjoyed mathematics and loved working things out in his mind
- Prepared intensely for exams and excelled
- Religious upbringing; adopted concept of impure thoughts and sin

Core beliefs

- I am odd, a misfit
- Apart from my family, people are cruel
- I am clever, I can work things out
- God is all powerful

Rules/assumptions

- Must have girlfriend to be accepted
- Must plan things meticulously or they won't go well
- Must say just the right thing to be liked by a girl
- Fantasies about meeting girls; help me feel better and prepare me for talking with them
- Must not think or do anything wrong or my soul will be tainted

Maintenance cycles (brief summary of each)

Socially: view of self as misfit activated → safety behaviours such as rehearsing lines, trying to 'act cool' and focus on self → stilted and cold → mixed reaction from peers → further reinforcement of social anxiety and social avoidance, spend more time with family (social anxiety model)
Obsessions: angry/envious of other men → 'They are bad' → shouldn't think this of people, my soul will be damaged → neutralise by grimacing or prayer → reinforce cycle (OCD model)
Fantasies: feel sad, lonely → 'must work out way of feeling better, doing better' → imagine and 'practise' social scenes where successfully meets girls (fantasies) → temporary relief but later frustrated angry at time 'wasted' → reinforce core belief, 'I am odd, misfit'

Figure 3.2   Jack's case conceptualisation

AN EVOLVING PICTURE

Psychiatric disorders may be largely stable and lifelong (e.g. OCD present from childhood). More often than not, they fluctuate in response to life events, stages of development, mood, drugs or even the seasons. When several problems co-exist this can lead to a bewildering picture, where depression may be the main problem one day, anger the next and anxiety another. New disorders such as schizophrenia or bipolar affective disorder can also emerge, depending on life stage or genetic susceptibility. The effect of CBT itself also influences the picture. For example, a low-priority problem like flight phobia can become a central issue in a patient with social anxiety, who with treatment has secured a job involving international travel. For fluctuating complex cases, a detailed narrative of the pattern over years combined with longitudinal data (e.g. diaries) can clarify what seems to be a disparate picture and pave the way for case conceptualisation. The case of Jude illustrates such a fluctuating picture.

THE CASE OF JUDE'S SUDDEN RECOVERY

Jude has been suffering from a relapse of depression for three months and commenced an antidepressant (citalapram) one month ago. She presents for CBT treatment and over the first three sessions she works with her therapist through the initial stages of Beck's (1967) depression model using the *Mind Over Mood* workbook (Greenberger and Padeskey, 1995). This seems to be going well and at the fourth session Jude denies any negative cognition or emotions and prefers to talk at length about her plans to start a business based on a brilliant new idea. Her therapist feels she has made a good recovery and discharges her to return if problems arise. Jude returns two months later and despite remaining on the antidepressant her mood has dropped dramatically over the previous two weeks. This time she is very agitated, can't sleep and feels worse than ever. Her therapist has great difficulty getting Jude to focus on the CBT work as her mind is 'buzzing'.

Various obstacles may present as a result of failing to recognise fluctuating and changing presentations. For example, therapists can easily mistake a transformation or shift in a problem for a remission. Patients can be discharged early or frustration can arise as therapists resort to a 'forced fit' – trying unsuccessfully to fit a new presentation to an old conceptualisation.

Pause for thought before reading on. Do you have any theories as to what might be happening with Jude?

JUDE CONTINUED

The therapist liaises with Jude's psychiatrist and together they realise that Jude's mood is 'cycling' between depression, mild mania (hypomania) and a mixed state (dysphoric hypomania) suggestive of a form of bipolar affective disorder (see Chapter 9). The psychiatrist agrees to review her medication and consider mood-stabilising drugs. Her therapist raises the case in supervision and decides to continue the CBT work but shifts to a bipolar disorder model (Scott, 2001).

By using a time-line ('Life Chart', Scott, 2001) of previous depressive episodes and collateral information from her family, it becomes apparent that Jude has experienced hypomanic episodes in the past, while on and off antidepressant medication which were viewed as normal recovery. Using the bipolar disorder model, Jude records her moods and becomes able to more clearly recognise and identify her mood state. She works hard to stabilise her lifestyle and daily routines. Later in the course of therapy she identifies and challenges the conditional belief involved in her ascent into mania (Mansell and Lam, 2003) and her tendency to work to exhaustion as 'to be good enough I must achieve great things'.

SUMMARY

Patient presentations can be complex. It is important for therapists to carefully and collaboratively consider with clients the focus of CBT. This begins with a thorough initial assessment of the presenting problem. Disorder-specific models and their associated protocols are most efficient and effective and the 'best fit' disorder-specific model should be used whenever possible or used sequentially in cases of co-morbidity. However, not infrequently none of the established models fit the presentation sufficiently to allow progress to be made or the case is simply too complex for a one track approach. Here the therapist can rely on the basic principles of Beckian case conceptualisation to illuminate a way forward. Though leaving the beaten track comes with perils and challenges, it is preferable to persisting with an ill-fitting model.

REFERENCES

Barlow, D.H. (ed.) (2001) *Clinical Handbook of Psychological Disorders* (3rd edn). New York: Guilford Press.

Barlow, D.H., Craske, M.G., Cerny, J.A. and Klosko, J.S. (1989) 'Behavioural treatment of panic disorder', *Behavioural Therapy*, 20: 261–82.

Beck, A.T. (1967) *Depression: Causes and Treatment*. Philadelphia, PA: University of Pennsylvania Press.

Beck, A.T. (1976) *Cognitive Therapy and the Emotional Disorders.* New York: International University Press.

Beck, A.T., Emery, G. and Greenberg, R.L. (1985) *Anxiety Disorders and Phobias.* New York: Basic Books.

Beck, A.T., Freeman, A., Davis, D.D., Pretzer, J.J., Fleming, B., Arntz, A., Butler, A., Fusco, G., Simon, K.M., Beck, J.S., Morrison, A., Padesky, C.A. and Renton, J. (2004) *Cognitive Therapy of Personality Disorders* (2nd edn). New York: Guilford Press.

Beck, J.S. (1995) *Cognitive Therapy: Basics and Beyond.* New York: Guilford Press.

Borkovec, T.D. (1994) 'The nature, functions, and origin of worry', in G. Davey and F. Tallis (eds), *Worrying: Perspectives on Theory, Assessment, and Treatment.* New York: Wiley. pp. 5–33.

Borkovec, T.D. and Costello, E. (1993) 'Efficacy of applied relaxation and cognitive behavioural therapy in the treatment of generalised anxiety disorder', *Journal of Consulting and Clinical Psychology*, 51: 611–19.

Clark, D.M. (1986) 'A cognitive model of panic', *Behaviour, Research and Therapy*, 24: 461–70.

Clark, D.M. and Wells, A. (1995) 'A cognitive model of social phobia', in R. Heimberg, M. Liebowitz, D.A. Hope and F.R. Schneier (eds), *Social Phobia: Diagnosis, Assessment and Treatment.* New York: Guilford Press.

Dugas, M.J., Gagnon, F., Ladouceur, R. and Freeston, M.H. (1998) 'Generalised anxiety disorder: a preliminary test of a conceptual model', *Behaviour Research and Therapy*, 36: 215–26.

Dugas, M.J., Ladouceur, R., Freeston, M.H., Langlois. F., Provencher., M.D. and Boisvert, J.M. (2003) 'Group cognitive behavioural therapy for generalised anxiety disorder: treatment outcome and long term follow-up', *Journal of Consulting and Clinical Psychology*, 71: 821–5.

Ehlers, A. and Clark, D.M. (2000) 'A cognitive model of post-traumatic stress disorder', *Behaviour Research and Therapy*, 38: 319–45.

Fairburn, C.G., Cooper, Z. and Shafran, R. (2003) 'Cognitive behaviour therapy for eating disorders: a transdiagnostic theory and treatment', *Behaviour Research and Therapy*, 41: 509–28.

Fennell, M.J. (2004) 'Depression, low self-esteem and mindfulness', *Behaviour Research and Therapy*, 42: 1053–67.

Fennell, M.J. 'Overcoming Low Self-Esteem'. www.overcoming.co.uk

Foa, E.B. and Kozak, M.J. (1986) 'Emotional processing of fear: exposure to corrective information', *Psychological Bulletin*, 99: 20-35.

Fowler, D., Geraty, P. and Kuipers, E. (1995) *Cognitive Behaviour Therapy for Psychosis: Theory and Practice.* New York: Wiley.

Gilbert, P. (2009) *Overcoming Depression: A Self-help Guide Using Cognitive Behavioural Techniques.* www.overcoming.co.uk.

Greenberger, D. and Padesky, C.A. (1995) *Mind Over Mood: Change How You Feel by Changing the Way You Think.* New York: Guilford Press.

Hawton, K., Salkovskis, P.M., Kirk, J. and Clark, D.M. (1989) *Cognitive Behaviour Therapy for Psychiatric Problems: A Practical Guide.* Oxford: Oxford Medical Publications.

Jacobson, N.S., Dobson, K.S., Traux, P.A., Addis, M.E., Koerner, K., Gollan, J.K., Gortner, E. and Prince, S.E. (1996) 'A component analysis of cognitive behavioural treatment for depression', *Journal of Consulting and Clinical Psychology*, 64: 295–304.

Jones, M.K. and Menzies, R.G. (1998) 'Danger Ideation Reduction Therapy (DIRT) for obsessive compulsive washers: a controlled trial', *Behaviour Research and Therapy*, 36: 259–70.

Kingdon, D.G. and Turkington, D. (2002) *A Case Study Guide to Cognitive Therapy of Psychosis*. Chichester: Wiley.

Kohlenberg, R.J. and Tsai, M. (1991) *Functional Analytic Psychotherapy: Creating Intense and Curative Therapeutic Relationships*. New York: Springer.

Kuyken, W., Padesky, C.A. and Dudley, R. (2009) *Collaborative Case Conceptualization: Working effectively with Clients in Cognitive Behavioral Therapy* (Chapter 1). New York: Guilford Press.

Lam, D.H., Jones, S., Bright, J. and Hayward, P. (1999) *Cognitive Therapy for Bipolar Disorder: A Therapist's Guide to Concepts, Methods and Practice*. Chichester, NY: Wiley.

Lam, D., Watkins, E., Hayward, P., Bright, J., Wright, K., Kerr, N., Parr-Davis, G. and Sham, P. (2003) 'A randomised controlled study of cognitive therapy of relapse prevention for bipolar affective disorder - outcome of the first year', *Archives of General Psychiatry*, 60: 145–52.

Linehan, M.M. (1993) *Cognitive Behavioural Treatment of Borderline Personality Disorder*. New York: Guilford Press.

Mansell, W. and Lam, D. (2003) 'Conceptualising the cycle of assent into mania: a case report', *Behavioural and Cognitive Psychotherapy*, 31 (3): 363–7.

Marks, I.M. (1987) *Fears, Phobias and Rituals*. Oxford: Oxford University Press.

Mayer, V. (1966) 'Modification of expectations in cases with obsessional rituals', *Behaviour Research and Therapy*, 4: 273–80.

McDonough, M. (2008) *Beyond Copied Letters – Corresponding Directly with Patients*. Abstract BABCP Conference, Edinburgh, July.

Morrison, A. (2002) *A Casebook of Therapy for Psychosis*. New York. Brunner-Routledge.

Öst, L.G. and Sterner, U. (1987) 'Applied tension: a specific behavioural method for treatment of blood phobia', *Behaviour Research and Therapy*, 25: 25–30.

Padesky, C.A. and Mooney, K.A. (2006) *Uncover Strengths and Build Resilience Using Cognitive Therapy: A Four Step Model*. Huntington Beach, CA: Center for Cognitive Therapy.

Rapee R.M. and Heimberg R.G. (1997) 'A cognitive-behavioral model of anxiety in social phobia', *Behaviour Research and Therapy*, 35 (8): 741–56.

Safran, J.D. and Segal Z.V. (1990) *Interpersonal Processes in Cognitive Therapy*. New York: Basic Books.

Salkovskis, P.M. (1985) 'Obsessional compulsive problems: a cognitive behavioral analysis', *Behaviour Research and Therapy*, 23: 571–83.

Salkovskis, P.M. (1989) 'Cognitive behavioural factors and the persistence of intrusive thoughts in obsessional problems', *Behaviour Research and Therapy*, 27: 677–82.

Scott, J. (2001) *Overcoming Mood Swings: A Self Help Guide to Using Cognitive Behavioural Techniques'*. London: Robinson.

Veale, D., Gournay, K., Dryden, W. and Boocock, A. (1996) 'Body dysmorphic disorder: a cognitive behavioural model and a pilot randomised controlled trial', *Behaviour, Research and Therapy*, 34: 717–29.

Wells, A. (1997) *Cognitive Therapy of Anxiety Disorders: A Practice Manual and Conceptual Guide* (Chapter 9).Chichester: Wiley.

Williams, J.M., Duggan, D.S., Crane, C. and Fennell, M.J. (2006) 'Mindfulness-based cognitive therapy for prevention of recurrence of suicidal behavior', *Journal of Clinical Psychology*, 62: 2001–10.

Young, J.E. (1994) *Cognitive Therapy for Personality Disorders: A Schema Focused Approach*. Sarasota, FL: Professional Resource Press.

4

PACING, TIMING AND ENDINGS IN CBT

BRIAN FITZMAURICE

LEARNING OBJECTIVES

By the end of this chapter the reader should:

• develop insight into suitability, assessment and timing issues within CBT;
• have knowledge of factors which can delay, inhibit or undermine engagement, e.g. legal cases, insecure relationships, secondary gain;
• be aware of the patient's personal readiness/capacity for change and its impact on progress and resources;
• be cognisant of pacing and the change methodology around termination of therapy issues.

INTRODUCTION

CBT has a rich heritage of time-limited, manualised approaches to a range of specific disorders (e.g. OCD, depression and panic) derived from research trials. While some may view it as lacking sensitivity to the individual's circumstances (e.g. Clarke, 1999), it provides a structure for both patient and therapist, which can be beneficial and time efficient. Agreeing specific deadlines may create some pressure to address the realistic challenges of therapy within a specific time-frame, thereby driving change. Conversely, the practitioner may experience this as similar to a 'train timetable', predicting how and when interventions should be delivered for each disorder, and increasing expectations that specific points of recovery will happen along that journey. The 'CBT train', however, may struggle to leave the station, run behind schedule or not arrive at its desired destination. The naturally collaborative therapist may become an anxious driver of the therapy process, feeling responsible for setting the speed, route and destination of therapy.

CBT for the patient is a journey of personal discovery and change. The patient seeks a reliable and experienced guide in their therapist, to support them through unfamiliar, challenging and often frightening new terrain. The therapist should be:

- familiar with the potential hazards that might lie ahead and help the patient prepare for, persevere with and ultimately complete as much of the journey as possible, within the available time resource;
- aware when the ambitions of the patient are unlikely to be achieved, or likely to result in little progress or even a deterioration in their condition.

CBT literature suggests that early improvements are strong predictors of good outcome. Similarly the patient's personal sense of responsibility for change, their capacity to articulate and differentiate emotions, and the quality of therapeutic relationships are all predictors of good outcomes (Myhr et al., 2007). This gives insight into patient characteristics, but not how or at what pace to work with them. Gaining insight into what maintains and optimises progress at different stages in CBT or when to consider ending therapy belongs to the art, rather than science of CBT.

The aim of this chapter is to explore how some common obstacles in each unique therapeutic journey can be understood and managed. The reader will not be provided with a perfect 'train timetable' or an instruction manual but with an aid to reflecting upon and addressing presenting pitfalls. Thus, therapists are encouraged to:

- identify suitable patients carefully at the outset and, where possible, use screening tools to assess suitability for short term CBT;
- incorporate a review process at the start, middle and end of therapy that not only reviews progress against explicit goals but also examines the process of therapy;
- examine our own beliefs about providing therapy.

In this chapter, obstacles will be explored within three sections loosely based around engagement, timing of interventions and termination, each with supporting illustrative cases.

ENGAGEMENT

Readiness for Therapy

CASE OF PAULA – READY OR SUITABLE FOR CBT?

Paula has presented just after the third anniversary of the stillbirth of her first child. Her husband started to drink heavily after the stillbirth and within months they decided to separate, which has left her feeling abandoned and uncared for. She told her therapist (John) that, 'I never did anything to deserve such misery,' and 'I've been let down by everybody and everything that I ever valued'. In the weeks prior to attending for therapy, she was made redundant, along with all her work colleagues. She acknowledges that work was a significant loss for her, as her boss had been extremely supportive in the aftermath of the stillbirth and separation. He gave her extra leave to help her cope with these adversities. She is concerned about how she will manage without the income, routine and the regular social contact at work. She wants to turn the clock back and start the last three years all over again. John feels extremely sorry for Paula. He has a desperate sense that he must do something to protect her from her chronic sense of helplessness and hopelessness.

There is often considerable variability in the empathic response therapists experience towards different patients, with some seeming to be more deserving of therapy than others. Experiencing different levels of empathy for patients is normal as there are some patients with whom it is a challenge to establish rapport. Conversely there are many patients whose narrative is so compelling that it rightly invokes very strong urges to help and comfort. In most instances a therapist would readily tune into the tragedy of a stillbirth and the deep pain and loneliness associated with the break-up of relationships. In the face of such adversity it would seem almost churlish to regard Paula as unsuitable for short-term CBT. Therapists might feel duty bound to provide whatever support is necessary, in such an instance and overlook factors that might suggest little prospect of real change through a time-limited therapy such as CBT. It would naturally be within John's duty of care to instil a sense of hope and to develop with Paula an understandable model of how her difficulties have evolved and are maintained. Should he feel an obligation to contract to provide 12 sessions of CBT focused on her low mood and present sense of hopelessness?

John recognises a very strong pull to provide treatment for Paula. In his experience previous 'superhuman' efforts to help very needy individuals did not result in very much progress or meaningful change. His heart sometimes overrules his head in these instances. He agrees, following discussion with his supervisor, to carefully consider Paula's suitability for CBT. Safran et al. (1990: 226–47) designed a ten-item suitability scale for short-term therapy, which has some predictive power in determining those likely to achieve better outcomes:

(a) accessibility of automatic thoughts – can patient report on their thinking in problematic situations?
(b) awareness and differentiation of emotion – can they label different emotional states in the past and present? Can they work when these emotions are present?
(c) acceptance of personal responsibility for change – how much can they see their own role in recovery?
(d) compatibility with cognitive rationale – does the patient sees the value of key tasks in CBT? e.g can they relate to the link between thoughts, emotion and behaviour or doing homework?
(e) alliance potential (in-session evidence) – can you both relate to each other in sessions?

(f) alliance potential (out-of-session evidence) – do past meaningful relationships, including previous therapies, indicate the potential for a good therapeutic alliance?

(g) chronicity – are the problems to be addressed relatively longstanding or entrenched?

(h) security operations – can patient tolerate anxiety-producing session content? Does patient seek safety by engaging in intellectualisation or avoidance?

(i) focality – can he/she remain focused and work on a problem in depth?

(j) general optimism/pessimism regarding therapy – can they see a way forward or can you instil a sense of hope?

When John reviewed his initial two sessions with Paula using this scale he concluded that chronicity (three years of problems), difficulties differentiating and reflecting on emotions, and poor accessibility of automatic thoughts might question her suitability for CBT. He also noted a limited sense of personal responsibility for change in Paula and a desire to unburden herself of emotions in sessions with little interest in exploring how she herself may contribute to maintaining her distress. After due consideration John was clearer about what he was able to offer Paula that would be realistic for both of them.

Determining suitability at assessment is far from a precise science but Myhr et al. (2007) have researched predictors of outcome prospectively. They summarise the literature as follows:

> While diagnostic category and demographic factors are helpful guides to suggest who might benefit from CBT (female, married, employed, with anxiety disorders do best!), it remains a challenge to determine the likelihood of benefit for any given individual. To this end, research has focused on selected psychological characteristics of an individual. Skills in problem-solving skills predict better outcomes (Moorey et al., 2001). The conviction that one can do things for oneself, related to Bandura's concept of self-efficacy (Bandura, 2004), has been associated with better treatment response in studies examining predictors such as 'mastery' (Bowen et al., 1994), self-directedness (Bulik et al., 1998), 'ineffectiveness', self-esteem (Baell and Wertheim, 1992). Conversely, low treatment expectations (Chambless et al., 1997) and lack of motivational readiness for change (de Haan et al., 1997) have been negative predictors, as has excessive perfectionism. (Zuroff et al., 2000)

Emotional Awareness and Expression

Besides being characterologically appropriate for therapy and ready to target specific problems, patients need to be emotionally ready. Myhr et al.'s (2007) work concluded that the factors most predictive of good outcome in the Safran et al. (1990) scale were the capacity to be aware of, or differentiate, emotion and the absence of 'security operations', the observed in-session psychological and behavioural operations that reduce anxiety and maintain self-esteem. Security operations naturally interfere with emotional awareness. One can only be aware of specific emotions if one can focus on them and tolerate the painful or frightening consequences. Often too limited a range of emotions are elicited in early sessions predicting some difficulty with engagement (see Chapter 7). The therapist should be adequately skilled in facilitating emotional expression in the patient. In so doing, the encountered difficulties reflect the patient's security operations or limitations in awareness and differentiation of emotions, rather than a deficit in the therapist's ability.

Paula in this instance did not enlist security operations and in fact was overwhelmed by the intense emotions experienced. John reflected on the concept of an Optimal Emotional Learning Zone (see Figure 4.1). Paula's high levels of arousal and anger would likely preclude significant new learning from regular CBT sessions or a capacity to undertake meaningful between session work. Before Paula would be able to engage in a meaningful CBT approach, the distress and disappointment experienced about her job loss may need to dissipate. She would benefit from having greater clarity about what she was capable of changing. Conscious that Paula's sensitivity to feeling rejected and abandoned might be activated by a decision not to offer individual CBT, John proposed that she might join the service's generic anxiety management group as a means of providing support during this difficult transition in her life. By utilising the concept of an Extreme Emotional Energy Zone (Figure 4.1.) with Paula, John was also able to validate the level of distress that she was experiencing and to suggest ways of containing and managing it, thus increasing her readiness for further work.

Therapist Objectivity and Readiness to Offer Therapy

It is not only the patient but also the therapist who needs to be ready to resume therapy and to engage collaboratively. Therapy might need to be slowed down with some patients, until the therapist has a clearer picture. It can be challenging to feel unable to offer CBT to therapy deserving patients who present with extreme distress.

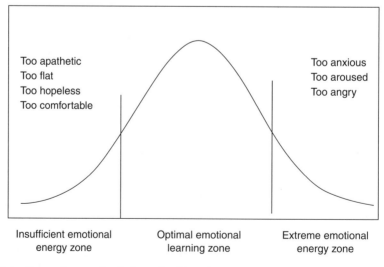

Figure 4.1   Curve of energy levels for optimal learning

Adapted from James et al. (2001) *Cognitive Therapy Scale – Revised Manual*, August. Northumberland, Tyne and Wear NHS Trust, UK.

Therapists may feel pressure to be seen to be 'doing something' for such a patient before they're ready. The following reflective questions may be helpful for the therapist:

- Where is the motivation for treatment coming from – therapist or client? Where is the responsibility for change?
- Is the client or therapist being pushed where he/she doesn't want to go?
- Is there a value in exploring what stage of change the client is at using the transtheoretical model of change (Prochaska and DiClemente, 1986)?

In Paula's case John rightly evaluated a limited sense of responsibility for change and that she was most likely to be in the pre-contemplative or contemplative phase in terms of readiness for change. Needleman (2003) proposes a growing body of evidence supports therapeutic effectiveness increasing when the therapist matches the intervention to the client's *stage* of change. Those in the *contemplation* stage are aware they have a problem and are seriously thinking about resolving it in the foreseeable future. However, they have not yet made the commitment to take action. There is ambivalence about giving up an old behaviour or replacing it with new behaviours or perhaps, as in Paula's case, there may be beliefs about low self-efficacy. Individuals in the *preparation* stage, in contrast, are developing specific plans for changing problematic behaviour, whilst in the *action* stage, overt behavioural changes have already started, or they may be restructuring their environment to support new behaviours. In a *maintenance* stage, new behaviours are stabilised to prevent relapse. To increase the likelihood of *maintenance*, Freeman and Dolan (2001) suggest adding pre-relapse, lapse and relapse stages to the Transtheoretical Model that might help guide therapists' interventions.

The converse of Paula's case can apply to the seemingly poor prognosis patient who, for example, has had multiple treatment failures and is then referred for CBT. Initial judgements about referrals can influence which patient is taken from a waiting list or which patient is prioritised or rejected in terms of offering CBT. The careful non-judgemental assessment considers potential suitability in the 'here and now'. A patient who has repeatedly relapsed into alcohol misuse and has remained stuck in difficult interpersonal relationships might cause initial therapist pessimism or aversion. Careful listening to the account of deep shame at a court appearance for drink driving however may enable the therapist to understand that the client has come to a turning point in their life. Therapist curiosity about the patient's rationale for seeking therapy, emotions and the context in which they arise is especially important in ensuring an unbiased assessment of possibly challenging chronic cases. In such cases, the assessment process for CBT ought to take place over two–three sessions to allow for the:

- appreciation of context;
- development of adequate empathy;
- capacity to consider suitability against objective criteria.

Planning further, more in-depth assessment sessions is preferable to prematurely contracting a number of sessions or deciding they are unsuitable for CBT. Such an in-depth assessment and feedback to the patient can in itself be useful therapeutically. The assessment process in CBT involves good interview skills, information gathering, synthesising and analytical questioning. Slowing the process down allows for proper use of these skills, so that assessment objectives are adequately achieved. Assessment should initially:

- Focus on the reasons for consultation/presentation, usually based on the central complaint or 'symptom story'. For example, Paula's therapist, John, felt uncertain about her motivation and central complaint. He therefore slowed down decision making and assessment by seeking supervision, before proceeding.
- Elaborate on the symptom story, incorporating a social and emotional story, before evolving it into the 'cognitive behavioural story' that guides intervention (see Figure 4.2). To clarify Paula's problem, John needed a more detailed contextualisation of it before developing it into a 'cognitive behavioural story'.
- Highlight the therapist's key role of empathically responding to emotions, which arise as part of that process and facilitate the ultimate articulation of a clearer 'emotional story'.

Unlike Paula, some clients can more readily express their internal world of emotions and thoughts, so that the rapport building and engagement process is achieved very smoothly. In such cases, it is vital that therapist develop skills for:

- Gentle clarification, summarising and checking the accuracy of their understanding about an individual's situation.
- Developing an appreciation of patients' social/personal context: this is particularly helpful in cases such as Paula's, where an individual struggles to convey what emotions

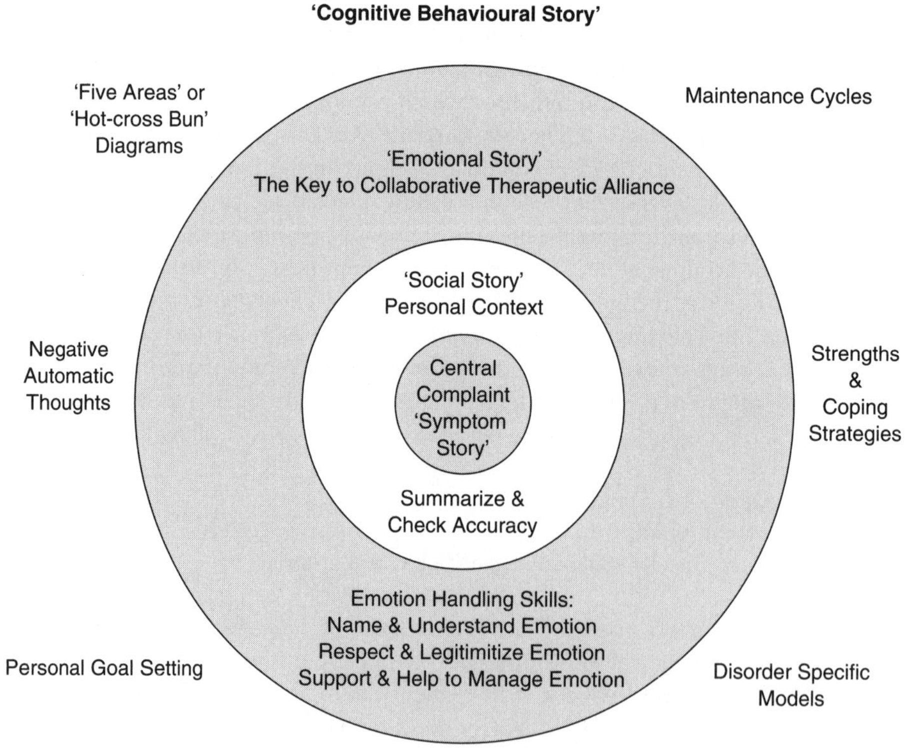

Figure 4.2 CBT assessment – building the story out from the central complaint

they are experiencing. It enables the therapist to empathically interpret information. John often found himself responding to Paula with statements such as, 'in that situation I guess I might have felt angry/ashamed etc' – and then checking with her if she had accurately understood their internal experience or his empathic response was correct.

The cycle of enquiring, summarising, responding to emotions and checking accuracy by eliciting clarification needs to be repeated many times. As the picture evolves, CBT elements/concepts can be incorporated to create the cognitive behavioural story that provides a logic and rationale for therapy. Rushing this process may negatively impact on the evolution of an early CBT 'case conceptualisation'. Once it is constructed and shared it can generate a major justification and logic for offering therapy and can be on its own, a strong driver for personal change, sometimes reducing the need for further sessions. If there is little clarity on a shared 'emotional story' or 'cognitive behavioural story' or alternatively, no evidence of clear behavioural change or goals after three or four assessment sessions, it is difficult to justify continuing CBT work. It then becomes important to suggest alternative supports and to instil hope in the absence of offering CBT sessions. The client's circumstances may change with time and the offer of re-assessment after six or 12 months may be helpful and appropriate, as happened in Paula's case.

Motivation for Seeking Therapy

CASE OF JAN – JUDGING TIMING AND SUITABILITY

Jan is a medical student who was involved as a passenger in a road traffic accident. She has taken two years out of her studies to recover and has symptoms suggestive of PTSD, along with chronic back and leg pain. She is unable to tolerate therapeutic doses of antidepressant medication, which significantly improved sleep and nightmares and lessened her anxiety levels. She is reluctant to be dependent on people and wants to be able to return to her studies and career to achieve personal independence. She tries to avoid becoming emotional in sessions. Jan has a legal case against the driver of the car which hit them. Whilst Jan has set specific goals for therapy to increase physical and social activity levels – she is unable to complete any homework tasks in either of these domains after eight sessions of trauma-focused CBT. Peter, her therapist, has now received a request for a legal report detailing Jan's diagnosis, response to treatment and prognosis. Jan wishes to prioritise legal issues and the report within their agenda setting, and finds it difficult to shift her attention to other areas. When she discusses these issues her emotions are palpable and Jan says that she cannot make progress until she knows what Peter is going to write in his report. Peter is now questioning whether Jan is suitable for CBT or if it was the right time for her to have engaged in this work.

Therapeutic progress can be affected by the motivation for seeking therapy. For many reasons, clients' problems can appear to not resolve, in spite of therapists' best efforts, leading to frustration. Legal cases such as that of Jan are not an uncommon example of non-change-focused motivation for seeking therapy, particularly if clients have a history of trauma, accidents or workplace bullying. Such cases can cast unhelpful shadows across the therapeutic process. The timing and expectations of therapy need to be carefully considered, including the detailed assessment of issues of secondary gain. Consideration would need to be given to the impact of a reduction or resolution of symptoms or disability upon the legal case and potential compensation. Explicit dialogue about such issues are generally best addressed prior to contracting to provide an agreed number of CBT sessions. Both client and therapist are then clear that litigation may potentially impact on the recovery process and it is necessary to openly negotiate management issues around this. The sequencing of goals may require that agreeing on the focus of therapy (i.e. legal or clinical) becomes the initial goal. Peter, for example, needed to clarify Jan's expectations, in spite of the discomfort and awkwardness associated with such a discussion.

Ethical Dilemmas

A specific, important issue, which needs to be addressed at the outset, is the capacity to provide a legal report as part of the therapeutic process. The CBT therapist, whilst aspiring to a non-judgemental stance in therapy, is obligated to provide an honest independent professional report to a court. The therapist who is usually entitled to payment for such a report may already be biased, based on a Rogerian unconditional positive regard for the patient. Several factors associated with the introduction of legal process may affect the therapeutic relationship, and when and how interventions are delivered, including:

- *Significant financial issues at stake*: Peter, for example, might experience a pressure to conform to Jan's account of events and that preferred by his legal representative.
- *The triangulated relationships (see Figure 4.3) which inevitably occur*: all parties (e.g. Peter, Jan and the legal advisers) are liable to be affected by any of the other's actions.
- *A conflict of interest*: perhaps, legal reports should preferably not be written by the treating therapist – if possible and practical, it might be helpful for Peter to ask a colleague or other team member to provide an independent report.

However, Peter could be seen as having a deeper understanding of Jan's experience than a clinician seeing her once off, for the sake of a legal report. Report writing may allow Peter to engage with and describe the complexity of this case, recognising the impact of the legal process, in a way that is helpful for Jan.

An important ethical question relates to the timing of the writing of the report. It is helpful for therapists to have clear guiding principles on how to deal with such requests, to avoid feeling compromised in the process of providing a report. Options may be to:

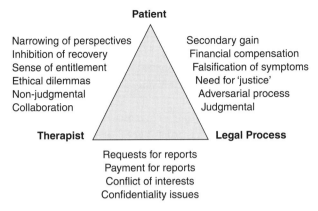

Figure 4.3   Legal triangulation – hazards for patients and therapists

1 limit report writing to the assessment phase, where no contract for therapy is agreed;
2 complete a report at the end of the therapy process.

In general the CBT therapist espouses a non-judgemental stance around issues of personal responsibility for change. Apportionment of blame or responsibility may need to be expanded, critically evaluated and commented upon by both therapist and client in the course of their work. Jan, for example, appears at times more interested in the need to experience a sense of justice, prioritising preparations for her court case over other activities. She has difficulty seeing a way forward without someone being held accountable for what happened in the road traffic accident and believes she is deserving of adequate compensation for the pain and suffering she has experienced.

The adversarial legal process necessarily tries to reduce events into clear cause and effect linkages to identify absolute responsibilities. Therapeutically, this approach is error prone, particularly to selective abstraction, focusing on one aspect of the presentation to the neglect of the others. The timing of the introduction of and focus on legal process can thus:

- *Inhibit therapist focus*: Peter might find it difficult to broaden perspectives as a method of addressing thinking errors that compound Jan's difficult emotional state.
- *Cause an energy diversion*: preparing for a court case is stressful, taking up time and energy that needs to be available for therapeutic change and recovery; while focused on the legal process, for example, Jan was unmotivated to collaborate therapeutically.

Exploring these issues before continuing therapy is beneficial. In the case of Jan, for example, Peter used a 'responsibility pie' to look at the different contributions to her disabling chronic pain. At first, she had estimated that the driver in the accident held at least 80 per cent of the responsibility for her current suffering. She then started to reflect on other contributory factors. This included a previously resolved sports injury to her back, her own reluctance to regularly use analgesic medication except when pain was extreme and regular conflict with her parents which intensified her experience of pain. In addition her lawyer advised her to avoid seeking work, to maximise any potential compensation offered or awarded. Jan understood many of these factors were beyond her control but only then was it possible to start focusing on therapeutic change.

Peter also emphasised the concepts of Maslow's Hierarchy of Human Needs (1943), which proposes that higher-order needs such as justice should be underpinned by the achievement of more basic needs. Jan readily recognised that her unstable tenancy was a significant worry and raised the prospect of her having to return to live with her argumentative and unsupportive parents. She could also see that her former peer group in college, from which she had cut herself off had previously given her a sense of belonging. This discussion of her needs created a lot of cognitive dissonance for Jan, about the status quo and her reluctance to undertake tasks between sessions. Timing of interventions and therapy progress are thus affected by a variety of factors, which need to be carefully assessed and conceptualised. An acknowledgement that CBT may sometimes be of limited value to the patient and even damaging, if other significant needs are ignored or not properly addressed, is also important.

PACING AND TIMING OF INTERVENTION

CASE OF GEOFF – PACING, SEQUENCING AND PRIORITISATION

Ann, a trainee CBT therapist coming to the end of a CBT training course, is working with Geoff, a middle-aged unemployed man with social anxiety disorder. Geoff is very reticent in sessions and appears to have very limited goals for therapy. He would like to be able to go to the library regularly, which he enjoyed during a previous period of unemployment. Despite his social circle being restricted to family members and his wife, he cannot identify any other social situations that he would target for a CBT focus. Geoff has attended three previous therapists and disengaged after three–four sessions on each occasion. Ann experienced some difficulties using a CBT model for social anxiety in a previous case and is very keen 'to get it right' with Geoff. She has limited time before she must submit a final recording of a CBT session to her course for assessment and is eager to get a good mark and do well.

Manualised CBT approaches for different disorders suggest the approximate number of sessions, and give guidance on how the treatment should be sequenced and prioritised. However, client work does not generally fit so neatly into a box. The individual's emerging story, aspirations, goals and progress are crucial determinants of the correct pacing, prioritising and sequencing of therapeutic work. In Ann's case, if she feels under pressure, there may be a temptation to rush through assessment and impose the first model that seems to fit with Geoff. Skills in problem identification and model selection will be crucial here (see Chapter 3). Even when the diagnosis is clear and a disorder specific model is chosen, the nature of therapy proposed may not be what the patient seeks or requires. When to intervene and with what interventions becomes crucial.

Therapists may need to suspend the manualised approach, hold back on the application of change methods and attend more closely to therapy process. Ann, for example, had plans for behavioural experiments, panic induction and work on core beliefs. Geoff, on the other hand was weighing up whether to disclose a history of sexual abuse. There was value in respecting what Geoff wanted rather than 'deciding' what he needed. This required time for identifying what it was that Geoff wanted and evolving a clear early conceptualisation. The value of early and evolving case conceptualisation is articulated and emphasised by Kuyken et al. (2009). They use the metaphor of a crucible bringing together an understanding of the individual's problem and goals with disorder-specific models of treatment. This can provide sufficient flexibility to hold together those two potentially competing dynamics, while also highlighting the individuals strengths and resilience in the same case conceptualisation. Ann, for example, discussed Geoff with her supervisor and they speculated that Geoff had difficulties with trust in most relationships. This seemed to significantly contribute to both his social avoidance and his early disengagement with previous therapists. Important considerations in such cases may include:

- *Rapport and trust*: Ann and her supervisor understood that a higher level of rapport and trust was needed before Geoff became comfortable setting an agenda for real change in social situations.
- *Guided discovery and collaborative conceptualisation*: Ann decided to use guided discovery, 'five-areas' diagrams and maintenance cycles to enable patterns in interpersonal relationships to be more explicit (see Chapter 5).
- *Exploration and validation*: Ann explored and acknowledged how difficult it was for Geoff to attend therapy. Geoff experienced significant feelings of shame, which emerged through a longitudinal conceptualisarion of his problems.
- *Collaborative decisions on the timing of interventions*: it was only after ten sessions of exploration, as above, that Geoff himself prioritised exposure based social anxiety work.
- *Acceptance of therapist motives*: as they proceeded to work on his social anxiety, Ann appreciated her own drive for a quick, comprehensive and 'perfectionistic' set of objectives that was different to Geoff's more limited goals based on her own academic needs.
- *Therapist/patient mismatch*: Ann was at times frustrated at Geoff's lack of ambition for himself and worried how her work would be evaluated by the examiners on her course; this highlights the possibility of a 'mismatch' in beliefs held by the client and therapist about what and when goals should be achieved, which can pose an obstacle to therapy.
- *Therapist self-reflection*: Ann for example, was able to reflect on her non-collaborative approach to goal setting and how she was pushing, setting and shaping the early

direction of her CBT sessions. This was an understandable and not unexpected position for a trainee completing a course to experience. Her supervisor normalised the tension associated with assessment that often prompts trainees to meticulously plan their sessions without due consideration to flexibility and appropriate pacing of sessions.

TERMINATION OF THERAPY

CASE OF ALISON – UNFORESEEN DISENGAGEMENT

Alison described difficult relationships with both her parents. Once she had moved out of home to go to boarding school as a teenager, she had strived for greater independence in life. She dropped out of university and adopted an alternative lifestyle, living in a large shared house called 'The Commune'. She had developed panic disorder and was extremely troubled that she was not able to manage this on her own. She had regularly used meditation and mindfulness as part of a healthy lifestyle. She feels defeated and frustrated at not overcoming the regular panic symptoms. 'I start to feel as weak as dishwater' and 'I feel as if I am falling into oblivion,' she told Joanne, her CBT therapist. Alison also acknowledged that she had some awareness of longstanding low self-esteem. She appeared to understand, and was reassured by a CBT model of misinterpretation of body symptoms as a trigger and maintaining factor for her panic. She rejected enquiry about underlying depression, evident in measures used at the time of assessment. She abruptly stopped attending her CBT with Joanne after six sessions and has not replied to telephone invitations to return to therapy.

Unplanned Endings

The termination of therapy can be either planned or unplanned. Joanne, for example, finds herself in a scenario familiar to all therapists, when a patient abruptly and unexpectedly disengages. This has many consequences for therapists, who may question what they have done wrong and wonder how they might have prevented this therapeutic impasse. If the client returns to therapy, it is an opportunity to understand more fully the factors, which contributed to the decision to disengage. In the absence of them returning, the therapist is left in a state of uncertainty. Therapists like Joanne may do well to reflect on positive research on early termination of therapy. Westmacott and Hunsley (2010) found several reasons for early termination, including:

- *feeling better.* 43 per cent of patients terminated because they felt better. Rather than termination of therapy being premature the patient may have been the better judge of the timing of termination;

- *subjectively believing that they have completed therapy* (13 per cent);
- *thinking the problem would get better without more professional help* (6.6 per cent);
- *wanting to solve the problem without professional help* (5 per cent).

This study indicates that the patient's own ongoing personal justification for continuing treatment may have dissipated in about two thirds of cases. Murdin (2000) further argues that therapists are not always good at recognising the right time for a patient to end therapy and, furthermore, asks whether the therapist is looking for something 'modest and attainable or an ideal, which will never arrive'. Only 20 per cent in this study indicated dissatisfaction with therapy or the approach of the professional. Whilst this study looks at the whole range of psychotherapies available, rather than specifically CBT, there is no reason to assume major differences.

Relational Schemas in Termination

Historically termination has often been viewed as a pivotal part of the therapy process. A psychodynamic perspective infers that, irrespective of whether therapy is short or long term, termination represents one of the most critical challenges to the therapist and can determine whether therapy turns out to be a success or a failure. This tradition paints a starker and more worrying picture for therapists as they try to understand patient disengagement. Joanne, for example, was also aware of a growing CBT literature focused on identifying and resolving 'ruptures' in the alliance as a critical component of CBT. Katzow and Safran (2007) suggest that when maladaptive relational schemas are triggered in therapy, 'ruptures' in the therapeutic alliance are likely to occur. Exploration of the 'rupture' theoretically allows opportunities to elucidate a dysfunctional cognitive-interpersonal style that the client might be enacting with the therapist (and in other interpersonal situations) (see Chapter 2).

Alison's interpersonal beliefs, expectations and appraisal processes may play a central role in perpetuating dysfunctional cognitive and interpersonal cycles. These cognitions may hold the possibility of working towards a more collaborative and mutually satisfying decision to end therapy. However, how could Joanne have put this into practice in normal CBT sessions, where her explicit and justifiable focus has mainly been on Alison's panic problems and goals to reduce frequency of panic symptoms?

Hypotheses around such issues might be generated in supervision and are worthy of reflection. In Joanne's case, rather than being the subject of speculation and discussion they were written down and incorporated into Alison's case conceptualisation. Evidence to support significant interpersonal patterns will ideally be evident in review of recordings used for supervision and through case discussion. As was the case with Joanne, the supervisory review of session recordings is crucial. If the therapist still struggles with the reasonable assumption that the patient is recovering or rediscovering her autonomy, a range of alternative possibilities may be considered in supervision, including intra- and inter-personal factors.

Intra-personal factors: Patient choice to terminate therapy early may be due to personal reasons. In Alison and Joanne's case, reflective questions included:

- Is Alison ending an undesired interaction with Joanne that profoundly challenges her need for privacy, containment of emotion or other and self-preserving mechanisms?
- Has Alison become frustrated at reaching a certain challenging point in therapy?
- Has Alison agreed to too many sessions or prompted the setting of too many goals?
- Does Alison wish to avoid exploration or conflict about how lifestyle/contextual issues may be maintaining her anxiety/low self-esteem?

Inter-personal factors: There may be relational reasons between therapist and patient and reflection may be helpful. Reflective questions in Alison and Joanne's case included:

- Is Alison testing Joanne's commitment to her?
- Are issues of relative power and status inhibiting the therapeutic relationship?
- Does Alison need to leave before the planned ending to retain her power in the relationship?
- Has their joint focus on CBT tasks or homework rather than on Alison's suffering triggered a sense of invalidation?

Should the patient not return to therapy to help answer such questions, there are several options open to the therapist, including:

- *Written communication*: this can normalise the break and acknowledge some of the possible reasons for termination as discussed earlier.
- *Empowering the patient*: giving the patient the decision to re-establish contact can do this. For example, Joanne's letter could indicate that an assumption would be made that she is no longer seeking therapy if she has not made contact by a certain date. In the absence of a response it is important to respect this implicit decision and update the referring agent of the client's status.

Keeping Alison's case open may not be justified in the absence of an explicit indication of her wanting to return to therapy. However, a review of previous session notes and reflection on the overall therapy process can be a rich learning experience for the therapist. In so doing, themes that might have predicted disengagement might be identified. Hypotheses may be generated as to how the therapy process might have been concluded in a more predictable manner with the clarity that objectives of therapy have been met. These hypotheses are nonetheless untestable and if issues are not obvious or easily identified one should probably assume the abrupt termination might not have been preventable or indeed retrievable. Such abrupt terminations might be better reframed as a 'normal' ending of therapy and as an integral step of any change process, similar to other unexpected breakthroughs in therapeutic work.

Where possible, it is good to seek feedback from clients who terminate early to clarify issues around this. A feedback survey to clients who drop out of treatment may offer further information on the disengagement process in a service.

Planned Endings

CASE OF GEORGE – WHAT IF I CAN'T COPE?

George is at the end of 18 contracted sessions of CBT with his therapist, Paul. The issues addressed are severe depression and marital conflict. George discontinued taking his antidepressant medication after four sessions of CBT. He attended regularly and is a model patient, completing all homework tasks and has now returned to work as a teacher. He achieved all the initial goals of therapy and feels confident about the future of his marriage for the first time in many years. He does retain some apprehension that his recovery could be impeded by events in the future. George specifically worries that if he becomes fatigued or has sleep disturbance for a few nights that he would rapidly crumble and be very quickly unable to work again. Paul feels very satisfied with their therapeutic work so far and is keen to protect the gains that George has made. His supervisor highlights Paul's strong drive to justify further sessions for George over several months to consolidate on relapse prevention work they are now completing.

In most cases, planned endings or 'clean breaks' from therapy occur without significant, identified difficulty for either therapist or patient, or any need for further sessions. However, further follow-up can be necessary, either with the treating therapist, an alternative clinician or another member of the clinical care team. Ideally, planning for termination should begin at the outset of therapy. Once a specific number of sessions are contracted or a specific interval of time has passed the therapist needs to flag up the approach of the agreed session limit. The therapist can do this unobtrusively during agenda setting. Some examples of helpful statements may include:

- 'We have now completed the '*nth*' of the '*x*' sessions we agreed at the outset.'
- 'We have '*n*' weeks to go before we have a review of progress as agreed.'
- 'We have '*n*' sessions left, so I think it would be useful to review how we are progressing and discuss how it feels to be coming towards the end of therapy.'

Orientation of the patient to the time-limited nature of therapy is important and helps reduce the client's anxiety or unease about finishing up in therapy. Ending psychotherapy within the patient–therapist dyad is an issue that can create anxiety for both client and therapist. The bond between the therapist and client can be strong, leading to the activation of schemas, so that termination of therapy becomes difficult. For example, in George's case, his dependence and incompetence schemas were triggered, leading to fears that he would not cope alone and that Paul would not be there for him. Careful planning can reduce the anxiety and challenge associated with endings in therapy.

Preparing to End Therapy

There is a rich legacy of literature stretching right back to Freud around termination of therapy. Some theories (e.g. psychoanalytic) conceptualise anxiety at termination as a re-enactment of important early intra-psychic conflicts or historic loss or separation experiences. The CBT therapist seeks to find and explore this within a shared longitudinal CBT case conceptualisation. For example, within their 18 sessions, Paul had collaborated with George on a shared conceptualisation, aspects which included core beliefs ('I am defective') and assumptions ('if I can sleep, then I can get through tomorrow'). They used this to guide and address relapse prevention strategies. The conceptualisation provided George with a memorable understanding of the origins of his problems, their likely triggers (including therapy termination) and maintenance, as well as their management (e.g. how they were more successfully managed during therapy). Therapy therefore provides the source of a written 'blueprint' for how to deal with problems and termination is an opportunity to review, reinforce and write out that blueprint for future reference. Carefully planned endings provide an opportunity to reinforce positive new beginnings and learn abilities to identify early signs of relapse.

For individuals with recurrent problems a 'pre-relapse' stage can often be clearly identified with typical triggers and the emotional, biological, cognitive and behavioural profiles of their unique 'early relapse signature' or early warning signs. Documenting these and identifying strategies that reliably manage pre-relapse is central to 'recovery' processes such as Wellness and Recovery Action Plans (WRAP) (Copeland, 1995). Clients in WRAP engage in 'crisis planning' and also enlist the help of others as 'spotters' identifying pre-relapse and use written advance directives to guide interventions that will prevent or manage relapse. Similarly the collaborative generation of a written relapse prevention plan in CBT creates a readily accessible reminder of the strategies that can be meaningfully applied by George if symptoms re-emerge

As part of relapse prevention, George needs to distinguish a 'lapse' from a 'relapse' as:

- *Lapses*: these are setbacks, which indicate the brief return of a symptom, problematic thinking or behavioural patterns (e.g. isolated episode of panic or gambling). In George's case, this might be one or two spontaneously resolving nights of insomnia without leading to a full relapse.
- *Relapses*: are a full return of the original cluster of symptoms with significant impairments in functioning.

In structuring relapse prevention in sessions, therapists may need to plan over a few sessions. A mistake made by some novice therapists is to leave relapse-prevention to the last session. This reduces its importance and limits the learning opportunities for the client. Having a clearly planned number of sessions and review points allows for the planning of relapse prevention two or three sessions before the end, the consideration of any anxieties and reviewing of learning that needs to be revisited. Therapists may need to consider work on developing skills and strategies for managing and neutralising lapses (Grant, P., 2005):

- *Identifying high-risk situations for lapses*: for example, Paul helped George to look at two possible lapses, either becoming fatigued or a return of poor sleep. They considered scenarios, which typically had a high risk of causing fatigue and sleep disturbance (e.g. when tired, staying at work longer to complete tasks and suspending all interests outside of work).
- *Learning coping skills*: Paul and George agreed that George would go for a walk on the way home from work – whatever the weather – which he always found invigorating. He would also avoid a previous habit of often taking a nap on his return home from work.
- *Rehearsing coping skills in challenging situations*: a carefully planned relapse prevention period allowed Paul and George to rehearse the strategies.
- *Addressing lifestyle balance issues*: these may include some of the coping strategies as was the case for George.

In George's case, a clearly planned review of therapy and relapse prevention lead to Paul seeking supervision about George's anxieties. Consequently, it was agreed that sessions would be spaced at four-week intervals to facilitate George's habituation to longer intervals between sessions in preparation for the ending of therapy.

Patients and therapist may need to guard against unrealistic optimism and expectations. It is natural for patients to have reservations and anxieties at termination and therapists like Paul may need to reassure the patient that having some sense of anxiety might promote healthy vigilance about his mental health rather than imply impending relapse. Such anxieties can persist and affect both therapist and patient. For example, George's perceived dependence might have been complemented by Paul's need to feel valued as a caregiver. Sometimes previously undisclosed difficulties can emerge at termination. In Paul and George's case, sensitive exploration of the perceived anxiety revealed that George's wife had a serious alcohol problem and constantly threatened to leave him when intoxicated. He had felt it would be disloyal to his wife to disclose this earlier. Although not in their shared case conceptualisation, George understood that his recovery from depression had been strongly linked with his improved capacity to manage her unpredictable and at times abusive behaviour towards him. In such cases, it is necessary to consider the follow-up support for the patient and whether the treating therapist is the best person to continue in the role, or if another clinician/service would be more appropriate. In George's case, he agreed to consult with his GP, who would see his wife and try to engage her in seeking help for her alcohol-abuse problems. If George himself needed further support, one to three monthly 'booster' sessions and/or telephone contact could be introduced to consolidate learning of functional approaches and to reduce the risks of relapse. Studies such as Clarke et al. (1999) suggest that booster sessions don't reduce relapse rates in adolescents who already had recovered with CBT but do appear to be helpful in achieving further recovery in patients not fully recovered at the end of initial CBT sessions.

CONCLUSION

Revisiting the analogy of therapy being similar to a train journey referred to at the outset of the chapter, it is helpful to consider that each patient embarks on their own personal journey. As a train travels from station to station, with individual passengers' journeys ending at different points, there are many possible endings for the therapeutic journey, planned or unplanned, final or temporary. Parts of every CBT journey must be taken alone, leaving the guiding therapist behind. Rather than aiming for a final and rather elusive destination of 'cure', therapists may need to aim for 'enablement'. For example, a therapist like Paul might need to acknowledge that it is 'good enough' just to take George 'far enough' and encourage him to complete the journey using the insights gleaned through therapy. Enablement isn't about planning or mapping out an entire journey. More effective ways of coping with key challenges can become available if chosen by the patient. Respect and a truly non-judgemental stance in CBT enable the patient freedom to complete their journey without further input or approval.

LEARNING ACTIVITIES

A Read *Oxford Textbook of Psychotherapy* (Gabbard et al., 2005):
   - Chapter 2 'Cognitive and Behavioural Therapies'
   - Chapter 5 'Cognitive Behavioural Group Interventions'
   - Chapter 11 'Cognitive Behavioural Therapy for Mood Disorders'

B Write down a three-column list of the type of cases that (1) you are regularly eager to take on for CBT, (2) you regularly avoid and (3) you regularly continue to see beyond the agreed number of sessions. Are there any explanations for this pattern?

C Draw up your own personal table of rules for dealing with patients who have legal cases.

REFERENCES

Baell, W.K. and Wertheim, E.H. (1992) 'Predictors of outcome in the treatment of bulimia nervosa', *British Journal of Clinical Psychology*, 31: 330–2.

Bandura, A. (2004) 'Swimming against the mainstream: the early years from chilly tributary to transformative mainstream', *Behaviour Research and Therapy*, 42: 613–30.

Bowen, R., South, M., Fischer, D. and Looman, T. (1994) 'Depression, mastery and number of group sessions attended predict outcome of patients with panic and agoraphobia in a behavioral/medication program', *Canadian Journal of Psychiatry*, 39: 283–8.

Bulik, C.M., Sullivan, P.F., Joyce, P.R., Carter, F.A. and McIntosh, V.V. (1998) 'Predictors of 1-year treatment outcome in bulimia nervosa', *Comprehensive Psychiatry*, 39: 206–14.

Chambless, D.L., Tran, G.Q. and Glass, C.R. (1997) 'Predictors of response to cognitive-behavioral group therapy for social phobia', *Journal of Anxiety Disorders*, 11: 221–40.

Clarke, G.N., Rohde, P., Lewinsohn, P.M., Hops, H. and Seeley, J.R. (1999) 'Cognitive-behavioral treatment of adolescent depression: efficacy of acute group treatment and booster sessions', *Journal of The American Academy of Child and Adolescent Psychiatry*, 38 (3): 272–9.

Clarke, L. (1999) 'Nursing in search of a science: the rise and rise of the new nurse brutalism', *Mental Health Care*, 2: 270–2.

Copeland, M.E. (1995) *Wellness and Recovery Action Plan*. Dummerston, VT: Peach Press.

de Haan , E., van Oppen, P., van Balkom, A.J.L.M., Spinhoven, P., Hoogduin, K. A. L. and VanDyck, R. (1997) 'Prediction of outcome and early *vs* late improvement in obsessive compulsive disorder patients treated with cognitive behaviour therapy and pharmacotherapy', *Acta Psychiatrica Scandinavica*, 96: 354–61.

Freeman, A. and Dolan, M. (2001) 'Revisiting Prochaska and DiClemente's stages of change theory: an expansion and specification to aid in treatment planning and outcome evaluation', *Cognitive and Behavioral Practice*, 8: 224–34

Gabbard, G., Beck, J. and Holmes, J. (2005) *Oxford Textbook of Psychotherapy*. Oxford: Oxford University Press.

Grant, P., Young, P. and De Rubeis, R. (2005) 'Cognintive and behavioural therapies', in G. Gabbard, J. Beck and J. Holmes (ed.), *Oxford Textbook of Psychotherapy*. Oxford: Oxford University Press. pp. 17–18.

James, I., Blackburn, I.-M, and Reichelt., K.A. (2001) *Cognitive Therapy Scale – Revised Manual*, August. Northumberland, Tyne and Wear NHS Trust.

Katzow, A.W. and Safran, J.D. (2007) 'Recognizing and resolving ruptures in the therapeutic alliance', in P. Gilbert and R.L. Leahy, *The Therapuetic Relationship in the Cognitive Behavioural Psychotherapies*. London: Routledge. pp. 99–103.

Kuyken, W., Padesky, C. and Dudley, R. (2009) *Collaborative Case Conceptualisation – Working Effectively with Clients in Cognitive Behavioural Therapy*. New York: Guilford Press.

Maslow, A.H. (1943) 'A Theory of Human Motivation', *Psychological Review*, 50 (4): 370–96.

Moorey, S., Holting, C., Hughes, P., Knynenberg, P. and Michael, A. (2001) 'Does problem solving ability predict therapy outcome in a clinical setting?', *Behavioral and Cognitive Psychotherapy*, 29: 485–95.

Murdin, L (2000) *How much is enough?: Endings in Psychotherapy and Counselling*. London: Routledge.

Myhr, G., Talbot, J., Lawrence, A. and Pinard, G. (2007) 'Suitability for short-term cognitive-behavioural therapy', *Journal of Cognitive Psychotherapy*, 21 (4): 334–45.

Needleman, L.D. (2003) 'Case conceptualization in preventing and responding to therapeutic difficulties', in R. Leahy (ed.), *Roadblocks in Cognitive Behavioural Therapy*. New York: Guilford Press. pp. 5–6.

Prochaska, J.O. and DiClemente, C.C. (1986) 'Towards a comprehensive model of change', in W.R. Miller and N. Heather (eds), *Treating Addictive Behaviors: Processes of Change*. New York: Plenum Press. pp. 3–27.

Safran, J.D., Segal, Z.V., Shaw, B.F. and Vallis, T.M. (1990) 'Patient selection for short-term cognitive therapy', in J.D. Safran and Z.V. Segal (eds), *Interpersonal Process in Cognitive Therapy*. New York: Basic Books. pp. 226–47.

Westmacott, R. and Hunsley, J. (2010) 'Reasons for termination psychotherapy: a general population study', *Journal of Clinical Psychology*, 66 (9): 965–77.

Zuroff, D.C., Blatt, S.J., Sotsky, S.M., Krupnick, J.L., Martin, D.J., Sanislow, C.A., III, et al. (2000) 'Relation of therapeutic alliance and perfectionism to outcome in brief outpatient treatment of depression', *Journal of Consulting and Clinical Psychology*, 68: 114–24.

5

SIGNIFICANT OTHERS

IMPACT ON CLIENT AND THERAPY

CRAIG CHIGWEDERE

LEARNING OBJECTIVES

By the end of this chapter, the reader should:

- be familiar with the way significant others can create therapeutic obstacles;
- evolve an idiosyncratic, CBT-based formulation of a relationship between a patient and significant other.

INTRODUCTION

Though CBT has historically focused on the individual seeking therapy, as far back as the 1960s and 1970s, it has been applied to the wider problems of families (e.g. Patterson et al., 1967) and couples (e.g. Weiss et al., 1973). CBT models have been evolved and adapted, and are now recognised as a significant adjunctive approach in the treatment of systemic problems (e.g. Nichols and Schwanz, 2001). The central therapeutic focus of these models is either schema change (Azar et al., 2005; Dattilio, 2005) or behavioural change in interactions, using interventions such as communication training, problem solving and behavioural contracting (Dattilio and Epstein, 2005).

The aim of this chapter is not the proposal of a new approach to the application of the CBT model to systemic problems, nor is it to offer a 'how to' guide to systems theory, family therapy or couples therapy. Literature exists, which does this more eloquently and comprehensively than is possible in this text (e.g. Schmaling et al.,

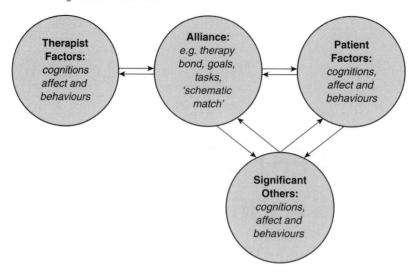

Figure 5.1   The therapeutic alliance, including the role of significant others

1989; Dattilio, 2005). Our objective is to highlight for CBT therapists who work individually with clients, the importance of considering the influence of extra-therapeutic relationships (i.e. those relationships outside of the therapeutic relationship, which impact on the attainment of therapeutic goals).

Through our experience of working with complex cases, such as those involving medically unexplained symptoms and childhood trauma, we observed therapeutic obstacles associated with the interplay of the patient, the therapist and significant others. This experience informs much of the discussion in this chapter. To expand on the model provided in Chapter 3, the therapeutic alliance comprises patient and therapist factors, which influence and are influenced by extra-therapeutic relationships (see Figure 5.1).

Three illustrative cases drawn from our work will be referred to throughout the chapter. The first case (that of Dion) will illustrate the theory. As the related theory in this area is broad and draws from a range of different modalities, we have chosen to restrict our brief theory discussion to the concept of schemas. We consider schemas to be a particularly important cognitive concept when taking a wider therapeutic perspective. The second and third cases, respectively, illustrate some of the obstacles associated with working with and without the presence of the significant other.

THE CASE OF DION – MY FAMILY OR MY THERAPEUTIC NEEDS?

Dion has recently re-established contact with his close-knit family. Unfortunately, his troublesome anxiety attacks have returned. When he has the attacks, he fears an unknown catastrophe. He believes himself to be 'vulnerable' and 'can't cope alone'.

He looks to his siblings for reassurance and support, which they actively provide. He speaks of them as having always been there to protect him throughout life and can't see how he would have survived without them. His family strongly believe 'families should need and support each other'. They have always seen Dion as the weak one in the family, who can't cope. They are therefore pleased he seems closer to them and is calling on them for the support they believe he has always needed. In therapy, Dion realises that the reassurance seeking is unhelpful but worries if he stops depending on family for this support, he might alienate or upset them. When he tries to resist seeking reassurance from them, some family members become upset. Arguments ensue and they accuse him of being distant, too independent and 'trying to destroy the family'. Dion is now not making progress in therapy because of his inability to challenge these fears and cope with the upset in the family.

SCHEMAS

Dion is attending therapy as an individual but is part of an inter-connecting 'system' of important family relationships. In therapy, both Dion and his therapist are aware of what is required for him to maintain therapeutic progress. The therapist hypothesises that Dion's goals are influencing and being influenced by significant others in his life, and that their schemas are reciprocal and pivotal. It is important to accept and explore this reciprocal influence and its effect on therapy. Neglecting to do so would result in Dion's family relationships becoming an obstacle to the achievement of his therapeutic goals.

Individual Schemas

We have found it useful to gain an understanding of the role of schemas (e.g. Beck, 1976; Beck et al., 1979; Young et al., 2003). In the Beckian perspective, schemas are attitudes or assumptions developed from previous experience and are associated with the development of levels of cognitions including core beliefs, conditional assumptions and negative automatic thoughts (Beck et al., 1979). In the Youngian perspective, schemas are 'broad, pervasive themes or patterns, which are comprised of memories, bodily sensations, emotions and cognitions regarding one's self and one's relationship with others. They are usually developed during childhood or adolescence and elaborated over a lifetime' (Young, 2006). Young et al. (2003) identify 18 maladaptive schemas (see Table 5.1) to which one responds in such ways as surrender, over-compensation or avoidance. A comprehensive description of the model and its application is beyond the scope of this chapter but the interested reader is directed towards *Schema Therapy: A Practitioner's Guide* (Young et al., 2003).

From Young et al.'s (2003) 18 maladaptive schemas, Dion would perhaps hold vulnerability, dependence or enmeshment-related schemas, which result in him needing others. In the Beckian perspective, Dion perhaps holds a cognitive triad (Beck at al., 1979) of beliefs about himself such as '*I am weak and vulnerable*' or '*I can't*

Table 5.1   Early maladaptive schemas

	Domain				
	Disconnection/ Rejection	Impaired autonomy/ Performance	Impaired limits	Other directedness	Over-vigilance/Inhibition
Maladaptive Schema	Abandonment/ Instability	Dependence/ Incompetence	Entitlement/ Grandiosity	Subjugation	Negativity/Pessimism
	Mistrust/Abuse	Vulnerability to harm/Illness	Insufficient self-control/ Self-discipline	Self-sacrifice	Emotional inhibition
	Emotional deprivation	Enmeshment/ Under-developed self		Approval or Recognition seeking	Unrelenting standards/ Hyper-criticalness
	Defectiveness/ Shame	Failure			Punitiveness
	Social isolation/ Alienation				

Source: adapted from Young, J.E., Klosko, J.S. and Weishaar, M.E. (2003) *Schema Therapy: A Practitioner's Guide*. New York: Guilford Press.

cope', while '*others* are strong' and 'protective'. The *future* is thus uncertain and frightening for him. His cognitive, emotional and behavioural responses to life events (e.g. the possibility of independence and his family's unhappiness) are an expression of the influence of his schemas.

Family Schemas

The theory of schemas has been elaborated and expanded, so that they no longer only apply to individuals. Families too can develop 'family schemas', which are jointly held belief systems that can become dysfunctional (Dattilio, 2005). For example, Dion's family jointly hold the belief that 'We need each other'. As with the individual who holds conditional assumptions, the family too can hold 'standards' (Schwerbel and Fine, 1992) or 'rules'. Dion's family, for example, hold the rule that 'We must not exercise our independence'. Consequently, when Dion tries to do anything without them, this schema is activated, resulting in upset within the family system, which impacts directly on Dion and his therapy. Dattilio (2005) discusses a covert variant of family or group schemas that are held by sections of the group, about or to the exclusion of one member. For example, Dion's family hold the belief that, 'Dion is the weak one, who cannot cope and needs support.' They, therefore, hold an expectation (Datillio, 2005) of what Dion's behaviour should be, in accordance with the group schema. When Dion's behaviour does not meet their expectations, disharmony ensues and they become upset. Dion has therefore taken the role of *the sick one*, towards whom the group schema and related behaviours are directed. His therapeutic goals are associated with the development of alternative, competing beliefs and behaviours, which present a challenge to the family schema. The consequent impact is the activation of family schemas and efforts to cope with the associated distress (i.e. their efforts to make Dion need them).

Generalisation of Schemas

Schemas can generalise to new relationships, including therapeutic relationships. Each member within a new relationship encounter will have their own schemas, born of their own past experiences (e.g. family relationships). Others will need to contend with the expression of these individual schemas and *vice versa*. To borrow from Young et al.'s (2003) conceptualisation, for example, Dion has three possible responses to the expression of his family's schema. He can either (1) surrender to his family's needs (e.g. comply, and become dependent), (2) overcompensate (e.g. become aggressive, 'manipulate') or avoid (e.g. social isolation, psychological withdrawal or use substances). Each of these responses would have a consequence upon his family relationships, so that that they are either (1) functional, (2) dysfunctional with a fragile surface-level harmony or (3) there is disharmony. The interpersonal challenges associated with each of these three positions may be reasons for Dion seeking therapy. The expression of Dion's and his family's schemas may also become evident in therapy, becoming obstacles. Figure 5.2 attempts to illustrate this description.

The basic principle of this model is one of circular causality or reciprocal effect (i.e. an individual's behaviour influences the behaviours of others and vice versa). Functionality, harmony and disharmony are based on the reciprocal effect of persons A and B's schema-based needs and behaviours. As illustrated in Dion's case, individual human needs are often mutually opposed, so that one person's needs create problems for another and *vice versa* (i.e. reciprocity). It is important for therapists of all levels of experience to have an understanding of the effects of this reciprocity on the patient and the goals of therapy. In therapy it is important to remember that:

1 there may be environmental/interpersonal factors needing therapeutic attention;
2 including significant others in the therapeutic process may be warranted;
3 implications for change in therapy will be influenced by significant others;
4 sometimes the goals of therapy can run counter to the needs of significant others.

INCORPORATING THE ABOVE IDEAS IN THERAPY

CBT specific interventions (e.g. Beck et al., 1976; Bennett-Levy et al., 2004; Kuyken et al., 2009) are still valid, though therapists may be called upon to be adept at holding multiple formulations simultaneously. These interventions will not be elaborated here. Instead, the focus will be on some ways in which extra-therapeutic relationship associated obstacles may become apparent in therapy.

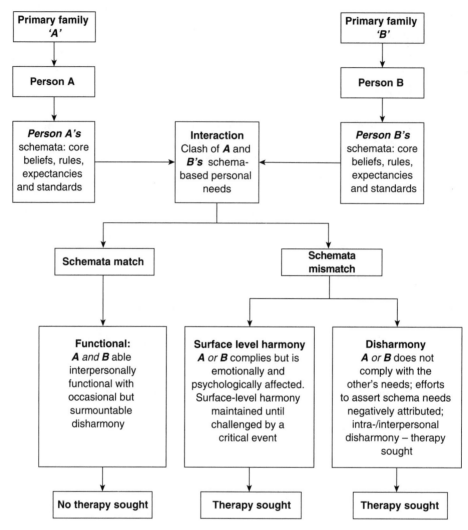

Figure 5.2   Simple schematic representation of Dion's formulation

Assessment

As with all other CBT approaches, a comprehensive assessment informs the initial formulation and treatment plan and has been expertly detailed by others (e.g. Kirk, 1989; Grant et al., 2008). Therapists are, however, encouraged to pay greater attention to the links within a system, thus heightening their awareness and understanding of wider influences, impinging on the client. In Dion's case, the therapist needed to be aware of the family culture and the family schema (e.g. 'we need each other'), group schemas (e.g. 'Dion is the weak one') and Dion's own personal schemas (e.g. 'I can't cope without my family' and 'If I assert my independence, then there will be disagreement'). A comprehensive assessment with consideration given to this can help clarify the necessity of involving others. At each stage, the maintenance cycle for the target problem is identified, including the role of significant others, leading to schema identification. Consistent with CBT theory, the effects of specific changes in one area may generalise to other similar problem areas.

HYPOTHESIS-BASED TREATMENT

Interventions need to be carefully planned and should be based on theory-driven hypotheses. Direct targeting of the cognitions and behaviours of a significant other, who is absent from the therapy room, is not possible when working with the individual patient, so it is necessary to:

- Clarify reasons for adopting a particular approach.
- Attend to the possibility that events outside the patient's control may be exerting a significant influence on the progress of the client.
- Focus interventions based on one of three objectives:
  a increasing coping skills;
  b challenging predictions;
  c targeting the significant other's cognitions and behaviours.

Novice therapists are often uncomfortable with coping-focused interventions. However, therapists need to accept that clients may live in objectively toxic circumstances. The task is then to help the client to consider ways of coping in such circumstances. This is in keeping with the general ethos of CBT, where increasing coping skills adheres very much to Salkovskis's (1996) distress equation:

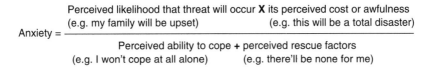

Figure 5.3   Dion's distress equation

Source: adapted from Salkovskis, P.M. (1996) 'The cognitive approach to anxiety: threat beliefs, safety-seeking behavior, and the special case of health anxiety and obsessions', in P.M. Salkovskis (ed.), Frontiers of Cognitive Therapy. New York. Guilford Press.

By developing skills and responses, the therapist increases the lower (coping) section of the equation as opposed to (upper) challenging danger perceptions. However, therapists need to be careful not to reinforce safety behaviours while strengthening coping abilities. To differentiate the two:

- Strengthening coping allows a person to enter and manage a situation, without maintaining negative cognitions and distress (e.g. Dion practised assertive responses, which allowed him to develop protective responses against his family's demands, without using safety behaviours to reduce his distress).
- Safety behaviours perpetuate the maintenance cycle, and generally have the objective of escaping from or avoiding uncomfortable arousal or cognitions (e.g. Dion's

avoidance of upsetting his family was reducing his anxiety in the moment but maintaining his distress and fear of upsetting them in the long run).

OBSTACLES ASSOCIATED WITH WORKING WITH THE INDIVIDUAL CLIENT

THE CASE OF JAMIE – SEEING ONESELF THROUGH THE CRITICAL EYE OF ANOTHER

25-year-old Jamie lives at home with his mother following the death of his father. He has been referred with depression and accepts the principles and rationale of a CBT therapeutic approach. He engages well with the interventions but does not experience any significant shift in mood. Apparently, his mother expects him to care for her and expresses a lot of anger if she doesn't get her way. She complains of being ill 'again' because of Jamie's depression. She then takes to her bed and blames Jamie, calling him selfish, evil and in need of psychiatric help. This is usually followed by uncomfortable periods of prolonged silence and tension in the house. Jamie becomes worried and sad. He believes he is to blame and that he needs to work harder on his depression. As Jamie is unemployed and is financially dependent on his mother, he is unable to leave home. Even if he did leave, he fears that his mother would become ill, be unable to cope and he would be responsible. In therapy Jamie blames himself for his mother's problems saying, 'I'm evil and bad. I did it again.' In-session work was only partially effective as the gains didn't last. Interactions with his mother were too emotional and he returned to the next session with his old thoughts back in place.

WHEN TO INVITE THE SIGNIFICANT OTHER

It is not always necessary to include the significant other and therapists may need to use their professional judgement, as well as a collaborative discussion with their client in making such a decision. Helpful hints for deciding when to include the significant other may include when:

- *The significant other's socialisation to the model may be helpful*: Jamie's mother, for example, could have been included as a co-therapist, giving her a role in his recovery.
- *The significant other's efforts to help are impeding progress.*
- *Updating an inaccurate internalised representation*: the presence of the significant other serves as a behavioural experiment for updating an internalised representation of the other, which has been frozen in time but is no longer true (e.g. Jamie's therapist initially suspected that there was a disparity between the schema-based image of his mother held by Jamie and how she really was now; he had considered inviting

her to therapy to help Jamie to realise that, though she had once been the 'ogre', she had in fact changed).

- *Reducing splitting*: therapists can sometimes see the patient as all good and the significant other as all bad. Bringing all parties into session can help to get them all on board with therapy, build alliance and reduce the splitting.

SPECIFIC OBSTACLES WHEN WORKING WITH THE INDIVIDUAL ALONE

The 'Interactional Dance' Obstacle

Due to the interpersonal effects of schemas, patients and their significant others may be locked in an 'interactional dance', so that responses to each other become second nature. Like expert dancers, who no longer need to think about the steps of their dance and appear to respond automatically to the slightest twitch from their partner, individuals may be so locked into their interactional styles that they respond automatically to each other. Jamie, for example, would believe that he was truly 'bad'. Verbal and other challenging would create acknowledged change in session. Between sessions, however, the emotion associated with interactions with his mother would prove too strong for Jamie, so that the therapeutic effect was easily undone, leading to him reverting to his old ways.

A useful approach which Jamie's therapist applied is what Padesky describes as the 'assertive defence of the self' (see Padesky, 1997). The phases of this approach include:

- *The schema-based accusation*: the therapist encourages the patient to defend themselves against their schema (e.g. Jamie's therapist took the role of the accuser, who confirmed the belief that Jamie was 'bad' and would indeed, bring catastrophe to his mother).
- *The self-defence against the schema*: the patient defends himself to dispute the schema (e.g. Jamie disputed the schema, giving evidence against it).
- *Grading of accusations*: the accusations were graded from being initially mild to stronger ones as Jamie's capacity for self-defence increased.

Jamie's ability to cope with his mother's accusations and triggering of his belief gradually increased, so that he was able to maintain therapeutic gains more successfully between sessions. This intervention increased Jamie's alternative perception of himself, as well as improving his coping skills for managing his relationship with his mother. He could apply the same defensive statements in interactions with her (i.e. assertiveness). He then had to resist appeasing her, leading to testing of her threats, thus reducing the danger perceptions associated with her statements and behaviours.

The 'Ghost in the Room' Obstacle

When it becomes clear that the other member of the relationship's behaviour is objectively unacceptable, an obstacle arises. How does therapy target that person's behaviours in his/her absence? This is akin to focusing on changing the cognitions and behaviours of a 'ghost', who is not visible and can not respond. Patients may have lifelong interpersonal difficulties associated with their significant others and vice versa, making it difficult for either party to change. Some patients may seek to invite the other person to therapy in the hope that the therapist can 'make them understand' and 'change' – an impossible task for therapists. Inexperienced therapists can often be caught in the 'omnipotence error' (see Chapter 3) in such cases, so that they think their role as therapist gives them the power to effect change. Unfortunately, not even our esteemed role as therapists endows us with the power to change long-established interpersonal patterns with a good telling-off!

In Jamie's case, his schemas were easily triggered and had generalised, so that he habitually responded to them in all interpersonal encounters. Jamie and his therapist used various CBT approaches, which increased his objectivity regarding his mother and empowered him, including the following:

The Intervention of 'Therapeutic Re-labelling'

The approach we have termed '*therapeutic re-labelling*' was useful with Jamie. It is aimed at patients like Jamie who have difficulty perceiving significant others' negative behaviours objectively. Since the aim of CBT is to consider alternatives, reduced ability to be objective poses a significant therapeutic obstacle. Therapeutic re-labelling generally consists of three main steps:

1   *identify a 'proxy' other*: encourage the patient to imagine a proxy other (e.g. a loved one). Consider what the patient would say, feel or do in the same situation on behalf of that loved one (e.g. Jamie's therapist said, 'If this was your girlfriend and her mother was saying these things, what would you say?');
2   *proxy re-labelling or 'blame' placement*: ask the patient to first label the behaviour on behalf not of themselves but of the proxy loved or important other (e.g. Jamie responded, 'I'd say she'd been unfair and bullying');
3   *Transfer insights onto real person*: transfer these words (e.g. unfair, bullying) to the real other or their actions.

The extract from an interview with Jamie illustrates therapeutic re-labelling, incorporating steps 1 and 2 above (i.e. identifying a proxy other and proxy re-labelling and blame placement).

THERAPEUTIC RE-LABELLING INTERVIEW WITH JAMIE

Therapist: Jamie, can you think of someone you really care about, that you would hate to see being hurt?

Jamie: Yes, of course.

Therapist: Who would that be?

Jamie: My girlfriend.

Therapist: If you heard your girlfriend's mother speaking to your girlfriend and saying what your mother said to you, how would you feel?

Jamie:	I'd be very angry! I'd want to protect her because it would be totally unfair. You know, it was a mistake?
Therapist:	Imagine your girlfriend was blaming herself for being selfish? I wonder what you'd say to her about her mother's reaction?
Jamie:	Unfair! I'd say she'd been unfair and bullying.
Therapist:	So, you'd call such behaviour unfair and bullying. Would you say the same might apply to your situation with your mother?

Therapeutic re-labelling can be difficult for those who personalise or fear betraying loved ones. It is easier for them to initially label the behaviour not the person. Encouragement is given to the client to practise 'retrospective re-labelling' of different behaviours after they have occurred. As this skill improves, 'prospective re-labelling' of the behaviours or significant other is then practised. The importance of re-labelling behaviours is that the 'other' – who might be perceived positively – is not all negative but has a 'tendency towards hurtful, unkind or other behaviours sometimes'. In doing this, in time the client develops a bank of *labels* for use when the 'other' behaves in ways that activate identified schemas. Therapists should take care to identify labels that result in a positive emotional impact. We recommend that readers access the compassionate-mind work of Paul Gilbert and colleagues, which outlines in detail other helpful techniques.

Interventions for Fostering Empowerment

Clients like Jamie may feel powerless to rid themselves of the burden of responsibility for the actions of others. They may be unaware that help is available, so they need support and education about available legal and social support routes. Indeed, research indicates that some clients may feel helpless or lack a sense of power to effect change by their own actions (Peterson et al., 1993). Jamie, for example:

- lacked the skills for recognising his own needs or getting them met;
- was easily derailed by the strength of his schema-based emotional effects of his mother's responses.

Clients like Jamie may need empowerment-focused interventions before proceeding with new learning in confronting the significant other. Jamie's therapist therefore drew on available CBT interventions to encourage him to start to act differently, thus collecting evidence towards a different relationship with his mother. These included:

1 '*Acting as if*' (see Fennell and Jenkins, 2004), which involves:
   - identifying a respected or admired other who behaves in the desired way in a similar situation;
   - rehearsing the desired behaviour;
   - practising the desired behaviour *in vivo*.

Use of the *as if* approach can be worked through in a graded hierarchy of targets, from least to most difficult. Therapist can initially role-play and model this technique. Modelling is useful as it takes into consideration the possibility that the patient might never have been free of their schema for long enough to consciously consider an alternative. Therapists need to be mindful of the danger that the client will state therapeutic goals with the significant other's needs in mind, which merely perpetuates the schema-based behaviours.

2 *Problem solving* (see Hawton and Kirk, 1989): the five main objectives of problem solving have been described and include:

  – identifying problems as causes of dysphoria;
  – helping patients to recognise the resources they possess for approaching difficulties;
  – teaching systematic methods of overcoming current problems;
  – enhancing a sense of control over problems;
  – equipping clients with a method for tackling future problems.

3 *Assertiveness*: this differs from assertive defence of the self, in that it is primarily a skills-development exercise as opposed to a belief-change intervention; it allows the patient to cope with an event by creating alternative behavioural responses.

4 *Performance of experiments*: (see Bennett-Levy et al., 2004): behavioural experiments can be very powerful in providing the client with extreme, schema-incongruent information.

By the end of treatment, Jamie was able to learn to confront his mother's accusations and to challenge his schemas. Though she continued to attack his 'badness' schema and he still experienced distress, his mood improved with his ability to see her behaviour objectively and separately from himself and to use his coping behaviours.

OBSTACLES IN JOINTLY WORKING WITH THE CLIENT AND SIGNIFICANT OTHERS

CBT therapy may at times necessitate inviting significant others into the therapy room. Both novice and experienced therapists may find this a daunting prospect. The inherent challenges of working with the 'ghost in the room' can be quite different when the significant other is present. The therapist needs to:

• be adept at not taking sides;
• recognise the multiple schemas that may be at play;
• have the ability to hold multiple formulations concurrently.

The case of Kim and Peter illustrates some likely obstacles and how a therapist can use existing CBT-based formulations to conceptualise and target maintenance cycles.

THE CASE OF KIM AND PETER – DIFFICULTY LETTING GO OF THE PROBLEM

Kim lives with her husband Peter who, after a number of years of inconclusive investigations and uncertain diagnoses for physical complaints, has been diagnosed with chronic fatigue syndrome. Both Kim and Peter know little about the illness and an internet search has failed to clarify exactly what it is. She supports him and wants the best for him. She knows how tired her husband gets and has given up her job to become his full-time carer. She now takes on most of the chores in the house to reduce the strain on him. Peter appreciates Kim's efforts and is truly grateful for her support. He has started CBT and is embracing a new way of thinking about his illness. Not only does he now worry that Kim will think he has been pretending, especially as she gave up her job to care for him, but he also fears losing her and the close relationship they share. The thought of telling her makes him feel very anxious and distressed.

The therapist in this instance needs to be able to identify both parties' maintenance cycles and to hypothesise how they link within the system. For example (see Figure 5.4), the therapist hypothesised that Peter's fear of upsetting Kim was affecting his ability to tell her about the goals of therapy. Likewise, Kim's fear of appearing uncaring and heartless was affecting her ability to meet her own needs, resulting in frustration. They both said nothing, resulting in Peter's continuing illness behaviours and Kim's continuing enabling of those behaviours, which then affected therapy.

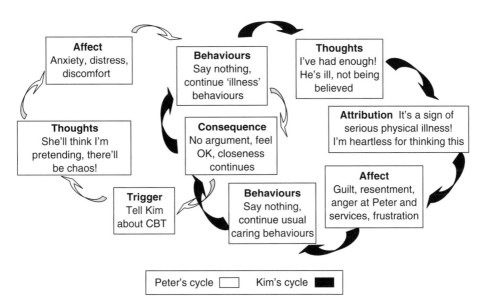

Figure 5.4   Idiosyncratic formulation of Peter and Kim's interaction

In sharing this idiosyncratic cross-sectional formulation, care should be taken to:

- resist being categorical but instead, convey that this is simply a hypothesis;
- resist appearing critical of either party;
- be collaborative, with all parties participating and taking ownership of the process.

Sharing such a formulation may create obstacles to progress, which the therapist may need to consider.

The 'Mouthpiece' Obstacle

Significant others may want to speak for the client. Clients like Peter or the earlier cases of Dion and Jamie can find themselves being overpowered by a significant other in session. The danger is that what the therapist gets (particularly at assessment) is the 'other's' perception of the problem rather than the client's, which influences the formulation and goal identification. Therapists can:

- collaborate with the patient around the decision to include the other in the session;
- facilitate the 'other's' awareness of the need to hear the client's voice (e.g. 'Kim, I am aware that you know Peter very well; however, for therapy to work, it is best that we get most of the information from him');
- highlight and explore the problem (e.g. 'Kim, I have noticed that you often speak for Peter. I wonder if this is what usually happens?' and so on); such explorations can lead to the identification of family schemas, attributions and standards;
- contract for future responses to the behaviour (e.g. 'I can really see that you want the best for Peter; however, it seems your very well-meant efforts can get in the way of us hearing what Peter wants. I'd like to propose that I gently highlight when that starts to happen).

Challenge to the Credibility of the Therapy or Therapist Obstacle

The patient who is attending therapy and invites their significant other is likely to have already accepted the credibility of the therapist and his approach. This was the case with Peter. Kim, who had not properly socialised to the CBT model, was still of the view that there was something seriously wrong with her husband's health. Consequently, out of love for her husband, she attended therapy with the aim of seeking 'proper' medical treatment for him. She had evidence collected from past medical investigations, the internet and support groups. The therapist's task then focused mainly on socialising Kim to the model. This was achieved through:

- *Collaboration*: Peter took ownership of a lot of the rationale giving, thus helping Kim to realise that the principles offered an explanation for his problems, which he found personally acceptable.
- *Combined and separate sessions*: some separate sessions were planned as Kim wanted time with the therapist without Peter present; as the therapy was for Peter, the issue

of combined or separate session time was clarified with him before Kim's arrival, thus maintaining the alliance.

- *Co-therapist role*: once Kim had understood and accepted the approach, discussions were held about how she could assist Peter in achieving his therapeutic goals; in that way her supportive and caring role was maintained in an optimistic and non-threatening way.

Therapists may need to assert their role as an expert and to underline the credibility of their modality. Some therapists are uncomfortable with asserting the 'expert' role. It is an important role, which needs to be gently asserted, especially when obstacles arise or therapeutic contracts are needed as with Peter and Kim. Besides the challenge to the therapy or therapist, therapists may need to be vigilant for the possibility of the significant other also seeking therapy and 'hijacking' the sessions. There is a danger of the focus shifting from the client to the significant other or competition for the therapist's attention. Kim, for example, wanted help with guilt, which she recognised as being troublesome. It was agreed that she could seek this elsewhere, with a different therapist.

Interpersonal Difficulties Being Played-out in the Session

Bringing the significant other into the therapy session raises the possibility of the interpersonal difficulties being played out in the session with the therapist. Therapeutically there can be several hazards associated with this:

- insufficient collaboration with the client can result in dissatisfaction;
- the therapist can then be perceived as taking the significant other's side;
- the significant other feels blamed, invalidated or not listened to, leading to reluctance to collaborate.

In this particular case, Peter and Kim's arguments about his illness quickly surfaced. The therapist had initially only invited Kim for an education and socialisation session in the hope that she would take on a greater co-therapist role with Peter. In session, it became evident that Peter had not been clear with Kim about the treatment rationale and their arguments quickly surfaced. In such situations, the therapist can follow the example of Peter's therapist by:

- *Resisting taking sides*: questions were at times directed at Peter and then at Kim and vice versa, thus creating a sense of balance and non-partisanship. Balancing questions by directing a question at one party and the next at the other is not always necessary. It can reduce exploration and create a disjointed session, which may seem contrived.
- *Providing emotional nurturance* (see Schmaling et al., 1989): as in Peter and Kim's case, parties may experience discomfort around emotional expression. Therapy should aim to facilitate and nurture such expression.
- *Encouraging positive realism*: unrealisitc expectations of each other and therapy should be explored in a positive and balanced way, through the use of Socratic questioning and guided discovery.

- *Identifying alternatives*: Peter and Kim, for example, were encouraged to express their apprehensions in session. These were then explored and CBT methods were then used to identify alternatives.
- *Practising communication skills*: Shmaling et al. (1989: 357–60) offer a brief and simple but informative discussion of communication skills to which we would direct the interested reader. Peter and Kim, for example, were unduly aggressive towards each other due to their frustration and unspoken emotions. Education and practice of active, empathic listening and assertiveness was introduced by the therapist.

The Blame Obstacle

Difficulties may arise if significant others do not view themselves as part of a problem and believe that someone else is 'the problem' and needs to change. If the significant other attends, the therapist needs to prioritise:

- education and socialisation to the model;
- reinforcing of the reciprocity assumption: i.e. each member's actions affect those of the others and vice versa, and co-operation or non-co-operation have consequences;
- reduced blaming: the respective members need to learn that the aim of therapy is not the placing of blame but the identification of maintenance factors;
- awareness of universality: all parties need to recognise the similarity of the human development experience through the use of formulation (i.e. everyone has a family of origin, which has shaped the way they think, feel and behave and this affects functioning in current relationships)

The desired effect of this is to reduce blaming of one individual, coupled with the realisation that each has unique perspectives and roles within the relationship. Besides issues of blame, both significant others and clients may not wish to attend because engaging in therapy would have unwelcome consequences for one or both parties, resulting in efforts to derail or sabotage the change process. There might be:

- *loss of material benefits* (e.g. social security or other benefits);
- *loss of emotional support* (e.g. the relationship might have become closer – as in Peter and Kim's case);
- *loss of personal credibility* (e.g. Peter feared being accused of pretending);
- *stigma associated with mental health diagnosis and treatment.*

If significant others refuse to attend therapy, it becomes impossible to undertake the socialisation and education process. In this instance, it may be best to revert to strengthening the resources of the client, empowering them and hypothesising the schemata of the 'other', in order to achieve a more objective view of their behaviours thus increasing detachment from them. The therapist can also take the role of holding initial responsibility until the client is strong enough to do so personally. The client could be given permission to say, 'My therapist said…'. Alternatively, if the client is finding it difficult to let go of the 'interactional dance', the family members can be given permission to say, 'The therapist said…not to respond, reassure you, etc.'

In this way, the therapist acts as a buffer, so that the emotional family relationships are preserved until the whole system is ready to face change.

SUMMARY

The CBT model already takes into account the contribution of significant others and environmental factors in the acquisition of problems. It seems logical and pragmatic to account for these in the treatment process. CBT therapists generally possess the skills and training necessary for considering the influence of extra-therapeutic relationships and the achievement of therapeutic goals. Literature is available for therapists to draw on to inform their practice and hone their skills in this area. It is not unreasonable for even an inexperienced therapist to identify extra-therapeutic influences and to intervene, thus increasing the chances of achieving and maintaining therapeutic change. Failure to consider the influence of extra-therapeutic relationships leaves therapy at the mercy of unexpected and complex interpersonal obstacles, which can impact on therapeutic gain.

LEARNING EXERCISE

THE CASE OF RONAN – WHEN THERAPEUTIC GAINS ARE NOT MAINTAINED

26-year-old Ronan lives with his parents. His sister Tilly lives alone. He has engaged with CBT and made progress in the past but always relapsed. He experiences distressing intrusive thoughts with accompanying images of sexually assaulting people. He strongly believes that he will carry out the thoughts and that he will be rejected by peers, who will think of him as weird and perverted. He avoids the thoughts and images and any associated triggers including socialising. At home, his family argue all the time and he discloses that he regularly gets kicked, punched or called a weirdo. When present, Tilly intervenes on his behalf. His parents both come from large families with a high expression of emotions, where the ability to stand up for oneself was valued. Ronan believes himself to be emotionally weak and a freak. Even though the problem started when he was being bullied and ostracised by some colleagues at work, Ronan believes that he has always been a rather anxious person, who worried about what people thought of him, though he recalls always having a small but good and supportive group of friends.

1 Reflecting on your clinical experience, have you ever worked with anyone whose circumstances in any way resembled Ronan's?
2 How did you or might you have included the significant others in therapy?
3 How would you evolve a preliminary hypothesis to formulate the maintenance of Ronan's problem?
4 Try to incorporate the significant other's maintenance cycle into the formulation.

FURTHER READING

Baucom, D.H. and Epstein, N.B. (2003) 'Couple therapy', in R.L. Leahy (ed.), *Roadblocks in Cognitive-behavioral Therapy: Transforming Challenges into Opportunities for Change*. New York: Guilford Press. pp. 217–35.

Dattilio, F.M (2005) 'The restructuring of family schemas: a cognitive-behavior perspective', *Journal of Marital and Family Therapy*, 31 (1): 15–30.

Schmaling, K.B., Fruzetti, A.E. and Jacobson, N.S. (1989) 'Marital problems', in K. Hawton, P.M. Salkovskis, J. Kirk and D.M. Clark (eds), *Cognitive Behaviour Therapy for Psychiatric Problems: A Practical Guide*. Oxford: Oxford University Press.

REFERENCES

Azar, S.T., Nix, R.L and Makin-Byrd, K.N. (2005) 'Parenting schemas and the process of change', *Journal and Marital and Family Therapy*, 31 (1): 45–58.

Beck, A.T. (1967). *Depression: Clinical, Experimental and Theoretical Aspects*. New York: Hoeber.

Beck, A.T. (1976) *Cognitive Therapy and Emotional Disorders*. New York: International Universities Press.

Beck, A.T., Rush, J.A., Shaw, B.F. and Emery, G. (1979). *Cognitive Therapy of Depression*. New York: Guilford Press.

Bennett-Levy, J., Butler, G., Fennell, M., Hackman, A., Meuller, M. and Westbbrook, D. (2004) *Oxford Guide to Behavioural Experiments in Cognitive Therapy*. Oxford: Oxford University Press.

Dattilio, F.M. (2001) 'Cognitive behavioural family therapy: contemporary myths and misconceptions', *Contemporary Family Therapy*, 23 (1): 3–18

Dattilio, F.M. (2005) 'The restructuring of family schemas: a cognitive-behavior perspective', *Journal of Marital and Family Therapy*, 31 (1): 15–30

Dattilio, F.M. and Epstein, N.B. (2005) 'Introduction to the special section: the role of cognitive-behavioral interventions in couple and family therapy', *Journal of Marital and Family Therapy*, 31(1): 7–13.

Fennell, M. and Jenkins, H. (2004) 'Low self-esteem', in J. Bennett-Levy, G. Butler, M. Fennell, A. Hackman, M. Muller and D. Westbrook (eds), *Oxford Guide to Behavioural Experiments in Cognitive Therapy*. Oxford: Oxford University Press.

Grant, A., Townend, M., Mills, J. and Cockx, A. (2008) *Assessment and Formulation in Cognitive Behavioural Therapy*. London: SAGE.

Hawton, K. and Kirk, J. (1989) 'Problem solving', in K. Hawton, P.M. Salkovskis, J. Kirk and D.M. Clark (eds), *Cognitive Behaviour Therapy for Psychiatric Problems: A Practical Guide*. Oxford: Oxford University Press.

Hawton, K., Salkovskis, P.M, Kirk, J. and Clark, D.M (1989) *Cognitive Behavioural Therapy for Psychiatric Problems*. Oxford: Oxford University Press.

Kirk, J. (1989) 'Cognitive-behavioural assessment', in K. Hawton, P.M. Salkovskis, J. Kirk and D.M. Clark (eds), *Cognitive Behaviour Therapy for Psychiatric Problems: A Practical Guide*. Oxford: Oxford University Press.

Kuyken, W., Padesky, C.A. and Dudley, R. (2009) *Collaborative Case Conceptualization*. New York: Guilford Press.

Nichols, M. and Schwartz, R. (2001) *Family Therapy: Concepts and Methods* (5th edn). Needham Heights, MA: Allyn and Bacon.

Padesky, C.A. (1997) 'A more effective treatment focus for social phobia', *International Cognitive Therapy Newsletter*, 11 (1): 1–3.

Patterson, G.R., McNeal, S., Hawkins, N and Phelps, R. (1967) 'Reprogramming the social environment', *Journal of Child Psychology and Psychiatry*, 8: 181–95.

Peterson, C., Maier, S.F. and Seligman, M.E.P. (1993) *Learned Helplessness: A Theory for the Age of Personal Control*. Oxford: Oxford University Press.

Salkovskis, P.M. (1996) 'The cognitive approach to anxiety: threat beliefs, safety-seeking behavior, and the special case of health anxiety and obsessions', in P.M. Salkovskis (ed.), *Frontiers of Cognitive Therapy*. New York: Guilford Press.

Schmaling, K.B., Fruzetti, A.E. and Jacobson, N.S. (1989). 'Marital problems', in K. Hawton, P.M. Salkovskis, J. Kirk and D.M. Clark (eds), *Cognitive Behaviour Therapy for Psychiatric Problems: A Practical Guide*. Oxford: Oxford University Press.

Schwerbel and Fine, M.A (1992) *Understanding and Helping Families: A Cognitive-behavior Approach*. Hillside: Erlbaum.

Weiss, R.L., Hops, H. and Patterson, G.R. (1973) 'A framework for conceptualizing marital conflict, a technology for altering it, some data for evaluating it', in L.A. Hamerlynck, L.C. Handy and E.J. Mash (eds), *Behavior Change: Methodology, Concepts, and Practice*. Champaign, IL: Research Press. pp. 309–42.

Young, J.E. (2006) 'Schema therapy: training in cognitive behaviour therapy for personality disorders', workshop held in Grosseto, Italy, 27, 28, 29 April.

Young, J.E., Klosko, J.S. and Weishaar, M.E. (2003) *Schema Therapy: A Practitioner's Guide*. New York: Guilford Press.

Part 2

PSYCHOPATHOLOGY-RELATED OBSTACLES

6

PERFECTIONISM

CRAIG CHIGWEDERE AND YVONNE TONE

LEARNING OBJECTIVES

After reading this chapter you should:

- understand the concept and effects of perfectionism,
- recognise clinical perfectionism in clients,
- understand a development and maintenance model of perfectionism,
- have knowledge of strategies for the management of perfectionism.

INTRODUCTION

THE CASE OF STEVEN – 'PLEASE, JUST GIVE ME A NEW FACE!'

Steven, a 22-year-old garage worker, presented for therapy with low mood and social avoidance behaviour. He dropped out of college due to self-consciousness about his appearance and belief that he 'was ugly'. Steven became particularly focused on his bone structure and facial appearance. Due to his self-consciousness and strong belief that he was 'ugly' he avoided meeting people and getting into relationships. He had also travelled abroad for a cosmetic surgery consultation, having been refused surgery locally. Steven felt pressured to come for therapy by his GP, who suggested this preoccupation with his physical appearance may not be due to an 'objective' physical imperfection. There was a family history of concern with appearance in that in her teenage years Steven's sister had suffered with anorexia nervosa. He described his mother as idealistic and liking the children to be well presented.

Perfectionism presents variously, in association with a range of disorders or as a discrete clinical entity. It can manifest in both clients and therapists. Its impact on disorder development, maintenance and treatment can be associated with therapeutic obstacles which are important to consider. The case of Steven illustrates perfectionism and its effects. Like Steven, most people are dissatisfied with some aspect of their appearance. This does not necessarily, make them pathologically perfectionistic. Though dissatisfied with perceived imperfections, they are able to function, pursue life goals and maintain relationships. However, Steven's dissatisfaction is extreme and troublesome in a way that fits with clinical perfectionism because:

- it is preventing him from functioning socially or in other ways;
- the strength of his view is based on a desire to meet a personal standard of appearance, which is clearly causing him distress and undue preoccupation;
- he continues to pursue these high standards in spite of the adverse effects.

This presentation fits with the definition of perfectionism as 'the overdependence of self-evaluation on the determined pursuit of personally demanding, self-imposed standards, in at least one highly salient domain, despite adverse consequences' (Shafran et al., 2002: 778). Shafran et al.'s definition highlights the *purpose* of perfectionism and the *mechanism* by which it becomes dysfunctional. Thus, perfectionism *per se* is not dysfunctional but becomes so when self-evaluation is overly dependent on the attainment of unrealistic high standards, whose pursuit is maintained at all costs.

Clients like Steven, who strive for perfection, may present for therapy with other symptoms, including depression, OCD, eating disorders and low-self esteem. Perfectionism may present an obstacle to therapy, which may require careful therapeutic attention. With illustrative case examples, this chapter will draw on relevant literature to explore perfectionism as a therapeutic obstacle.

DEFINITION OF PERFECTIONISM

A number of useful definitions of clinical perfectionism are available (Hamachek, 1978; Hollender, 1978; Burns, 1980; Shafran et al., 2002). Hamachek (1978) describes a perfectionist as someone 'whose efforts, even their best ones, never seem good enough, at least in their own eyes. It always seems to these persons, that they should and could do better' (p. 27). Shafran et al. (2002) offer a cognitive behavioural definition of perfectionism quoted earlier under the case of Steven. Perfectionists can be similar to high achievers, hence the description of perfectionism as normal or abnormal (Hamachek, 1978). Table 6.1 differentiates normal and abnormal perfectionism.

Thus, as in the case of Steven, the perfectionist will usually set unrealistic goals and remain in a state of dissatisfaction and distress. The perfectionism is all-consuming, with an inability to recognise adverse effects on ability to form relationships and engage socially or professionally until crisis-point. There is consequent unhappiness, self-criticism and perception of self as a failure, when unrealistic standards are not satisfactorily met. Thus, it is understandable that perfectionism interferes with enjoyment of life, is accompanied by constant worry, and contributes to low self-esteem and mood disturbance.

Table 6.1   Normal versus abnormal perfectionism

Criteria	Abnormal (clinical) perfectionism	Normal perfectionism
Stress	Higher	Lower
Effect of stress	Obstacle to goal achievement	Spur towards goal achievement
Driver	Fear of failure	Need to achieve
Effect of driver	High stress, unhappiness, self-criticism, avoidance of tasks	Motivation, engagement with tasks
Goals	Unrealistic	Achievable
Standards	Personally set, unachievable, global	Less precise, situation specific

Cognitively, Hollender (1978) highlights how the perfectionist engages in selective attention, so that one is 'constantly on the alert for what is wrong and seldom focuses on what is right'. The analogy of the client as 'slave to standards' is appropriate here. Perfectionists become their own 'unrelenting slave master' who is never satisfied and continues to expect more. When the standard is achieved, there is likely to be further criticism, due to the cognitive bias towards what has not been achieved or completed to the perfectionist's satisfaction (Shafran et al., 2002). They are continually looking out for and finding evidence for 'imperfection'. Consequently, they behave in ways that maintain the perfectionism. This issue was particularly pertinent in the case of Steven. He spent hours studying his image from different angles in the mirror. He avoided social contact, due to fear that others would view him as ugly. He became intermittently depressed, due to his strongly held view that he was 'visually unacceptable to others'. He strongly believed that the only help he needed was a cosmetic surgery consultation with a surgeon, who would alter his face to his desired shape.

As with other disorders, which are associated with high standards such as OCD, the expression of the perfectionism can be either overt or covert. Overt perfectionism might present as observable behaviours, such as Steven's seeking of cosmetic surgery and over-attendance to appearance. Covert perfectionism might be more subtle and not so easily observed. An example might be the attention paid to other people's responses, selective attention to evidence of failure to meet standards and choices made on the basis of fear of such failure. Either way, perfectionism might at some point appear to be adaptive but will ultimately become disruptive and dysfunctional. An example might be the singer, whose fear of creative failure drives him to practise and become exceptional but is then unable to perform, for fear of not meeting a high personal standard.

CO-MORBIDITY

Perfectionism, though widespread, commonly occurs alongside or as part of another Axis I or II disorder (e.g. OCD, anxiety, depression and eating disorders). Literature indicates that perfectionism is a predictor of poor treatment outcome and interferes with the therapeutic relationship. Shafran et al. (2002) suggest that the negative effect of perfectionism on treatment of a psychiatric disorder will be more likely, where there is an overlap between the domain affected by the perfectionism and the psychiatric disorder. For example, a social phobic fear of negative evaluation of his appearance by others in Steven, might be exacerbated by his unrealistic standards of acceptable appearance. Shafran et al. suggest that eating disorders may be unique in that perfectionism does not merely co-occur with the psychiatric disorder but the disorder is in fact an expression of perfectionism in control of eating, shape or weight. Perfectionism has been shown to co-exist with eating disorders (Fairburn et al., 1997; Fairburn et al., 1999), muscle dysmorphia (Grieve et al., 2009), procrastination (Flett, et al. (1992), depression (Hewitt et al. 1998; Arpin-Cribbie et al., 2008), OCD (OCCWG, 1997; Frost et al., 2002) and social anxiety (Ashbaugh et al., 2007). Comprehensive assessment of its presence and impact is therefore important.

ASSESSING PERFECTIONISM

The thinking of perfectionists is in general, overly self-critical. This is evidenced by black and white and self-belittling statements in response to perceived failure to meet unrealistically high standards. This detail may be identified early at assessment or may emerge as a clinical entity over time. Assessment of the perfectionism can be difficult when it is so closely identified with a psychiatric disorder that it can be masked by it. Historically, perfectionism has been viewed as a uni-dimensional construct. More recently, researchers have considered perfectionism as a multi-dimensional construct, consisting of self-oriented (i.e. expecting exacting standards of oneself), other-oriented (i.e. expectations of high standards of others) and socially oriented perfectionism (i.e. a belief that others expect unrealistically high standards of the individual) (Hewitt and Flett, 1991; Shafran et al., 2002). Very helpful measures, both uni-dimensional (e.g. the Dysfunctional Attitude Scale (DAS) Weissman and Beck, 1978) and multi-dimensional (e.g. the Multidimensional Perfectionism Scale (MPS) Hewitt and Flett, 1991) have been developed and are very useful in assessment. These measures can be useful in cases where co-morbidity exists and perfectionism seems to emerge as a theme. This aids formulation and clarifies if therapy should focus on the perfectionism as a clinical entity in its own right or the co-morbid presentation.

FORMULATION ISSUES

Perfectionists evaluate themselves on the basis of the achievement of standards in specific domains (Shafran et al., 2002). This implies that the standard does not have to be objectively high but the over-dependence on its achievement leaves the individual highly vulnerable, if it is not achieved. Perfectionistic clients, therefore, make behavioural or cognitive (overt or covert) efforts to achieve their set standards. Failure to achieve these results in specific types of punitive, belittling and self-critical thinking. Attainment of the standard itself is often not enough, as the bar is likely to be raised due to attending to what has not, rather than what has been done well. They are therefore likely to present with black and white thinking, selective abstraction, magnification and minimisation thinking errors. They may also practise emotional reasoning as the distress from their negative biases and not the objective facts is seen as the supporting evidence for their view that they have failed to meet their standards. They are therefore constantly responding to their perfectionistic fears confirming their sense of having just avoided the worst (i.e. the near miss). This not only maintains the belief in the helpfulness of perfectionism but also the accompanying distress. Clients will often present for treatment as a result of the consequent distress associated with the struggle of striving to satisfy their perfectionistic traits. The resultant consequences may include depression, social isolation, physical distress, poor concentration, or behavioural inhibition (e.g. repeated checking or avoidance).

OBSTACLES ASSOCIATED WITH PERFECTIONISM

Obstacles in Engagement

The perfectionist's experience and distress is often associated with negative responses of others, being teased or treated as somehow odd and so on. Engagement can thus, require very careful handling as clients may be vigilant for a negative response. Steven for example, was reluctant to engage, as he believed the therapist would not share his perception (i.e. an image of himself as 'imperfect and ugly') or would think of him as somehow 'crazy'. It was therefore imperative that the therapist engage with him by:

- *acknowledging the source of his distress*: the therapist non-judgementally accepted Steven's distress and perspective without reinforcing it;
- *avoiding argumentation or trying to 'make him see sense'*: the therapist resisted putting forward an argument that he was actually 'a handsome young man', who was overly self-critical and suffering major adverse consequences, due to his perfectionist view of the 'ideal' self. It is thus important to:
  - *Clarify a mutually agreed focus of therapy*: Steven and his therapist identified not only the goals of therapy but also the negative consequences of the perfectionism, thus increasing motivation.
  - *Respect and consider the client's perspective and work creatively*: while avoiding argumentation, it is necessary to creatively use CBT interventions in a way that reduces reliance on perfectionism and broadens sources of self evaluation (e.g. Steven learnt to draw on a broad range of sources to reinforce his sense of self-worth, thus reducing his reliance on appearance).

The adverse consequences of perfectionism (e.g. functional impairment) and the need to attain goals may motivate clients to seek therapy. Therapists need to be aware that:

- *Client goals can be driven by perfectionism* (e.g. Steven's desire to have support with his need to access cosmetic surgery).
- *Therapy can be sought to please others*: the client themselves may not be motivationally ready to 'take action' against the perfectionism but others who are impacted upon

by it may make the patient seek therapy, thus presenting a challenge to the engagement process.

- *Perfectionism may be perceived positively*: the initial task of therapy can be to help clients identify the negative consequences of behaviours they consider positive and necessary; Steven, for example, avoided work or socialising and spent endless hours looking through magazines at male models, studying their bone structure apparently in preparation for possible cosmetic surgery, which he considered the only way to 'look acceptable'.
- Literature (e.g. Shafran et al., 2002) indicates that even when the standard is met, the perfectionist is unlikely to be satisfied and may respond by 'raising the bar' even higher. It is unlikely that surgery would satisfy Steven. Making Steven aware of this became one of the initial challenges of therapy and effort to engage him in therapy. In this endeavour therapists can consider specific themes in their assessment and engagement efforts. Some useful themes for consideration are:

  - high standards (strong value system) associated with a salient domain (e.g. physical appearance);
  - the personal adverse consequences of striving to meet that standard (value system);
  - the efforts to meet the standards;
  - the response (cognitive, affective and behavioural) to successful or unsuccessful attainment of the standard;
  - the consequences of relinquishing the high standards.

Proceeding with Engagement and Strengthening the Alliance

As the perfectionism might represent a source of the evaluation of self, rather than a straightforward standard that needs to be achieved (Shafran et al., 2002), letting go of it and its associated responses may pose risks to self identity. Without striving to meet the high standard, Steven for example would be left at the mercy of these strongly held negative beliefs that he is ugly and unacceptable, resulting in increased distress. It is important to:

- *respect where the client is at*: the client's perfectionism is an effort to cope with distress; Steven, for example, is merely trying to cope with his own sense of unacceptability;
- *develop a good and strong therapeutic alliance*: therapy requires a good therapeutic alliance and engagement of the client before undertaking such challenging interventions;
- *use gentle and collaborative cognitive behavioural methods*: foster alternative sources of self-evaluation and alternative beliefs about standards while challenging maintaining behaviours.

It is likely that the therapist may be the first person to whom the client has disclosed aspects of their perfectionism. Clients with perfectionism may engage in behaviours of which they are ashamed or guilty. Forging a good therapeutic alliance with the client is imperative in order for disclosure to occur and continue. The therapist needs to be empathic, accepting and non-judgemental, paying attention to the emotions associated with the perfectionism. A thorough assessment of the perfectionism will be important, so that the therapist can offer a comprehensive, client specific, accurate and acceptable 'maintenance rationale'. Clients may be reluctant to relinquish aspects of their perfectionism, so skill in using engagement focused interventions, such as motivational interviewing (Prochaska and DiClemente, 1986) is helpful. Therapists need to be sensitive to the readiness, or otherwise, of the client to make radical changes. The initial focus may need to be on engagement in therapy and reducing distress rather than on being 'less perfect', unless the client is clearly aware of the need to reduce their demanding standards. Steven, for example, was not ready to make the acceptance of his perceived imperfection a goal. The recognition of this as a possible obstacle was necessary for continuing engagement with him. Thus, the goal of therapy was lowered to one he could achieve. The extract (below) from a discussion between Steven and his therapist illustrates the type of discussion, which might encourage engagement, helping the client and therapist to identify the initial objectives of therapy.

EXTRACT FROM A DIALOGUE BETWEEN STEVEN AND HIS THERAPIST

Therapist: I gather from your GP letter you are uneasy about attending today?

Steven: Yeah, I can't see how talking about my worry about my appearance can help. I need plastic surgery to solve the problem.

Therapist: Sounds like this issue has been troublesome for a long time and you have put a lot of time and energy into trying to find a solution to the problem. That must be difficult for you.

Steven: How would you like to look like this and not be able to go out socially without people looking at you strangely?

Therapist: It must be distressing to hold such a strong negative view of your appearance that it has impacted on your life in such a big way and caused you so much restriction.

Steven: Yeah, my mum keeps telling me I look fine but then she would say that.

Therapist: Aside from your mum, who else that knows you shares her view?

Steven: The GP and my friend Jean – they both think I look OK and I keep pointing out the way my jaw juts out but they don't agree.

Therapist: From what you say, it seems you have a particular view on what shape a jaw should be and others differ in this view. Due to the intensity of this belief you are hiding away and this has caused you a lot of distress and futility in recent months. Given that you have already decided to go down the cosmetic surgery route, I wondered if we could meet together to explore the strength of these beliefs, the idealistic ideas you have of how you should look, maybe checking out some ideas on how to reduce your distress while you wait for the surgery consult.

Steven: Yeah, I suppose that might be worth doing, so ok

As Steven agreed to continue therapy, the risk of him dropping out was averted. This was achieved by the therapist engaging in a modified treatment plan focusing on supporting him to consider orthodontic work rather than surgery. In addition, therapy focused on his avoidance and distress, rather than disputing idealistic views pertaining to his appearance, which would have created a therapeutic obstacle.

THERAPIST CAUTIONS IN ENGAGEMENT

There are issues of which the therapist needs to be aware when working with perfectionism. The therapist's own behaviours and beliefs may create obstacles to therapeutic progress and awareness of these is imperative. Therapists may have perfectionistic traits themselves, leading to an unhelpful *over-identification* with the client. Therapists may expect too much of the client in terms of outcome, leading to frustration for both parties when high expectations are not met. Therapists should heighten their self-awareness when working with perfectionism. The case of Sarah and her therapist (below) illustrates the type of difficulty that can arise as an obstacle to progress towards goal achievement.

THE CASE OF SARAH: HOW MUCH IS ENOUGH?

Sarah is a mother of two, whose husband is a critical recovering alcoholic. To cope with the criticism and tensions in the home and in her relationship, she becomes busy and obsessively cleans, which gives her relief. Her husband says he can't relax as she is cleaning around him and there is conflict as she feels unappreciated by her children, who leave the home untidy after all her efforts. Sarah and her therapist have conflicting views on the need for such high standards of cleanliness when the family relationships are suffering and her health is being affected.

Objective Reality Error

Though perfectionism may be born of early experiences, it is maintained by self-imposed and 'policed' standards. It is therefore a very personal problem, underpinned by personal values. Therapists can make the mistake of seeking a universally accepted standard – *the objective reality error* – which the clients then perceive as a criticism of their personal values, thus affecting engagement and impeding treatment. Therapists need to accept the client's position, without necessarily agreeing with it. In Sarah's case, the therapist could make the error of trying to convince her that it is reasonable for her children to be untidy, which is in conflict with her value. In the case of Steven, despite not sharing his view that he needed orthodontic treatment, the therapist validated his experience and helped him to feel supported. In this case, the therapist was flexible in matching the client's need, which prevented the perfectionism becoming an obstacle to treatment.

The Perfect Therapeutic Goal

Our experience is that novice therapists can be motivated by perfect therapeutic goals. CBT literature is often written in a way that gives inexperienced therapists the impression that the employment of a series of techniques will lead to the perfect therapeutic outcome – the cure or eradication of a problem. This is not always the case; with perfectionism the trait can remain, though the client's functioning and distress may improve. It is therefore sometimes necessary to make improved functioning and distress reduction the primary goals of therapy. In such instances, the reduction of the perfectionism trait becomes a bonus. For example, Sarah might not be able to change her perfectionist traits. She might, however, be able to become more comfortable with her children's lower standards. She might learn to see it not as evidence of her *failure* but a sign of their youth, thus reducing the pressure to meet her high standards. In Steven's case, at the end of treatment he continued to have strong views on his appearance but was better able to cope socially, he had secured employment and was not obsessing on a daily basis. His belief ratings and ability to cope improved and he was not now seeking surgery, agreeing to orthodontic dentistry work instead.

TREATMENT OF PERFECTIONISM

Due to the high co-morbidity with psychiatric disorders, varying treatments may be appropriate depending on the presenting case. We advise referring to the relevant treatment protocols depending on the co-existing psychiatric disorder. A specific empirically grounded treatment for perfectionism is still lacking (Glover et al., 2007). However, CBT-based treatments have been published, including a randomised controlled trail (Riley et al., 2007), a case series (Glover et al., 2007), a group-based approach (Ashbaugh et al., 2007) and a richly detailed single-case study (Hirsch and Haywood, 1998). These and other studies can provide some direction towards appropriate interventions for perfectionism. Glover et al. (2007: 89) recommend a four-stage treatment:

- a personalised formulation in terms of clinical perfectionism: perfectionism as an obstacle to formulation;
- broadening the client's scheme for self-evaluation: therapy as a source of confirmation of perfectionism;
- using behavioural experiments to test competing hypotheses;
- using cognitive behavioural methods to address personal standards, self criticism and cognitive biases that maintain clinical perfectionism.

We will use these stages as the source of our discussion of obstacles associated with perfectionism.

PERFECTIONISM AS AN OBSTACLE TO FORMULATION

Due to the difficulty in engagement associated with perfectionism, Glover et al., (2007) recommend that the personalised formulation be carried out at the end of the assessment interview. However, due to the likelihood of perfectionism being masked by or co-existing with another disorder, it can be very challenging to formulate the perfectionism, co-occurring disorder or both. Co-existing Axis 1 disorders may appear atypical in their presentation. Sarah, for example, can be formulated as an OCD, a perfectionism presentation or a combination of both.

As mentioned earlier, co-morbidly of perfectionism with other disorders is high. It is not within the scope of this chapter to outline all the co-morbid variations. It is worthwhile within this chapter to examine perfectionism in the context of one of the common co-morbid disorders – OCD. Perfectionism has been recognised as a belief domain in OCD (Frost et al., 2002). The Obsessive Compulsive Cognitions Working Group (OCCWG) (1997) have grouped these belief domains as follows:

- inflated responsibility;
- over-importance of thoughts;
- over-estimation of threat;
- importance of controlling thoughts;
- intolerance of uncertainty;
- perfectionism.

Perfectionism in OCD is defined as '… the tendency to believe there is a perfect solution to every problem, that doing something perfectly (i.e. mistake free) is not only possible but also necessary, and that even minor mistakes will have serious consequences' (OCCWG, 1997: 678). Clients with OCD will tend to evaluate thoughts in terms of an absolute, complete or perfect way (e.g. 'I need to be absolutely certain this is done correctly and there is no chance I have made a mistake or there might be consequences'). It will be necessary and possible for therapists to differentiate perfectionism and the co-occurring disorder such as OCD, based on the motivation for the maintenance cycle. For example, in this example of OCD and perfectionism:

- OCD might be associated with an effort to reduce anxiety or feared catastrophe;
- perfectionism might be associated with a fear of not meeting a personally defined standard, which might imply failure.

In identifying perfectionism in OCD, therapists may need to be vigilant for the client who 'tries too hard' to get things right. They may over-control their thoughts, try to create the perfect living environment (as in the case of Sarah) or strive to meet the perfect partner and so on, which then creates problems. Similar differentiations would need to be derived for other disorders; however, for co-existing presentations like depression and low self-esteem, where self-critical statements may be an aspect, extreme care needs to be taken.

PERFECTIONISM AS AN OBSTACLE IN THERAPY

THE CASE OF MILA – 'BUT THEY WILL FIND OUT I'M A FRAUD!'

Mila, an architect, graduated at the top of her year in university, feels professionally and socially surpassed by her academically inferior peers. She lost a job in the past and attributes this to her employers having discovered that she was not as good as she made herself out to be. She will now cancel job interviews, fearing that she will not be perfectly prepared. She fears being found out as 'a fraud', who is not as good as expected. She no longer socialises with peers or family as she needs to be in control. Her marriage of one year's duration is suffering. She and her husband never socialise, as she can never be sure that social experiences will be 'the best they can be.' Mila is frustrated and depressed at being in a job for which she is over-qualified. She believes that perfectionism is protecting her from being found out and reducing her standards will result in failure.

Clients' perfectionism is often motivated by an abiding fear of failure. The negative consequences of this fear of failure create an impediment to functioning and the achievement of goals, as in the case of Mila. Emotionally, she is frustrated and depressed. Socially, she is struggling and her marriage is suffering. Professionally, she is not realising her full potential. In spite of this, Mila continues to believe that her high standards are helpful and protective.

Therapy as a Source of Potential Failure for the Perfectionist

The centrality of a fear of failure in perfectionism presents a very particular therapeutic hazard. Therapy itself presents a great potential for failure, in such areas as:

- *Homework*: clients may return to therapy with great frustration and distress, because goals have not been achieved to expected standards. For example, in therapy, Mila had idealistic standards about their need to be 'less perfect'.
- *Goal achievement*: they may expect themselves to reach ideal goals rapidly and become frustrated. Mila for example, believed that she had failed, because distress reduction was not achieved quickly and perfectly enough.
- *Expectations of self and others*: the goal-achievement hazard described above is most likely if the perfectionism is self-oriented. If the perfectionism is socially oriented, clients may feel under pressure to be the 'perfect client'. If the perfectionism is other-focused, therapists too can fail in the eyes of the client, as they may be expected to meet very high standards, especially when the perfectionism is other oriented.

Hirsch and Hayward (1998) describe the 'perfect patient', whose improvement was signified by a reduction in the need to do homework perfectly or in some cases not doing it at all. As a cue for perfectionism, therapists can be vigilant for the client who never seems to 'be satisfied' or seems critical of themselves, therapeutic modality, service or the therapist themselves.

As was done with Mila, regular, clear and collaboratively derived behavioural analyses will be vital. The careful reviewing of homework using guided discovery to identify the presentation of the 'perfectionistic bias' and its alternatives will help to motivate towards change. Therapists need to look for evidence supporting the belief in failure as well as to be aware of the focus of the perfectionism (i.e. self, other or socially oriented). Mila, for example, due to her reliance on a perfect outcome, returned to therapy claiming that the week had been a 'disaster'. Thus, the homework had created an opportunity for her to fail to achieve a perfect outcome. Clients don't leave their perfectionism at the clinic room door. They continue to be perfectionists in the process of therapy too. Therapy is, therefore, a laboratory for testing out what really happens outside of the therapy room. The view of 'self as a failure unless specific standards are met' is self-perpetuating (i.e. keeps itself going) and self-fulfilling (i.e. creates its own evidence). Therapy not only presents opportunities to identify the cycles that maintain perfectionism but also creates opportunities for the reinforcement of the fear of 'imperfection' (e.g. failure). In illustration of the effect of the use of the behavioural analysis and Socratic questioning, Mila's therapist concluded that her perceived 'disastrous' events were really only disastrous in the context of her perfectionism. The homework had created an opportunity for Mila to try to be perfect and to potentially fail. Thus, the tasks of therapy can be used to shed new light on the effects of this perfectionism.

Novice therapists can be overwhelmed by the perfectionist's awareness of the multitude of areas in which perceived failure occurs. Some therapists resist being specific in therapy with perfectionists, for fear of giving the client opportunities to practice more perfectionism. However, the aim of therapy is to encourage learning and when learning situations are focused and specific, there is greater likelihood that the client will make the correct interpretation. It is often easier and more achievable for the client to practise alternatives with a specific situation than to be unfocused and try to 'just be less perfect', which makes therapy a risk to 'the self' of the perfectionist.

Perfectionist Images, Expectations and Behaviours

Perfectionists may hold ideal images and outcomes based on experience, which they then try to meet. The media, idealised others or even fictional characters may be emulated with the expectation that such an ideal can be achieved. An extreme example might be the priest who is not satisfied with being a good priest but, instead, strives to be as good as Jesus or God himself. Subtle versions of this can be difficult to formulate for the client, especially if they are close to what is socially acceptable, such as a teenager striving to be fashionable and acceptable or Mila's belief in the need to be prepared, based on her past experience. A helpful approach is to focus on specific situations and perform behavioural analyses as already discussed. This is a useful way to identify the reinforcement of feared outcomes by:

- maintenance cycles;
- perfectionist expectations;
- behaviours.

An example would be a behavioural analysis of Mila's homework. Rather than a general discussion of the week, the therapist identified a shopping trip with her sister and school friend as a therapeutic opportunity. Mila had organised the trip with an 'ideal' image of them all laughing and laden with shopping bags, like the characters from the film *Sex and the City*. In reality, the trip was relaxed and her companions 'were not buying in every shop'. Mila became frustrated, tearful and angry. Not meeting the standard in her mental image resulted in her feeling a failure, causing distress. Analyses of the evidence that the trip was a 'disaster' were conducted, considering evidence from Mila herself, as well as from each of her companions. Mila identified a typical 'self-fulfilling prophecy' associated with her perfectionism. She realised that events generally go well, until she perceives herself as not meeting a personal standard, which is set in her mind and then she becomes distressed. Her efforts to meet this expectation then result in the perception that her feared outcome (i.e. failure) had been realised. During the homework, her reaction of anger and tearfulness made the event 'imperfect' and resulted in criticism of herself as a failure and 'disaster' at organising events. The cycle was repeated both within and outside the therapy room. Failure to be focused and specific in treatment leads to lack of opportunities for identifying the self-fulfilling prophecy of perfectionism. This reduces the motivation for change, and leads to frustration for therapist and client and difficulty in identifying goals.

Perfectionism as a Source of Distress Relief

Perfectionism can be perceived by clients as a source of distress relief. Failure to meet perfectionist standards or deliberate attempts to relinquish them can leave the client at the mercy of the distress. Clients' resistance of perfectionism is thus a key to associated core beliefs and arousal, which can be masked by the perfectionist behaviours. Perfectionists can often be unaware of or deny any associated distress, particularly if they have a long history. This is akin to obediently living under a repressive law for so long that it feels normal. Only when one steps out of the 'norm' does that 'norm' seem wrong. It may thus be necessary to help perfectionists to find alternative ways of coping with or tolerating associated distress (see Chapter 8).

PLANNING OF INTERVENTIONS

A core hypothesis in the formulation of perfectionism is that perfectionists' self-evaluation is based on a limited number of domains (Shafran et al., 2002). It is therefore necessary to use CBT interventions to broaden the domains for self-evaluation. Without doing so, the client is likely to remain vulnerable to any perceived failure to achieve limited, self-imposed demanding standards. Planning of interventions can be helped by hypothesising the means by which they may achieve desired goals as follows:

- *Behavioural experiments*: experiments function as a means of gathering information, identifying the effects of perfectionism and evolving alternatives (Glover et al., 2007) as well as practising new and more helpful strategies to confirm or disconfirm beliefs.
- *Examination and challenging of perfectionist cognitions*: their function is the reduction of the client's conviction regarding their rigidly held beliefs and an increase in the belief ratings for more flexible beliefs. (Hirsch and Hayward, 1998)

In their single case study, Hirsch and Hayward (1998) detail the main perfectionism specific interventions, which have been elaborated on by others (e.g. Shafran et al., 2002; Grieve et al, 2009). These interventions are used in conjunction with standard CBT techniques, such as focus on maintenance factors and having clearly identified goals. Strategies include the examination of perfectionist beliefs, such as all or nothing thinking and developing new and alternative assumptions and beliefs. They also suggest the examination of the disadvantages of perfectionist beliefs and cognitive biases and their modification. Usual CBT interventions include identifying alternative and more balanced ways of expressing perfectionist statements, cost–benefit analyses of the perfectionist thinking and behaviour as well as the continuum technique (Padesky, 1994) as a way of reducing rigidity, absolutism and introducing the notion of degrees of perfectionism. To reinforce the new, more flexible beliefs, specific incidents that are in keeping with them are recorded regularly by the client. Thus, as treatment progresses, the focus is increasingly on reinforcement of more flexible thinking.

PERFECTIONISM AND THE IMPLICATIONS FOR CHANGE

Clients with perfectionism can often find that they structure their lives in a way that allows them to practise perfectionism. They may seek employment that makes their perfectionism acceptable. For example, the client with perfectionism in a body image domain might seek employment in the fashion industry or in the physical fitness industry, while one who has perfectionism about getting things right intellectually might become an accountant, etc. The clients may function well or even excel for some time. In that way their perfectionism is not dissimilar to helpful high standards. At some point, however, the perfectionism begins to interfere with the performance of tasks, so that the accountant takes too long to do his duty and clients complain, the fashion model becomes so overly thin that that they look ill and are unable to find work and the fitness instructor spends so much time working out that he is unable to help his clients. Only then does the client seek help. Unfortunately, they can find it challenging to set appropriate goals because of the personally accumulated past evidence that perfectionism *is* helpful. They may believe that their achievements have been realised as a result of the perfectionism, which they may simply view as 'a high standard'. They may even have received compliments for these high standards in the past. This perception of perfectionism as positive and functional can create a tension between therapeutic and personal need. It is wise for therapists to be aware of the impact of this on goal setting and motivation for change, which may help to prevent this becoming an obstacle in therapy.

Cognitions about the usefulness of perfectionism need to be identified and tested. Cognitive distortions may include black and white thinking and the evaluation of self in terms of goal achievement. Performance then becomes a very important theme resulting in a high vulnerability to distress (i.e. low mood, anxiety, etc.) if those goals are unmet. Unlike the individual with high standards, who aims to do well and would be disappointed if they don't, the perfectionist rates their worth not only by the achievement of the goal but also by the extent of the achievement (Shafran et al., 2002). Mila, for example, might not simply be content with succeeding in getting a job that she applies for. She would also need to be the best candidate and becomes depressed and frustrated if she 'feels' this not to be the case. Simply having a good time with her companions is not enough; she wants everyone to carry handfuls of shopping and be laughing hysterically all day or else it is all a disaster! Indeed perfectionists can sometimes seem to be controlling of others to achieve personal satisfaction. Perfectionists may thus engage in emotional reasoning, ignoring objective evidence in favour of their 'felt sense' that they have failed, which is distressing.

THE BROODING TRAP

Clients like Mila and Steven can get caught up in what has been described as the 'brooding trap' (Flett and Hewitt, 2008). This involves ruminating over what is not done well and how what has been done could have been done better. This type of 'brooding' is often associated with depression and depressive rumination. It may be difficult for this type of brooding to be separated from other types of repetitive thinking, so that the therapists are 'side-tracked' by diagnosis (see Chapter 9). Without being able to recognise perfectionism, clients may be deemed as experiencing depressive ruminations or OCD. Therapists in practice may focus on the wrong disorder and use the wrong interventions particularly in cases where co-morbidity is a problem (see Chapter 3).

The brooding trap can also affect therapists. It may be attached to their need 'to get things right' and have their clients think highly of them. This is an example of 'other-oriented' perfectionism presenting as therapists who have a strong desire to please their clients. This is something to reflect on ourselves as therapists.

SUMMARY

Although there is no universally accepted treatment model for perfectionism, there is an evolving body of literature and research. Perfectionism presents as a clinical entity in its own right or co-existent with other disorders. Clearly, it merits attention in its own right. Becoming familiar with and recognising perfectionism, as well as being skilled with intervention approaches, provides a useful additional tool in working with a range of clients, where perfectionism can become a problem and obstacle in therapy.

LEARNING EXERCISE

- Consider the patients you have worked with. Identify any possible presence of perfectionism that you may have missed.
- Attempt to re-work that patient's formulation, taking account of the perfectionism.
- What impact do you think that perfectionism may have had on therapy progress towards goals?
- What would you do differently with a similar patient?
- Over the next month, identify one patient on your current case load and include perfectionism-focused interventions in your work.

REFERENCES

Arpin-Cribbie, C.A., Irvine, J., Ritvo, P., Cribbie, R.A., Flett, G.L. and Hewitt, P.L. (2008) 'Perfectionism and psychological distress: a modelling approach to understand their therapeutic relationship', *Journal of Rational Emotive Cognitive Behaviour Therapy*, 26: 151–67.

Ashbaugh, A., Antony, M.M., Liss, A., Summerfeldt, L.J., McCabe, R.E. and Swinson, R.P. (2007) 'Changes in perfectionism following cognitive behavioural treatment for social phobia', *Depression and Anxiety*, 24: 169–77.

Burns, D. (1980) 'The perfectionist's script for self-defeat', *Psychology Today*, November: 34–52.

Fairburn, C.,G., Shafran, R. and Cooper, Z. (1999) 'A cognitive-behavioural theory of anorexia nervosa', *Behaviour Research and Therapy*, 37, 1–13.

Fairburn, C.G., Welch, S.L., Doll, H.A., Davies, B.A. and O'Connor, M.E. (1997) 'Risk factors for bulimia-nervosa: a community-based case-control study', *Archives of General Psychiatry*, 54: 509–17.

Flett, G.L. and Hewitt, P.L. (2008) 'Treatment interventions for perfectionism – a cognitive perspective: Introduction to the special issue', *Journal of Rational Emotive Cognitive Behaviour Therapy*, 26: 127–33.

Flett, G.L., Blankstein, K.R., Hewitt, P.L. and Koledin, S. (1992) 'Components of perfectionism and procrastination in college students', *Social Behaviour and Personality*, 20: 85–94.

Frost, R.O., Novarra C. and Rheaume, J. (2002) 'Perfectionism in obsessive compulsive disorder', in R.O. Frost and G. Steketee (eds), *Cognitive Approaches to Obsessions and Compulsions*. New York. Pergamon. pp. 91–105.

Glover, D.S., Brown, G.P., Fairburn, C.G. and Shafran, R. (2007) 'A preliminary evaluation of cognitive-behavioural therapy for clinical perfectionism: a case series', *British Journal of Clinical Psychology*, 46: 85–94.

Grieve, F.G., Truba, N. and Bowerbox, S. (2009) 'Etiology, assessment and treatment of muscle dysmorphia', *Journal of Cognitive Psychotherapy: An International Quarterly*, 23 (4): 306–13.

Hamachek, D.E. (1978) 'Psychodynamics of normal and neurotic perfectionism', *Psychology: A Journal of Human Behaviour*, 15: 27–33.

Hewitt, P.L. and Flett, G.L. (1991) 'Perfectionism in the self and social contexts; conceptualisation, assessment, and association with psychopathology', *Journal of Personality and Social Psychology*, 60: 456–70.

Hewitt, P.L., Flett, G.L., Eidiger, E., Norton, G.R. and Flynn, C.A. (1998) 'Perfectionism in chronic and state symptoms of depression', *Canadian Journal of Behavioural Science*, 30: 234–42.

Hirsch, C.R. and Hayward, P. (1998) 'The perfect patient: cognitive behavioural therapy for perfectionism', *Behavioural and Cognitive Psychology*, 26: 359–64.

Hollender, M.H. (1978) 'Perfectionism, a neglected personality trait', *Journal of Clinical Psychiatry*, 39: 384.

Obsessive Compulsive Cognitions Working Group (OCCWG) (1997) Cognitive assessment of obsessive compulsive disorder', *Behaviour Research and Therapy*, 39: 887–78.

Padesky, C.A. (1994) 'Schema change processes in cognitive therapy', *Clinical Psychology and Psychotherapy*, 1 (5): 267–78.

Prochaska, J.O. and DiClemente, C.C. (1986) 'Transtheoretical psychotherapy: towards a more integrative model of change', *Psychotherapy: Theory Research and Practice*, 19: 276–88.

Riley, C., Lee, M., Cooper, Z., Fairburn, C.G. and Shafran, R. (2007) 'A randomised trial of cognitive behaviour therapy for clinical perfectionism: a preliminary study', *Behaviour Research and Therapy*, 45: 2221–31.

Shafran, R., Cooper, Z. and Fairburn, C.G. (2002) 'Clinical perfectionism: a case report', *Behaviour Research and Therapy*, 40: 773–791.

Weissman, A.N. and Beck, A.T. (1978) 'Development and validation of the dysfunctional attitude scale', paper presented at the annual meeting of the Association for the Advancement of Behaviour Therapy, Chicago.

7

WORKING WITH INTOLERANCE OF AROUSAL

CRAIG CHIGWEDERE AND MICHAEL MCDONOUGH

LEARNING OBJECTIVES

After reading this chapter, the reader should be able to:

- conceptualise arousal intolerance and avoidance;
- recognise arousal intolerance in therapy;
- identify how arousal intolerance can present an obstacle to therapeutic progress;
- identify some interventions for overcoming experiential intolerance and avoidance.

INTRODUCTION

Psychotherapy achieves change by targeting subjective and behavioural experiences. Facing subjective experiences can be very difficult for some patients, which presents a considerable therapeutic obstacle. The case of Mark, with whom we worked in therapy, illustrates this problem.

THE CASE OF MARK – DRINKING TO FEEL BETTER

Mark has an alcohol problem. Since stopping drinking, whenever he feels anxious he wants to drink to numb or take the feelings away. The anxiety is accompanied by images of catastrophe, from which he tries to distract himself by keeping busy. He was supposed to have attended a support group for an hour as part of his CBT homework. He tells the therapist, 'I didn't do the homework because thought of the feelings that it would bring up was too much. I feel red-raw! I know that the feelings won't kill me but I can't cope with them. Even just thinking about them now terrifies me! Can we talk about something else, please?'

Mark appears to have an intolerance of, or difficulty with, appropriately experiencing thoughts, emotions and/or bodily sensations. Like many people with intolerance of arousal, he tries to 'avoid' subjective experiences, hence the term experiential avoidance (Hayes et al., 1996). Such intolerance and avoidance are not uncommon in therapy, as either discrete problems or secondary to another presentation. Indeed, theorists such as Hayes and colleagues in acceptance and commitment therapy (ACT) (e.g. Hayes et al., 1999) and Linehan (1993) and colleagues in dialectical behaviour therapy (DBT), see such intolerance as central to many psychological problems. Using clinical experience, particularly from the authors' work with dissociation and non-epileptic seizures and drawing on the work of others (e.g. Hayes et al., 1996; Goldstein et al., 2010), this chapter describes an approach to working with intolerance of arousal, which has been helpful for many of our patients. This is not a subject that is routinely taught on CBT courses but can affect therapy, which makes it important that it is included in the current text. Besides the case of Mark already provided, we will draw on three other cases, each illustrating a specific aspect of our discussion of arousal intolerance, including assessment and formulation and treatment obstacles associated with two different hypothesised broad presentations of arousal intolerance.

RECOGNISING INTOLERANCE

Many mental-health problems involve subjective discomfort but this does not necessarily constitute the intolerance of focus in this chapter. Such arousal intolerance can be difficult to identify but it is most easily recognised through the conscious or unconscious measures employed to cope with the unwanted subjective experiences. In Mark's case, he wanted to avoid what he described as feeling 'red raw'. The measures taken to avoid the feelings are often disproportionate to the presenting trigger, so that the issue being avoided is more the subjective arousal than the situation or its consequences.

In conscious intolerance of arousal, the individual 'does' something effortful (planned or unplanned) to cognitively, emotionally, physiologically or behaviourally avoid or reduce the arousal. Mark, for example, would try to change the subject, to keep busy or to avoid engaging with his homework task, which tallies with Hayes et al.'s (1996) definition of experiential avoidance as '… the phenomenon that occurs when a person is unwilling to remain in contact with particular private experiences (e.g. bodily sensations, emotions, thoughts, memories and behavioural predispositions) and takes steps to alter the form or frequency of these events or the contexts that occasion them' (p. 1155).

Avoidance of subjective experience can also be unconscious and automatic. Examples include dissociative experiences such as non-epileptic seizures and depersonalisation, which bring clients out of the awareness of what is happening in their bodies as an adaptive or automatic protective response. Research evidence is growing to illustrate that in dissociative responses there can be an automatic reduction of activity in the motor centres of the brain (e.g. Kanaan et al. 2007). Reduced autonomic responses to unpleasant but not to pleasant stimuli has been illustrated in patients with dissociation, though their startle response is increased, suggesting that they have a selective inhibition on mechanisms associated with emotional processing (e.g. Sierra et al., 2002). Such inhibition is outside of awareness.

A HYPOTHESIS FOR MAINTENANCE

THE CASE OF PAUL'S PANIC – 'I KNOW I WON'T DIE BUT IT HURTS!'

Paul has a history of panic disorder. He has had successful CBT treatment no longer catastrophically misinterprets bodily sensations but has relapsed following a relationship break-up. He now knows that he will not have a heart attack or pass out but is fearful of the bodily sensations. He now avoids some everyday situations and wants to get rid of the sensations themselves because 'they are intolerable'. Paul also notices that if the sensations are present for any length of time he detaches from them, becomes less aware if his body and feels separated from it. The detachment began with his first panic and gradually worsened. There is no identified trigger situation but he describes a car accident sometime prior to the onset of the panic and detachment.

It is crucial for therapists to have a coherent and acceptable explanation for patients. Without such a rationale for presenting problems, therapy and collaboration will be very challenging. One useful explanation is based on associative learning theories (Mowrer, 1947, 1960).

In Paul's case, the preliminary formulation was that he was intolerant of sensations that were related to his panic. The unconscious experiential avoidance of detachment, which he experienced during his first panic, then continued. The therapist hypothesised that sensations or reminders of the panic had become *conditioned stimuli*, which trigger the *conditioned response* of arousal. There was then the consequent voluntary behavioural avoidance and an automatic, involuntary avoidance through detachment or depersonalisation. Paul was well until a critical event (the relationship break-up) raised the reminders of panic and induced subjective experiences similar to those to which he has become sensitised. Experiential avoidance through detachment brought temporary relief from the sensations but in fact served to maintain

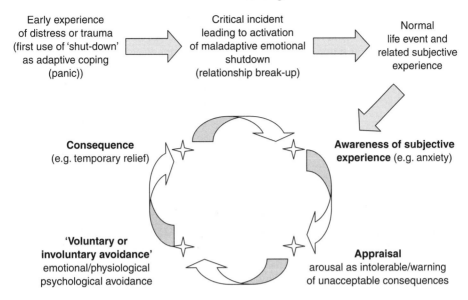

Figure 7.1   Conceptualising emotional shut-down

their intolerability. Perhaps the subjective experience functioned as a warning system or cue for voluntary and involuntary avoidance, resulting in a 'shut down' response (detachment in Paul's case) rather than increased arousal response, as in panic. This maintenance cycle is described in Figure 7.1.

SHARING THE RATIONALE WITH THE PATIENT

Use of analogies, such as those from the Second World War, when soldiers on the frontline went blind after witnessing trauma, or the detachment behaviour of animals such as possums, can be helpful. It is important to instil hope, to avoid making the person feel that they are being perceived as mad, condescended or disbelieved. The maintenance cycle can be diagrammatically illustrated, with the therapist sitting shoulder-to-shoulder with the patient or using a white board. The cycle is explained slightly differently for voluntary and involuntary avoidance as illustrated below. In Paul's case, the second explanation was offered.

Voluntary Experiential Avoidance

'Paul, it would seem that the situation, such as the motorway or a confrontation, is only a key to unlock the real danger, which appears to be the feeling of discomfort, to which you have become very sensitive and which you naturally want to reduce. Unfortunately, these sensations have over time become triggered by a multitude of situations which you encounter regularly in your daily life. Sadly, the success of the measures you take to make yourself feel better, such as avoiding roads, confrontation and thinking about the feelings, means that you will have to use those measures again and again in order to feel better. By so doing, the feelings become increasingly frightening and you become more sensitive to them. It might be helpful for us to find a way for you to become more comfortable with these feelings. This would reduce the fearfulness of the situations that trigger them. How does that sound to you?'

Involuntary Experiential Avoidance

'Paul, for reasons that we don't understand, it seems that once you have experienced this emotional "shut-down", the body can become very sensitive to normal feelings. These normal feelings or sensations are interpreted by the system, as a warning of the onset of something terrible, so that in future the body automatically "shuts down" for the sake of safety. This mechanism would have been useful, for example in Stone Age times, when there was a lot of danger from predators. Most of the predators that would have presented a danger to us, such as lions and tigers, would prefer to kill for themselves, so being still and appearing dead would have reduced the chances of being attacked. "Shutting down" emotionally would have reduced fight-or-flight-related emotional and bodily reactions, which may have reduced the risk of drawing the attention of the predator. Sadly, even though we're no longer surrounded by predators, our fear-response system has not been updated. Unfortunately, the body does not distinguish between situations. It reacts only to the feelings, which may be entirely harmless.

Once the shutting-down response is "switched on", for example by an accident, it becomes a way of avoiding all intense feelings that may lead to pain or distress. The body therefore begins to shut down, seemingly at random in response to any arousal feelings, which may be caused by a variety of unrelated and harmless situations. So, it is possible that when you feel bodily sensations that are similar to those you felt at the time of the accident, your body automatically associates them with the onset of pain and distress and shuts down to protect itself. Your avoidance of distressing situations might then not only maintain but increase the fearfulness of the avoided situations, so that the next time you are confronted with them, they are more likely to cause bodily sensations, resulting in more shutting down. How does this sound to you?'

Poor rationale giving can become an obstacle to therapy, with several risks. The patient might:

- not give the therapy much credibility and not go along with it;
- be at odds with the therapist concerning the rationale for the problem;

- find it difficult to engage with exposure and behavioural experiments;
- relapse because of the intolerance, if it's not resolved.

The therapist might:

- 'skirt around' the intolerance of arousal in the hope that targeting those symptoms that he/she understands (e.g. the drinking and low mood) will affect the emotional shut-down;
- take a 'hit and miss' approach;
- become frustrated;
- refer patients like Paul onto someone else.

OBSTACLES RELATED TO ASSESSMENT

The Search for Predisposing and Precipitating Factors

One of the first obstacles to confront the therapist is often a search for the reason for the intolerance of arousal. Patients can seek an explanation for their experience and the therapist can get bogged down in trying to find a clear causal event. It is not necessary to seek a traumatic predisposing or precipitating event. However, if important causal events are identifiable, they may be those that at the time of occurrence resulted in the individual feeling powerless to control outcome. These may include being overprotected, bullied, seriously ill, sexually abused or terrified. The only recourse for the body during the experience or later recall might be to 'shut-down' cognitively, emotionally or somatically or to behaviourally avoid, as a means of escaping the subjective experiences. Emotional processing of the event is then impeded. Our approach would be to:

- Resist 'mining' for causal events if they are not remembered by the client. Instead offer the maintenance rationale in Figure 7.1 as the target of intervention. This reduces the likelihood of false memories.
- Focus only on the current presenting problem if a traumatic event is not identified through the normal course of therapeutic questioning (assessment and treatment can often continue very successfully with the identification and targeting of the current maintenance cycle alone).

In the case of Paul, for example, besides the mention of the car accident, there was no single clearly identifiable traumatic event prior to the first panic experience. The therapist resisted searching for an early trauma, such as sexual or physical abuse. In our experience, traumatic events in dissociation do not have to be objectively but only subjectively traumatic. Thus, if the person experienced the event as traumatic, and their system responded by 'shutting down', then it is possible that ongoing dissociation can become a part of the presentation.

Poor Emotional Engagement with the Patient

Standard cognitive behavioural treatment interventions are likely to have a very superficial effect without reducing the intolerance and avoidance issues. Due to the distress associated with arousal:

- patients may develop an automatic response of 'tuning out' experiences (e.g. in talking about his panic, Paul would occasionally 'tune out' and not be emotionally present);
- assessment can be more challenging and take longer than with a patient with normal access to subjective experiences;
- patients may find it difficult to recognise or focus on changes in sensations and emotions (e.g. Paul found it difficult to identify many of his panic sensations, because he had been 'shutting down' and not experiencing them for so long);
- patients may be unable to habituate or engage emotionally with interventions;
- it can be difficult to use exposure tasks or behavioural experiments;
- patients can be labelled as 'resistant'.

Therapist Reaction

Therapists need to be aware of their own responses to engaging in a relationship in which the usual 'rules' associated with awareness and tolerance of one's own subjective experiences do not apply. Patients with intolerance of arousal often struggle to maintain healthy social relationships. The same will be the case in therapy. This was not the case with Paul but the supervision-derived example of a trainee therapist describing her response to assessing an anxious patient with apparent avoidance of arousal (below) illustrates the effect of a poorly understood problem.

A Trainee Therapist's Response to Shut-down

I was so frustrated. Her daughter said she is drinking and awful to live with because of her anxiety. She is unable to do anything alone, not even to cross the road and yet can't tell me a single thing she feels, emotionally or physically! She won't even say she is anxious. She just says, 'I don't know'. I started to think that I was doing it all wrong and I felt like I was failing as a therapist. I felt deflated when I left her.

REFLECTIVE EXERCISE

- What is the trainee experiencing?
- Have you ever felt anything similar?
- What did you do to deal/cope with those emotions and the situation?
- What would you do differently if you found your self in a similar situation?

EMPATHY AND ALLIANCE

Empathy is essential when working with experiential intolerance. Rogers (1980) described it thus: 'This means that the therapist senses accurately the feelings and meanings that the patient is experiencing and communicates this understanding to the client' (p. 116). Therapists working with experiential intolerance need to work very much from the knowledge of their own subjective experiences and then to connect these to the work with the patient. In the case of Paul the therapist was aware of a sense of frustration and, on reflection, realised that this was because of Paul's avoidance of the very arousal necessary for accurate problem assessment and formulation. Second, through reflection in supervision, the therapist was able to recognise the presence and effect of his own schemas. Therapist empathic responses therefore function as:

- a barometer for therapist factors being activated;
- an indicator of those things which the patient is intolerant of.

Therapists too can suffer from intolerance (for the role of the therapist in the therapeutic relationship, see Chapter 2). Therapists may need to develop the skills of empathic awareness and expression, which may helpfully be shown by:

- *Normalising*: 'How would someone else feel in that situation?'
- *Pointing out incongruence*: 'I accept that you say that you don't feel ...; however, you seem [sad, angry, etc.] to me.'
- *Pointing out the natural*: 'That seems very [sad, frightening, etc.]'.
- *Experiential self-disclosure*: 'When you say that, I am aware of a sense of [sadness, anger, etc.]'.

OBSTACLES IN TREATMENT

The Treatment Assumption

Based on the maintenance hypothesis discussed earlier, we can assume that increasing tolerance to subjective experiences will lead to a reduction in their fearfulness and the related avoidance. B.F. Skinner, in his 1962 debate with Carl Rogers, discussed the notion of exposure to emotional stimuli, such as failure and frustration, as well as gradual exposure to physiological and visual stimuli, in order to make them more tolerable (Kirschenbaum and Henderson, 1990). Like Skinner we assume that interventions which increase exposure to subjective experiences will raise their tolerance or acceptance. Whole-treatment approaches have been developed focusing on the notion of acceptance. Of particular importance would be the work of Hayes and colleagues in Acceptance and Commitment Therapy (ACT) (see Hayes et al, 1999) and mindfulness (see Segal et al., 2002).

OBSTACLES ASSOCIATED WITH VOLUNTARY AVOIDANCE

Difficulty Engaging with Exposure and Behavioural Experiments

Returning to the cases of Mark and Paul, any therapeutic efforts were likely to be affected by their arousal intolerance. CBT interventions to tackle their anxiety needed to involve activity that would raise subjective arousal, so that this could be faced and tolerance increased. Patients with arousal intolerance may not engage with exposure tasks and experiments. It is pointless to continue to educate the patient by reiterating the rationale and the harmlessness of the arousal. Therapists may therefore become aware that patients are presenting with:

- awareness that catastrophic consequences will not occur but still be distressed;
- lack the 'emotional' stamina for tolerating discomfort;
- perceptions of their subjective arousal as somehow abnormal.

In both Mark and Paul's cases, there was an awareness that catastrophic consequences were unlikely to occur. This is akin to panic without concious catastrophic misinterpretation. Therapists can be confused and thrown by this type of presentation, which does not fit with the usual disorder-specific models. There may, however, be misinterpretations of normal subjective experiences at the onset of distressing arousal, accompanied by thoughts such as those described by Mark. He would think 'It is happening again' or 'This is going to be distressing', which then triggered fear and efforts to avoid or reduce the arousal. Based on the treatment assumption, in such cases the therapist will need to:

- *Perform exposure as a behavioural experiment*: Paul and his therapist, for example, performed information gathering behavioural experiments to identify the normal progress of arousal. This meant that he had to expose himself to the arousal.
- *Model the normality and tolerability of the arousal*: it is often important for therapists to take part in the exercises with patients, so that they can model and compare normal arousal, which the client might be perceiving as abnormal. Paul and his therapist planned a therapist-assisted exercise in the gym, with the therapist participating and comparing arousal sensations. Therapists need to be aware that arousal might differ in severity due to fitness levels.
- *Raise and encourage tolerance of the arousal*: exposure exercises may involve inducing somatic arousal, to increase 'emotional stamina' for the experience of discomfort. In Paul's case, he and his therapist both ran on a treadmill for increasing durations from one minute to more than ten minutes.
- *Undertake exposure tasks*: 'sit' with the sensations as part of gradual, repeated and prolonged exposure to them. As is the principle with exposure, the exercise is planned as a homework task to be repeated regularly. Though for Paul, it did not reduce the fear of the arousal, in time it made it more acceptable and normal.

Examples of exercises for normalising and increasing tolerance of sensations include:

- *Activity*: engaging in physical activity that is avoided, including sport, physical work, walking upstairs, to raise autonomic arousal. The intensity of the activity can be graded starting with less intense to more intense amounts with gradual increases in duration.

- *Normal bodily sensations*: experientially intolerant patients can at times misinterpret normal sensations such as pins and needles, dizziness, visual disturbances, and will focus on these, without being aware of the effect of self-focused attention. Focusing on a specific body-part (e.g. encouraging the patient to close their eyes, focus on the tips of the fingers, thumb, the inside of the mouth, and describe sensations present there) will help the patient to realise that these sensations are normal, present all the time and not an indication of distressing arousal. Other ways of triggering sensations may include:
  - going from darkness into sudden light or vice versa;
  - taking the arm from an elevated position and letting it suddenly hang limply;
  - activity (e.g. running on the spot, hyperventilation).

- *Focused attention*: patients that experience dissociation can be encouraged to fixate on a dot or stare without blinking to induce dissociation-like sensations

Note: when planning experiments and exposure tasks, it is often worth asking yourself as a therapist, 'Would I do this exercise myself'. If the answer is no, then it is either something you need to work on for yourself or something that is unrealistic to expect of a patient!

Unacceptability of Arousal

Patients can find it difficult to tolerate arousal because of the sense that it is unacceptable. Consequently, focusing on that arousal in exposure or experimentation becomes difficult without efforts to control it somehow, hence the efforts to avoid through experiential avoidance (Hayes et al., 2006). There is also evidence that some forms of arousal do not respond very well to prolonged exposure and experimentation. Images, thoughts and emotions associated with guilt, anger and shame, for example, may not respond so well to prolonged exposure (Grunert et al., 2007). Anecdotally, the same may be the case for thoughts and emotions that result in an increased sense of hopelessness or induce depression. A need to control the arousal can make exposure very uncomfortable because, as in our experience with both Mark and Paul, the associated intolerance:

- increases attention to the arousal;
- makes it appear to take abnormally long to reduce without intervention.

It can be helpful to increase acceptability rather than aiming for habituation. Interventions based on mindfulness may be very helpful to increase acceptability and reduce the striving for controllability (Segal et al., 2002; Hayes et al., 2006). To model mindfulness with specific intolerable sensations in session, we have found it helpful to encourage patients to 'watch' sensations without attaching meaning to them. This was done with Paul as illustrated in the example of watching sensations in session exercise (below). The therapist helped him to simply 'watch' the feelings. Note how the therapist resists engaging Paul in the fear or going into great detail about its meaning.

EXAMPLE OF WATCHING SENSATIONS

Paul and his therapist have just completed a cycling exercise together in the gym. As a result he has become aware of the arousal and is getting anxious:

Therapist: Paul, can you just tell me what you're feeling?
Paul: I feel hot.
Therapist: Ok, Paul, you're feeling hot. Anything else … ?
Paul: I'm feeling sweaty, very sweaty and hot.
Therapist: Right, sweaty and hot. You know, that's similar to how I feel. I think that's quite normal after exercise. What are you feeling now?
Paul: Shaky, I'm feeling shaky and hot now, my heart is beating.
Therapist: Ok, just keep telling me what you are feeling. What are you feeling now?

Once patients are able to reduce their avoidance and to allow the sensations to be, it can be easier to engage in behavioural experiments, exposure and normalising interventions. This was the case with Paul but it may be useful to consider the difference between exposure and normalising interventions. Table 7.1 offers some differences.

OBSTACLES ASSOCIATED WITH INVOLUNTARY EXPERIENTIAL AVOIDANCE

In involuntary avoidance the person might have little awareness of the intolerable experience. The avoidance method is thus a form of 'automatic subjective shutdown'. Interventions for increasing tolerance will therefore need to be preceded by measures that increase experiential awareness. We will refer to the case of Christine to illustrate this and the associated obstacles.

Table 7.1   Differentiating exposure and normalising interventions

Principle	Exposure	Normalising
Grading	Difficulty based	Time based
Frequency	Always repeated	Does not have to be repeated
Duration	Prolonged until habituation	Depends on patient tolerance
Focus	Focused on arousal	Focused on all sensations

THE CASE OF CHRISTINE – 'I'M NOT BOTHERED!'

Christine is a 38-year-old survivor of childhood sexual abuse. She has some memory of pain and fear but generally recalls little else from the abuse. She describes memories of anticipatory anxiety, when she would hear her abuser approaching. She finds her emotions and physical sensations difficult to describe. Five years ago she ended a ten-year physically, emotionally and sexually abusive marriage. She describes herself as a practical person, who just gets on with it. She has been experiencing episodes of collapse and loss of awareness, which started during the bitter divorce case. All available neurological investigations have failed to identify an organic cause for the episodes. She denies having been aware of stress during the divorce and court case but recalls having difficulty sleeping and concentrating. She finds it difficult to accept the psychological rationale for her symptoms. She has been attending CBT sessions for nine weeks and both Christine and her therapist are beginning to feel frustrated. Christine attends for the tenth session accompanied by her partner, who reveals that their home had been broken into, while Christine was there alone and he was away on a business trip. Since then, Christine had been finding it difficult to be alone at home. On further questioning, Christine acknowledges that she had been finding it difficult to enter the room associated with the burglary but denies any arousal or fear. She denies being bothered by the incident, simply saying, 'I just can't go into the room, I don't like it but I'm not afraid. It doesn't worry me.'

If a patient is unaware of the subjective experience, it is almost impossible to target that experience therapeutically. Patients like Christine, who are 'shut down' to the point of having little access to arousal, may have trouble recognising the reasons for their avoidance. Holmes et al. (2005) state that people can continue to have subjective experiences and behavioural responses but may be consciously unaware of the arousal. In their trauma model, Ehlers and Clark (2000) describe the notion of avoidance without arousal, where patients avoid without necessarily recognising the subjective arousal. This type of involuntary avoidance can create therapeutic obstacles in various ways including:

- *Collaborative information gathering*: in Chrsitine's case, had her partner not been present, her involuntary avoidance might have been missed. She did not perceive the situation as a problem, because she was 'dealing with it' by involuntarily shutting down her emotions as a form of avoidance thus, not experiencing any arousal.
- *The learning and accessing of descriptive language*: the importance of language in human experience and inference and attribution making has been illustrated in research (e.g. Dymond and Barnes, 1995). Thus, patients may need to learn to put language to emotions and their relevant contexts in order to correctly attribute

them and appropriately respond to those contexts. Patients like Christine with long-standing experiential avoidance may lack the words to describe their feelings.

- *Goal identification*: the patient, as was the case with Christine, may maintain that the situation is not problematic and refuse to make it a therapeutic target

With patients like Christine, behavioural analyses, necessary for formulation and the planning of interventions may be very challenging. It may therefore be necessary to:

- *Seek corroborative information*: corroborative information from a reliable observer/informant helps to link behavioural responses to the unrecognised subjective experiences.
- *Encourage the learning of an emotional vocabulary*: with such patients, as in the case of Christine, learning an emotional vocabulary might be necessary as new sensations are recognised. Without such an emotional vocabulary, recognition of what one is feeling would be difficult. This would impact on interventions and become a therapeutic obstacle. As was done with Christine, the patient might be encouraged to:
  - maintain a diary of avoidances, noting any sensations, including the most subtle that may be present at the time;
  - name the sensations in therapy, thus becoming *foundations* upon which to build a 'sensory vocabulary';
  - practise recognising the named and described sensations and emotions.

Specific exercises may be helpful in the development and increasing of an awareness of arousal, which can then be used for the development of an emotional language through naming. The therapist can initially perform these with the patient, identifying similar sensations and naming them, as the patient might not be able to differentiate them. Exercises may include:

- *Using a stimulation object*: Christine was encouraged to listen to emotive music, watch films, to look at pictures of personal emotional relevance and to identify the emotions that arise. One picture for Christine was a picture on a coffee tin from her childhood, which made her emotional.
- *Tactile sensory stimulants*: holding a block of ice or another sensory stimulant and naming the sensations.
- *Surveys*: approach different people to identify the range of feelings that can be experienced in the situation. Christine was unwilling to do this although, as is often the case with severely 'shut-down' patients, she was unable to clarify the reasons. She was, however, able to go into a meeting with her partner, who was also her business partner. She was able to compare his description of his feelings of tension and anxiety and to recognise some of these in herself. This helped with naming the specific sensations as well as to normalise and make them more acceptable.
- *Assisted entering of feared situations as exposure*: as Christine had trouble recognising arousal but her partner did not, she was encouraged to practise going into the fear-provoking room at home and to maintain a diary of emotions and sensations that could indicate the presence of anxiety. Her partner was enlisted as co-therapist, so that if Christine was aroused but unaware, he could help her to identify the feelings, the evidence of which he could see.

'Shutting down' completely

Some patients may completely shut down, so that they are no longer aware of their surroundings or unable to respond to the environment (e.g. in dissociative non-epileptic seizures) (Goldstein et al., 2010), as illustrated in Christine's case. If discussing specific topics or experiencing sensations in therapy triggers the 'shut-down' response, conducting therapy becomes highly challenging. The person:

- is unable to engage in therapy at all;
- difficulties and the experience of arousal can become 'therapeutic taboos', so that therapy focuses only on superficial events, avoiding the difficult ones;
- the patient never really learns to identify what they're thinking or feeling if they are unconscious of those subjective experiences;
- formulation and behavioural analyses become impossible.

In cases of patients like Christine, who experience total 'shut-down' it is important to identify:

- triggers and arousal-based warning signs;
- behavioural responses that may maintain the shut-down response;
- responses that may 'compete' with or make it difficult for the arousal-based warning signs to continue and develop into 'shut-down'.

Identify Triggers and Arousal-based Warning Signs

Maintaining a diary of the shut-down experiences (Table 7.2) will help to clarify the link between experiences/environment, the arousal and the conditioned 'shut-down' response. Note how the column titled 'Episode' states that there was no awareness. This can become an obstacle if awareness of the episode becomes the primary focus

Table 7.2   Episode monitoring diary

Date/Time	Situation	Awareness	Episode	Awareness	Response
	What you were doing/thinking, where, with whom	Anything you were aware of (e.g. hot, cold, sad, tired, bored worried) before the episode (rate intensity out of 100)	What you were aware of during the episode itself (e.g. sounds, smells, nothing at all)	Anything you were aware of after the episode (rate intensity out of 10)	What you did after the episode
10 October 10 a.m	Alone at home, walking into spare room	Slightly hot and sweaty (10), shaky (20), heart beating a little (40)	Nothing, everything went black	Tired and sleepy for half an hour, slight headache	Took tablets for pain, lay down on the bed. Avoided the spare room

of therapy. The first ('Awareness') column is what the shut-down is an escape from, so learning to identify and tolerate this makes greater therapeutic sense in line with the 'intolerance of arousal' rationale.

Though it can be difficult, it is usually possible to identify a pattern to the warning signs in the 'Awareness' column. Considering sensory changes is likely to be more fruitful than considering situational changes. Sensory changes could be as broad as sensations associated with anxiety, stress and tension, sensations associated with feeling relaxed or sensations associated with excitement. Situations will usually seem to have little commonality. This is because the episodes occur in response to sensory changes, which are triggered by a diverse range of situations (e.g. increased heart-rate can be triggered by running, watching an exciting film or having an argument). A good example of this is the patient who would collapse due to feeling an increase in body temperature. She experienced episodes in the bath, in a scout hut on a hot summer day and at a party whilst dancing. The situations were disparate but the arousal was the same (i.e. she felt hot). In Christine's case, she was able to become aware of specific perceptual disturbances, which occurred in virtually all anxiety and stress-related situations. She would become aware of a sense of distance, as though there was something between herself and the world. She would then experience what felt like water running down the side of her head. Soon after this, she would collapse and lose awareness of her surroundings. It was important to identify responses that would compete with some of these sensations. These grounding or competing responses may include:

- *controlled breathing*: diaphragmatic breathing exercises;
- *relaxation*: progressive and cued relaxation involving tensing and relaxing (see Clark, 1989);
- *distraction and refocusing*: focusing attention away from the arousal onto a neutral stimulus and describing it in detail. The competing response should be 'warning specific' (i.e. should distract from the specific, identified warning signal for the 'shut-down'/dissociation).

An example of a distraction and refocusing grounding exercise is as follows:

Instruction to patient: Imagine you are on the phone and describing this room to someone who has never seen it before, or imagine you're describing it to someone who is blind. You want to be able to describe it in such detail that the blind person or the person at the end of the phone is able to picture or draw the room as closely as possible to what it looks like now.

The patient is encouraged to attempt the distraction and refocusing exercise. If this is difficult for the patient, the therapist can demonstrate, picking up details of colour, markings, shape, smells, texture, size, decorations, etc. The patient tries again.

Other things to focus on include:

- the environment (trees, the inside of buses and trains, people, etc.);
- pictures of loved ones, holiday places, etc.;
- reading;
- music;

- engaging in exercise, dancing, etc.;
- number games (e.g. subtracting serial 7s such as $200 - 7 = 193, 193 - 7 = 186$, to reach 0).

The patient is then encouraged to practise the grounding/competing responses daily, so that their use can become second nature, requiring minimum effort. With Christine, at the first sign of the onset of the warning signs, she was encouraged to use the competing response or grounding technique. She was given permission to stop activities (including sessions), use the competing responses and then continue with the activity, once the warnings have reduced. As control improved, leaving situations became less necessary. Initially this was practised when the warning signs were *not* present, so that the skill of using them was developed without the pressure of needing to actually control an event. Many patients and therapists make the mistake of only practising with the actual warning signs or sensations present. This is too difficult and akin to a pianist only practising his scales in front of a paying audience. A second mistake is to aim to control the sensation or to make it go away. This does not work and makes the whole exercise feel rather contrived. As in Christine's case, patients should be encouraged to simply practise the response and be told that 'the arousal will respond at it's own pace, because trying to control it only increases awareness of it'.

TRAUMATIC EVENTS AND MEMORY

THE CASE OF PAULINA: 'WHAT HAPPENED TO ME!'

30 year-old Paulina attended therapy with a ten-year-history of panic disorder. Initially, she feared collapse during the panic. With the help of her therapist, she began to believe that this was not a likely consequence and was doing well. Her GP-prescribed anxiolytic medication for the anxiety was now being reduced by her psychiatrist. Her panic resurfaced with the reduction of the medication but without the accompanying catastrophic predictions of collapse. CBT was no longer effective and her therapist began to get frustrated. One night she had a nightmare and suddenly recalled that she had been sexually assaulted at the age of 16. Her panic increased and she began to experience increased somatic symptoms, which could not be explained medically.

Traumatic events as in the case of Paulina, may be associated with poor recall of specific past events. This requires careful handling. The trauma model (see Ehlers and Clark, 2000; Kennerly, 2000 for model and interventions) may be appropriate. It makes sense that if intolerance of arousal can be experienced as a protection against intolerable subjective experiences, what better protection is there than not to remember associated events at all? People with subjective intolerance may be amnesic of specific events, may have incomplete memories or may feel that their day-to-day recall of events is affected. Paulina's therapist hypothesised that she had compartmentalised her traumatic assault experience, because it was too much for her to cope with. She had therefore 'forgotten' it but continued to experience the associated arousal. The medication was helping to mask the associated distress and its reduction allowed the full experiencing of the memories and arousal. She then started to experience more diffuse symptoms of 'shut-down', such as loss of sensation. Until her trauma recall, therapy had ceased to be effective, because the amnesic response. Thus:

- recall of CBT sessions or important events can be affected. Paulina's therapist, for example, could do little until the memory surfaced;
- learning from the sessions becomes difficult, requiring much repetition;
- distress associated with recalling the memories could be high and require very gradual and carefully planned targeting.

Once it presents, poor memory may have a range of consequences, which maintain and exacerbate it. As in Paulina's case, these may include:

- *The effects of medication*: the medication may have become part of the maintaining factors for Paulina's amnesia, because it prevented emotional processing of the original trauma. Stopping the medication resulted in the resurfacing of the trauma memory, so that it now required active attention and processing.
- *Anxiety, depression or other psychiatric problems*: the co-morbidity of dissociative and psychiatric problems such as depression and anxiety is high (de Araujo Filho and Caboclo, 2007). Though these may improve with the increased control of the dissociation or shut-down and its effects, it may be necessary to target them first. Once the depression or anxiety has lifted, the memory problem might also resolve. Sometimes, however, there may be other maintainers or exacerbators of poor memory, including:
  1 concern about one's capacity to recall, so that associate anxiety reduces recall ability;
  2 unrealistic 'expectation' of ability to recall, so that there is excessive focus on detail;
  3 safety behaviours, which then have a paradoxical effect, thus reinforcing the belief that memory is truly affected (e.g. memory aids and keeping unnecessarily detailed notes).

These need to be assessed and will become the focus of the usual CBT interventions.

Unrecalled Events

Sometimes therapists or patients may wish to search for an explanatory past trauma. We would adopt the approach taken by Paulina's therapist, which was to resist searching for a trauma unless there is evidence of one. Important early events usually become evident in the normal process of assessment and therapy. If there is a past event that is vague or not fully recalled, it might be best to consider acceptance, based on ACT principles (Hayes et al., 1999) or to use imagery reprocessing and rescripting interventions (e.g. Wild et al., 2007). Therapy could easily get 'stuck' on trying to dig up unknown past traumatic causes for current distress. If there is a clearly recalled and unresolved event however, it would need to be targeted therapeutically. Literature is well established on treating the effects of traumatic events (e.g. Ehlers and Clark, 2000; Kennerly, 2000).

SUMMARY

Intolerance and avoidance of arousal can occur as a discrete problem or secondary to a broad range of psychiatric disorders. Its symptoms and effects are varied but, whatever they are, they can impede therapeutic progress. Interventions for resolving the effects of intolerance and avoidance of arousal require creativity on the part of the therapist and his/her patient. This chapter has introduced the idea of intolerance of arousal and suggested a rationale for its maintenance and treatment.

ACTIVITIES

1 How might you explain voluntary and involuntary intolerance and avoidance of arousal to a patient?
2 Consider a disorder of your choice. With examples, how may intolerance and avoidance of arousal present in that disorder?
3 How might you go about treating the intolerance and avoidance of arousal in the examples you provided in Activity 2?

REFERENCES

Clark, D.M. (1989) 'Anxiety states', in K. Hawton, P.M. Salkovskis, J. Kirk and D.M. Clark, *Cognitive Behaviour Therapy for Psychiatric Problems: A Practical Guide*. Oxford: Oxford University Press.

de Araujo Filho, G.M. and Caboclo, L.O.S.F. (2007) 'Anxiety and mood disorders in psychogenic non-epileptic seizures', *Journal of Epilepsy and Clinical Neurophysiology*, 13 (4), Sup. 1: 28–31.

Dymond, S. and Barnes, D. (1995) 'A transformation of self-discrimination response functions in accordance with the arbitrarily applicable relations of sameness, more-than, and less-than', *Journal of the Experimental Analysis of Behaviour*, 64: 163–84.

Ehlers, A. and Clark, D.M. (2000) 'A cognitive model of post traumatic stress disorder', *Behaviour Research and Therapy*, 38: 319–45.

Goldstein, L.H., Chalder, T., Chigwedere, C., Khondoker, M.R., Moriarty, J., Toone, B.K. and Mellers, J.D. (2010) 'Cognitive therapy for psychogenic non-epileptic seizures', *Neurology*, 74 (24): 1986–94.

Goldstein, L.H., Deale A.C., Mitchell O'Malley, S.J., Toone, B.K. and Mellers, J.D.C. (2004) 'An evaluation of cognitive behavioural therapy as a treatment for dissociative seizures', *Cognitive Behavioural Neurology*, 17 (1): 41–9.

Grunert, B.K., Weis, J.M., Smucker, M.R. and Christianson, H.F. (2007) 'Imagery reprocessing and rescripting therapy after failed prolonged exposure in post-traumatic stress disorder following industrial injury', *Journal of Behaviour Therapy and Experimental Psychiatry*, 38 (4): 317–28.

Hayes, S.C., Strosahl, K. and Wilson, K.G.(1999) *Acceptance and Commitment Therapy*. New York: Guilford Press.

Hayes, S.C., Luoma, J.B., Bond, F.W., Masuda, A. and Lillis, J. (2006) 'Acceptance and commitment therapy: model, processes and outcomes', *Behaviour Research and Therapy*, 44 (1): 1–25.

Hayes, S.C, Wilson, K.G., Gifford, E.V., Folette, V.M. and Strosahl, K. (1996) 'Experiential avoidance and behaviour disorder: a functional dimentional approach to diagnosis and treatment', *Journal of Consulting and Clinical Psychology*, 64: 1152–68.

Holmes, E.A., Brown, R., Mansell, W., Fearon, R.P., Hunter, E.A., Frasquilho, F. and Oakley, D.A. (2005) 'Are the two qualitatively distinct forms of dissociation? A review and some clinical implications', *Clinical Psychology Review*, 25: 1–23.

Kanaan, R.A., Craig, T.K., Wessely, S.C. and David, A.S. (2007) 'Imaging repressed memories in motor conversion', *Psychosomatic Medicine*, 69: 2002–5.

Kennerly, H. (2000) *Overcoming Childhood Trauma*. London: Robinson.

Kirschenbaum, H. and Henderson, V.L. (1990) *Carl Rogers: Dialogues*. London: Constable.

Linehan, M.M. (1993) *Cognitive-Behavioral Treatment of Borderline Personality Disorder*. New York: Guilford Press

Mowrer, O.H. (1947) 'The dual nature of learning – a reinterpretation of "conditioning" and "problem solving"', *Harvard Educational Review*, 17: 102–48

Mowrer, O.H. (1960) *Learning Theory and Behaviour*. New York: Wiley.

Rogers, C.R. (1980) *A Way of Being*. Boston: Houghton Mifflin.

Segal, Z.V., Williams, J.M.G. and Teasdale, J.D. (2002) *Mindfulness Based Cognitive Therapy for Depression: A New Approach to Preventing Relapse*. New York: Guilford Press.

Sierra, M., Senior, C., Dalton, J., McDonough, M., Bond, A., Phillips, M.L., O'Dwyer, A.M. and David, A.S. (2002) 'Autonomic response in depersonalisation disorder', *Archives of General Psychiatry*, 59: 833–8.

Wild, J., Hackman, A. and Clark, D.M. (2007) 'When the present visits the past: updating traumatic memories in social phobia', *Journal of Behaviour Therapy and Experimental Psychiatry*, 38 (4): 386–401.

8

SHAME AND GUILT

YVONNE TONE

LEARNING OBJECTIVES

After reading this chapter you should:

- be aware of how shame and guilt impact on therapist, client and therapy;
- have an understanding of the skills needed to negotiate barriers to disclosure and therapeutic progress due to shame and guilt experiences;
- have knowledge of management interventions.

INTRODUCTION

Therapists can never predict entirely what underlies the client's presenting problem. This chapter describes the various ways shame and guilt can create obstacles in therapy and explores management strategies.

Clients present in different ways to therapy. Some are reticent and struggle to disclose the details of their problem; others may be hostile and defensive. Shame-based experiences from past events can present in a covert way. The experience of shame can evoke strong feelings, which can impact on therapeutic process. If not acknowledged and worked through in an empathic way this may lead to disengagement of the client, non-compliance and/or poor outcome. The case of Petra is an example of a client struggling in this way.

THE CASE OF PETRA – THE 'I CAN'T TALK ABOUT IT' CLIENT

Petra presents for therapy with panic attacks, referred by a concerned friend. On a recent weekend away she had taken alcohol while socialising in a nightclub with her friends. Later, three men offered her and a friend a lift home. During the journey, Petra became upset and felt 'trapped.' She started hyperventilating and wanted to leave the car, feeling 'very unsafe,' but unsure why.

During the session Petra continually looked up at the clock, appearing uncomfortable. She avoided eye contact with the therapist and continually expressed the view that the incident in the car was 'no big deal'. Though appearing uncomfortable she laughed off the story and suggested she was wasting the therapist's time. She stated that she was not sure why she was attending the session, as she had nothing to say.

Twenty minutes into the session, Petra said she felt better and wanted to leave. The therapist respected her wish and offered her a further appointment, but Petra said she was uncertain if she could come again. The therapist commended her on taking the first steps towards exploring her feeling of panic and for seeking help even if it was only to ease her friend's concerns.

Petra walked out of the consultation appearing uneasy and relieved to be leaving. Petra clearly has an anxiety problem. Her attendance, however, was at the behest of her friends. She was reluctant to discuss what brought her to therapy, making engagement difficult. Therapeutic obstacles related to shame and guilt themes can emerge in therapy. Both novice and expert therapists need to develop skills in their management.

RECOGNISING SHAME AND GUILT

Shame and guilt have common features (see Table 8.1). Though shame and guilt have similarities and overlapping areas, clinically there are significant differences between them. Lewis (1971) describes them as distinct emotional experiences that differ along cognitive, affective and motivational dimensions. Lewis hypothesises that they are mainly distinguished by the role of 'the self'. In Lewis's hypothesis, shame experiences tend to relate to global negative evaluations of the self (e.g. 'who *I* am'), whereas guilt experiences involve a more descriptive condemnation of a particular behaviour (e.g. 'what I *did*'). Thus, in Lewis's hypothesis shame and guilt experiences do not differ greatly in relation to the context or situation in which they arise but, rather, in the construal of self-referent experiences. For example, with Petra, it emerged a past experience made her believe she was 'a bad person'. She displayed some shame-congruent attributions relating to a global evaluation of herself (e.g. 'I'm stupid, I'm vulnerable, I can't take care of myself'). More of Petra later.

Table 8.1 Common features of shame and guilt

- Both fall into the class of 'moral' emotions.
- Both are 'self-conscious' or self-referential.
- Both involve internal attributions of one sort or another.
- Both are experienced in interpersonal contexts.
- Negative events contributing to shame and guilt experience are similar, and frequently have a moral theme.

Tangney, J.P. and Dearing, R. (2002) *Shame and Guilt*. New York. Guilford Press.

Kevin, another client, illustrates the guilt presentation.

THE CASE OF KEVIN – 'I'VE DONE SOMETHING WRONG'

Kevin struggled with intrusive thoughts of causing harm or inadvertently 'doing something wrong'. He ruminated on a childhood event when, at the age of nine, a friend and he stole books from outside of a shop. He experienced thoughts that he was 'bad' and felt guilty for having done something he deemed 'morally objectionable'. He worried and repeatedly prayed to make restitution. He sought reassurance from his wife, the local priest and work colleagues. When visiting toy shops with his young daughter, he became fearful that she might damage the toys she touched, 'causing harm'. He became strict with her, leading to further feelings of guilt.

Kevin's presentation exhibited guilt-congruent attributions relating to the evaluation of certain behaviour (i.e. '*What I did* was wrong and morally objectionable'). He struggled with guilt feelings and feared he or his daughter would do something wrong.

CO-EXISTENCE OF SHAME AND GUILT

Though discussed as distinct concepts, our experience is that guilt and shame can co-exist. For example, with Kevin the feeling of guilt was more predominant, driven by a fear he might not be 'saved' on the basis of wrong doing. Kevin's strong moral code had been threatened leading to experience of guilt and the need to engage in reparation. He also experienced shame that his problem was impacting on his daughter. He considered that he was exerting control over her freedom to explore the world in a safe and unencumbered way (a guilt-related evaluation of behaviour). He also exhibited shame in the global evaluation of himself as a person (i.e. I am a bad father for behaving in this way). Besides her shame-related attributions, Petra too had guilt-related attributions relating to the evaluation of an event (i.e. 'I *did* a stupid thing, *I let them* use me').

Table 8.2   Dimensions of shame and guilt

Focus of evaluation	Shame: global self	Guilt: specific behaviour
The 'actor' *vs* the 'act'	'I' did a horrible thing	I 'did' that horrible thing
Degree of distress	More painful than guilt	Less painful than shame
Phenomenology	Shrinking, feel small, worthless	Tension, remorseful, regretful
Operation of 'self'	Self 'split' – observing and observed self	Self intact
Impact on 'self'	Self impaired by global devaluation	Self unimpaired by global devaluation
Concern vis à vis 'others'	Concern with others evaluation of self	Concern with one's effect on others
Motivational features	Desire to hide, escape or strike back	Desire to confess, apologise or repair

Source: Lewis, H.B. (1971) *Shame and Guilt in Neurosis.* New York. International Universities Press.

It is important to tease out clients' cognitions to identify whether they relate to the 'evaluation of the self' or the 'evaluation of a behaviour'. Our experience is that this can be a challenging task because of the possible co-occurrence of shame and guilt as illustrated in the cases of Kevin and Petra. Therapists thus need to focus on the meaning of the experience along with an intuitive 'felt sense' of the behaviour being bad or wrong (i.e. guilt) or if it is likely to lead to negative and embarrassing self-evaluation or evaluation by others (e.g. shame). The ability to separate shame and guilt experiences can be useful in managing such challenges. Lewis (1971) helpfully describes dimensions of shame and guilt (see Table 8.2).

Alternative descriptions of guilt and shame have been offered. Gilbert (1998) describes an alternative evaluation of shame on two conceptual dimensions:

1   'internal shame' focusing on negative self-evaluation;
2   'external' shame associated with fear of others' judgement.

Petra, for example, displayed some 'internal' shame-associated attributions (e.g. 'I'm stupid, I'm vulnerable, I can't take care of myself'), related to her shame experience and attributions about what happened ('I'm bad, I did a stupid thing, I let them use me'). Feelings of shame can involve an acute awareness of what might be described as 'a flaw or unworthy part of oneself'. This response is usually out of proportion to the event, as was the case with Petra. Tangney et al. (1996) recognise shame as a particularly intense negative emotion, involving feelings of inferiority, powerlessness and self-consciousness, all of which were troublesome for Petra. Tangney and Dearing (2002) highlight that feelings of shame and guilt will inevitably emerge in therapy. Tangney et al.'s (1996) position on the association of inferiority powerlessness and self-consciousness resonates well with conceptualisations of shame and guilt by other authors. For example, Gilbert (1992), drawing on the work of Lewis (1986), usefully contrasts the experience of shame and guilt from the perspectives of self and other (Table 8.3). Gilbert posits that shame is mostly interpersonally driven, with a constant interplay between the self and how others perceive us. Guilt relates more to self action, hurting others and the need to make amends or reparation.

Table 8.3 Shame and guilt experiences of self and others

(a) Shame experiences

Self (unable)	Other (able)
1 Object of scorn, disgust, ridicule, humiliation	The source of scorn, contempt, ridicule, humiliation
2 Paralysed, helpless passive, inhibited	Laughing, rejecting, active, uninhibited, free
3 Inferior, smaller, weaker	Superior, bigger, stronger
4 Involuntary body response, rage, blush, tears, gaze avoidance	Adult and in control
5 Functioning poorly, mind going blank, desire to hide, conceal	Functioning well but experiencing contempt
6 Self in focal awareness	Other in focal awareness

(b) Guilt experiences

Self (able)	Others (unable)
1 The source of hurt, let down or failure	Injured, needful, hurt
2 Intact and capable	Incapable, needing
3 Focus on self actions and behaviours/ feelings	Focus on let down/injury from other and own needs/ losses
4 Efforts to repair	Efforts to elicit reparation or rejection/contempt leading to shame

Source: Gilbert, P. (1992) *Depression: The Evolution of Powerlessness*. London. Routledge. p. 226.

CLINICAL PRESENTATIONS OF SHAME AND GUILT

Shame experiences can be pervasive and associated with a range of concerns. The associated thoughts, feelings and behaviour cycles can vary, depending on the client's experience. Shame and guilt issues are not limited to a single presenting area or disorder. The breath of shame and guilt topics have been described in literature and research (e.g. Weiner and Schuman, 1984; Hook and Andrews, 2005). Shame and guilt rarely present clinically as the main reason for seeking help. Clients usually seek therapy in relation to another disorder, such as anxiety, depression or an eating disorder. Shame and guilt can present in a variety of ways and be associated with virtually any psychological problem. It is beyond our remit to offer a comprehensive review of how they can present clinically. We will therefore confine ourselves to outlining three presentations where clinicians are likely to be confronted with shame and guilt. An anxiety, depression and body-shame presentation are described as broad illustrative examples.

SHAME AND GUILT AS AN ANXIETY PRESENTATION

Anxiety presentations have been variously associated with shame and guilt. It is not surprising that shame should be associated with low self-esteem, social anxiety and other presentations in which social evaluation plays an important role. Gilbert (2000), referring to social rank theory, argues that emotions and moods are linked to the degree to which one feels inferior or superior to others, and identifies shame as being associated with social anxiety. Guilt has been shown to be associated with obsessional presentations in particular, as well as social anxiety (Stekettee et al., 1991). Responsibility appraisals, uncertainty and guilt intolerance in OCD forms a basis for the theoretical model of OCD (Salkovskis, 1985).

In post-traumatic stress disorder (PTSD), Lee et al. (2001) proposed a treatment model which acknowledges the role of shame and guilt. PTSD symptoms associated with guilt and shame may not respond very well to prolonged exposure approaches but can be managed by imagery reprocessing and rescripting (Grunert et al., 2007). Treatment of anxiety can be complicated by the presence of non-fear emotions, such as shame, guilt and anger (Grunert et al., 2007).

Imagery rescripting and reprocessing therapy has also been shown to be helpful with social anxiety (Wild et al., 2008) and in OCD (Kearns, 2010). The compassionate mind approach of Gilbert (2009) has also been shown to be helpful. Therapists therefore need to take special care when working with guilt and shame in anxiety. The case of Petra presents a useful illustrative example of shame associated with an anxiety presentation. A presentation such as this can be very challenging for a therapist not recognising the presence of shame.

SHAME AND GUILT AS A DEPRESSIVE PRESENTATION

The DSM IV (American Psychiatric Association, 1994) highlights 'feelings of worthlessness or excessive or inappropriate guilt' as a symptom of a major depressive episode (APA, 1994: 327). Cognitive theorists suggest shame is probably a more pathogenic emotion involving themes of loss, hopelessness and or helplessness (Overmeier and Seligman, 1967). The presence of guilt and shame can complicate and exacerbate the themes of loss normally associated with depressive presentations, requiring careful consideration in assessment and treatment. Shame (Andrews, 1995; Thompson and Berenbaum, 2006) and guilt can also be predisposing factors for depressive presentations.

CLIENTS DROPPING OUT FROM THERAPY

Clients prematurely disengage from therapy for a number of reasons. When this happens, therapists can experience a range of emotions with associated questions. The loss of a client through suicide is possibly the most upsetting and challenging issue for a therapist. The percentage of clients lost to treatment through suicide has been estimated between 15 and 50 per cent (Chemtob et al., 1988; Knox et al., 2006). The distress associated is multiplied when the therapist witnesses the distress of the client's family and friends. Often, the methods of enquiry can result in great shame and guilt, especially when families or organisations appear to want to blame someone. At such times, when the need for support from colleagues and employers is at its greatest, therapists can feel alone due to the shame associated with speaking about one's distress. Supervision, peer support and personal therapy can be of great help at such times.

THE CASE OF DAVE – THE SHAME OF BEING DEPRESSED

Dave is a 24-year-old computer scientist. He recently had a major depressive epi-sode requiring hospital admission. Dave's mother suffered intermittently with depression for years, as did two of his cousins.

His family, particularly his father (a successful lawyer), attach a high value to achievement. His sister is a medical student, and Dave himself began working in a very successful and competitive computer company immediately after he finished his undergraduate degree. He is very keen to impress his father in this way, and made a difficult transition from living in the country to the city in order to take up his current job. He spent most weekends back at home in his first two years of work.

Dave describes himself as 'shy and not confident'. After two years of working long hours on the job, he feels stressed and fatigued. During a presentation to peers and clients he went blank, became distressed and left the room. The shame he felt about this triggered his depressive episode and hospitalisation. He now feels unable to return to work, as he believes the company are intolerant of psychologi-cal problems. He worries his colleagues will see him as 'weak and incompetent'.

Reflect on the following exercise:

REFLECTIVE FORMULATION EXERCISE

Review the case of Dave:

1 What factors would you say predisposed Dave to shame-related problems?
2 What factors precipitated Dave's problem?
3 What factors are maintaining Dave's shame experience and low mood?

In Dave's case, he experienced feelings of shame and guilt at not living up to his family's expectations. Failure to meet expectations of self or others can present a critical precipitating event for the onset of depression with underlying shame and guilt. Such clients, as was the case with Dave, can put themselves under extreme pressure to achieve specific standards, leading to stress. This in turn affects their abil-ity to perform, thus creating a self-fulfilling prophecy, by making it more likely that the guilt and shame-inducing experiences they are trying to prevent actually hap-pens. The experience of depression itself can complicate the treatment of shame and guilt because depression has been shown to predispose patients to the accessing of negative experiences more than positive experiences (Teasdale and Fogarty, 1979). Once patients become depressed, they may be more likely to recall events that sup-port the feelings of guilt and shame, thus increasing their experience. It is important that clinicians monitor such clients closely due to the association between guilt and shame related cognitions and suicidality (Hastings et al., 2002). Typical of such clients, Dave described feelings of frustration and anger towards himself for not meeting expected standards. This turning of the defect inward towards oneself can predispose patients to self-harming or parasuicidal behaviours due to the consequent experience of guilt. It may thus be necessary to consider a multidisciplinary treatment approach for the safety of both client and therapist. If the depressive component is severe and impeding the psychotherapeutic assessment and treatment of shame and guilt, therapists may need to engage the services of a medically qualified colleague to consider pharmacological interventions. The severe depressive affect could impede the accessing of experiences that are not consistent with the guilt or shame, as per Teasdale and Fogarty (1979).

In line with Gilbert's (1998) notions of internal and external shame and guilt, patients meeting the 'internal' hypothesis may become distressed when they break their own rules. External shame- and guilt-related distress may be experienced, as in the case of Dave, when others' expectations are not met. Novice therapists may become confused and miss the shame aspect, merely considering that a client like Dave's depression is due to low-self esteem or social anxiety because of the fear of negative evaluation. Shame and guilt issues therefore need careful evaluation to tease them out from other differential diagnoses.

SHAME AND GUILT AS BODY IMAGE DISTURBANCE

THE CASE OF JENNY: 'I'M FAT, UNATTRACTIVE AND ASHAMED OF MY BODY'

Jenny, a 29-year-old nursing assistant, was referred by her GP for low mood and anger issues. In her childhood, her father drank heavily and was verbally abusive to the whole family when drunk. Her parents separated when she was 15. She currently lives with her mum and younger sister, who are both slim and very fashion conscious, while she suffers from weight gain and an increase in downy facial hair resulting from polycystic ovaries. Jenny recently broke up with her boyfriend following an on-and-off volatile relationship in which he would occasionally hit her and verbally abuse her. She is upset about this break-up, and feels that her boyfriend did not understand her illness. She has a rigid belief that she will never meet another man as she is 'fat and ugly'. She has difficulty socialising unless she is wearing long, loose clothing, scarves and heavy make-up. Jenny also recently requested to work night shifts at the hospital in order to 'hide myself away' from people. She told her GP that she has superficially cut her upper arms to 'ease the numbness'. In her initial session, she is tearful and reluctant to engage. She is openly pessimistic about the helpfulness of therapy, and is angry and dismissive.

The case of Jenny illustrates the third possible presentation of shame and guilt – the body-image disturbance. The discussion so far has related to shame and guilt as focused on emotions and behaviours. The focus of shame and guilt is broad and can include a focus on personality traits, the experience of illness and social background. Personal appearance, body image (Carr, 2002) or body shame (Gilbert and Miles, 2002) is an important clinical focus of shame. Body image shame can have significant effects on sufferers including anorexia and bulimia nervosa (Troop and Connan, 2003) and muscle dysmorphia (Grieve et al., 2009). Sufferers can experience great distress at not meeting what they consider to be personal or social standards of appearance, suggesting a link between guilt and shame to the issue of perfectionism (see Chapter 6). This extreme level of unacceptability of a perceived shameful defect can globalise to a perception indicative of the unacceptability of the entire self of the individual. Consequently individuals can go to extreme measures to become more acceptable. The resultant emotional and social impact can be extremely disabling. The focus on appearance can affect interpersonal interaction so severely that one becomes angry, anxious or depressed due to misinterpretation of others' reactions relating to the 'personal defect'.

As with many body-image clients, Jenny was distressed, angry and extremely self-critical. Consequently, she believed that the only reason the therapist was nice to her was that she was 'being paid to be'. This made engagement extremely challenging and it was at times difficult to work out what Jenny needed from therapy. A key element of a shame-based experience involves exposure of perceived undesirable qualities about oneself or one's actions (Gilbert, 1992). In Jenny's case, she was ashamed about having facial hair, being overweight and feeling unattractive. She believed others, including the therapist, viewed her this way and her experiences were fuelled by criticism and rejections in the past. Attending therapy itself was therefore a significant challenge for her, which could have easily become an obstacle. There are therefore various ways in which shame and guilt can present as obstacles in therapy.

OBSTACLES TO DISCLOSURE OF SHAME AND GUILT

Clients may find it difficult to be open about issues of shame and guilt for a variety of reasons. Hill et al. (1993) highlight negative feelings towards therapists and Hook and Andrews (2005) identify trust issues as reasons for client non-disclosure. Consideration to the association between shame and guilt and what clients 'don't tell us' is important. Some of the main reasons for non-disclosure are:

- too ashamed,
- lack of trust in the therapist,
- fear of negative judgement,
- too painful to talk about,
- too guilty,
- treatment too short,
- too private.

Hook and Andrews (2005) conclude that shame was by far the most frequently endorsed reason for non-disclosure. Petra experienced shame about a past experience and was reluctant to disclose the incident due to fears of negative judgement. It is important to support clients in a respectful empathic way towards disclosure. An open explorative enquiry can be useful. Therapists can use statements such as:

- 'Sometimes it is difficult for clients to disclose things to their therapist. Have you any troubling issues around your experience that you have not been able to discuss in therapy before?'
- 'Would there be any other issues or past experiences of a distressing nature you have not been able to discuss in therapy before?'

SHAME AND GUILT AS OBSTACLES TO ENGAGEMENT

It is clear that patients with shame and guilt can have great difficulty engaging therapeutically. Consider the case of Jenny: not only did she need to manage issues of shame (i.e. facial hair and weight) but also her emotions of low mood and anger. Along with this, she needed to manage how she was perceived by others, including the therapist. Therapy itself thus presents significant challenges to shame and guilt clients, not least because it requires them to be open about the very shame and guilt which they make great efforts to escape from or control. There are therefore many ways in which guilt and shame can become obstacles to engagement, including difficulty:

- *Accessing therapy*: clients can feel great shame and guilt at accessing therapy due to the problems associated with having to discuss the problem. They may also fear the stigma associated with seeking psychological help. Thus, clients often attend therapy at the behest of someone else or due to an associated distress (e.g. depression or anxiety).
- *Describing the problem*: clients may feel shame and guilt talking about their problem, so the therapist is unable to conduct a full assessment. Clients may talk about associated depression, anxiety or another problem, but not necessarily the shame or guilt, so that these issues are often missed in assessment. They may be unaware of it as a problem.
- *Eliciting the goals of therapy*: clients can have difficulty expressing what they want from therapy because considering a better self can be a source of shame and guilt.
- *Expressing or controlling emotions*: clients may have difficulty coping with their emotions, so that they are expressed inappropriately or as a defence. They may have experienced negative responses from others in the past so they may then easily misinterpret therapist responses as disingenuous, mocking or as having some other ulterior motive. This can make collaboration and the forming of a therapeutic relationship challenging.

The case of Petra illustrates some of the above. An inexperienced therapist may have seen Petra as 'unsuitable for therapy' as she could not elicit clear goals, had difficulty discussing what brought her to therapy, and was reticent and avoidant in session

(Safran and Segal, 1996). The therapist, on the basis of Petra's non-verbal behaviour, reticence and discomfort, wondered if Petra was exhibiting signs of a shame-based experience. This clearly warranted further exploration. There may be many causes of the shame including the stigma of attending a mental-health service. Some of the shame-based behaviours for therapists to look out for with clients are:

- withdrawing from interaction;
- becoming guarded in disclosure;
- becoming hostile or angry;
- engaging in self-loathing;
- deliberate self-harm episodes;
- resisting therapy;
- coming late for sessions;
- wanting to leave the session prematurely;
- not having anything to say;
- cancelling or missing an appointment;
- downcast eyes, averting gaze;
- restlessness, fidgety behaviour;
- nervous laughter;
- covering the face;
- slumped closed posture.

The challenge for the therapist was to engage this client in the process of what Gilbert (2007) suggests as facilitating the experience of 'feeling safe enough' to engage in what can often be painful therapeutic work. This involved adjusting the pace of therapy to suit Petra's needs. The sessions were shortened in response to her distress and discomfort in sitting with the therapist in session. Ways to improve engagement with clients experiencing shame or guilt include:

- *Assessing specifically for guilt and shame*: the likelihood of missing shame and guilt experiences is high. The therapist should assess for it as if they suspect that it may be a problem.
- *Expressing concern*: genuine concern for the wellbeing of the client. To do so, it may be necessary to spend time just listening and 'being present' and expressing compassion and empathic understanding (Gilbert and Leahy, 2007: Chapter 1).
- *Altering the pace of therapy*: assessment and problem identification may take longer. An 'eagerness to diagnose' can result in unhelpful triggering of shame and guilt before trust has been developed.
- *Fostering safety*: the initial aim should be the fostering of a process that will feel safe for the client's expression of their shame and guilt.
- *Enabling creativity*: the therapist tried to be creative in enabling Petra describe the source of her distress (e.g. using writing to describe the shame related experiences).
- *Normalising*: Petra's therapist shared appropriate disclosures and anonymous anecdotes of other clients who presented with shame experiences.

In instances where the therapist is uncertain about the presence or extent of the guilt and shame presentation, the use of a validated measure can be helpful. There is an increase in empirical work on measuring shame and guilt experiences. The Tests of

Self-Conscious Affect (TOSCA) (Tangney et al., 1996) is a useful measure, which assesses (1) emotional states (e.g. feelings of shame and guilt in the moment) and (2) emotional traits (e.g. shame proneness and guilt proneness). Other useful measures include the Internalised Shame Scale (ISS) (Cook, 1989) and the Guilt Inventory (Kugler and Jones, 1992). The Beck Depression Inventory (BDI) (Beck et al., 1961) also contains an item about guilt experiences. Low self-esteem may also increase ones vulnerability to shame proneness or repeated experiences of shame may contribute to low self-esteem and the experience of depression.

SHAME AND GUILT AS OBSTACLES TO THE USE OF CHANGE METHODS

Gilbert (1992) discusses exposure to the undesirable qualities about one's self or one's actions as a key aspect of the experience of shame and guilt. CBT works through the use of specific change methods (Blackburn et al., 2001) to mediate change by targeting cognitive, behavioural and affective maintaining factors. Hence in therapy, as illustrated by the example of the Cognitive Therapy Scale – Revised (CTS-R) (Blackburn et al., 2001), a therapist is expected to elicit cognitions, behaviours and emotions. Anything that reduces access to those maintaining factors will be likely to reduce the effectiveness of the change methods. There are various ways in which shame and guilt can present obstacles to the application of change methods.

Verbal Challenging

Therapy relies very much on the use of language both verbal and non-verbal. When certain emotions, such as shame and guilt, are present, it can be difficult for a client to access the thoughts (language) associated with the affect or distress. Efforts to reduce the experience of the distress increase not only emotional but also cognitive distance from that distress and its triggers. Getting a client to talk about the problem means they have to face (in imagination and in vivo) the triggers of shame and guilt and the associated distress. Verbal challenging may be difficult because patients are unable to describe their problem. Socratic questioning, a well-utilised technique of CBT intervention, becomes impossible because the client is unable to name problems or their alternatives. In three of our illustrative cases, Petra was unable to speak of her problems and minimised them. She also did not see herself as having a problem and had only attended at the behest of others. Jack felt he was a bad person who had committed an unacceptable act, which he could not mention for fear of being judged and because it was too distressing to think about. Jenny was angry and defensive as she struggled to put words on her experience.

Homework-task Completion

Homework can become difficult for clients with shame and guilt to engage in tasks that cause them distress. They may be able to do so with the assistance and encouragement of the therapist in session but at home they have to face the shame and guilt alone. Homework tasks are therefore often challenging and not completed.

Exposure Tasks

Exposure is mediated by the experience of habituation (Marks, 1987). For habituation to occur, a client needs to have the ability to maintain repeated and focused contact with the arousal, long enough for it to reduce spontaneously. Shame and guilt can make it difficult for clients to face their fear stimuli. Even when they are able to face the fear stimulus, distress might remain if the shame and guilt are not resolved. In our three cases, Jenny's shame at her facial hair and weight was more distressing than her anxiety, which was secondary to the shame. Initial targeting of the problem with exposure achieved habituation but did not impact on the distress associated with the problem. The shame and guilt remained. Thus, shame and guilt needed specific targeting. Likewise with Dave, initial prolonged imaginal exposure to his traumatic event had only limited impact on his low mood until the shame was targeted specifically. With Petra, the panic did not reduce until shame-specific interventions such as alternative emotional processing and rescripting were utilised.

Behavioural Experiments

Shame is often associated with events that have actually happened. Behavioural experiments (Bennett-Levy et al., 2004) target danger predictions (i.e. the top half of Salkovskis's (1996) equation; see Chapter 5 in this volume), to reduce the overestimation of predicted adverse outcomes. If the event has already happened and the shame is being experienced in relation to that event, targeting future predictions may have a reduced effect.

The following specific CBT interventions may be required:

- imagery rescripting and reprocessing;
- identification of personal attributes (Blackburn and Twaddle, 1996);
- identifying the role of schemas.

The role of schemas can explain the reticence and strength of emotion associated with thinking about shame and guilt, including identifying alternatives. Blackburn and Twaddle (1996) discuss this issue in relation to a fragile self-esteem, which is associated with shame and guilt. Dave, for example, was given an explanation using Beck et al.'s (1979) longitudinal formulation of the development and maintenance of emotional distress. Through this explanation it was possible to then consider how his shame may have been linked to a core belief-based desire to satisfy familial demands for achievement. Only then was it possible to implement specific interventions to weaken the effects of the schemas.

Increasing Sense of Self

Once both client and therapist hold a shared understanding of the problem through formulation, it is possible to apply change methods to reduce the impact of the shame and guilt. With all of the illustrative clients we used methods for increasing awareness and acceptance of positive attributes of the self, as described by Blackburn and Twaddle (1996). For example, the therapist worked with Jenny to identify specific attributes that were *acceptable* to her *as true* but not related to the specific domain of physical appearance on which she was so focused (e.g. hardworking, resilient, reliable). This is because most clients can identify positive personal attributes, which are acceptable to them but may not attend to them. Instead they attend disproportionately to attributes that support their shame and/or guilt. Indeed, Jenny attended only to her downy facial hair, her weight and her failed relationship. There was evidence of discounting positives, so Jenny's therapist worked with her to identify attributes of herself, which were not necessarily accepted as wholly true but were *plausible* (e.g. I am likeable, fun, tenacious). They then worked to identify those attributes which Jenny considered unacceptable but which others observed (e.g. intelligent, fun, likeable, strong). This last part involved the collection of perspectives of others including the therapist. It was then possible to plan exposure tasks, behavioural experiments, self-monitoring exercises and evidence gathering to challenge thoughts and support positive evidence. For example, Jenny was asked to collect information, which supported her acceptable attributes and those that were plausible, thus increasing attention to positive attributes of herself. This was explained using the analogy of a set of scales, with one side containing evidence for the unacceptable attributes and the other, the acceptable attributes and plausible attributes. She had been inadvertently increasing the evidence to support the unacceptable attributes by focusing on them so much. She needed to practise recognising the alternative attributes thus, balancing the scales, so that negative events would not unbalance the scales too significantly.

Evidence of acceptability   Evidence of unacceptability

Figure 8.1   The weight-scale analogy

Targeting of Shame- and Guilt-related Emotions

Specific shame- and guilt-focused interventions and bibliotherapy can be utilised, including those derived from compassionate mind (Gilbert, 2009), Acceptance and Commitment Therapy (ACT) (Hayes et al., 2004) and imagery rescripting and reprocessing therapy (Lee et al., 2001; Grunert et al., 2007; Wild et al., 2008), mindfulness (Segal et al., 2002) and emotion regulation strategies from Dialectical Behaviour Therapy (DBT) (Linehan, 1993).

GENERAL OBSTACLES DERIVED FROM SHAME AND GUILT

Therapeutic Relationship

Shame and guilt can interfere with the ability of the client to form a therapeutic relationship with the therapist (see Chapter 2). For example, in the case of Petra, she was defensive, challenging and mistrustful, believing her therapist was only working with her because it was her job to do so. The challenge for Petra's therapist, as is usually the case with such clients, was to work with the client on gaining insight into how their symptoms and behaviour function as strategies to manage their experience of threat and shame. Patients can be so focused on the threat of possible shame or guilt that they are unable to engage interpersonally. As in the case of Petra, therapists need to be sensitive and present to clients' distress. It was imperative that Petra's therapist attended closely to her verbal and non-verbal cues (e.g. the poor eye contact, darting looks at the clock). The therapist was vigilant for signs of avoidance or distress in Petra's telling of her story. This included attending to indirect expressions of shame (e.g. 'there is something wrong with me for seeking therapy'). Lewis refers to this as 'listening with the third ear'.

Past trauma, Shame and Guilt

Clients often describe the experience of past traumatic events, about which they carry shame and guilt. These would require careful attention to encourage emotional processing, reframing and reattribution. Inability to attend to past trauma can often leave the client with the shame or guilt unresolved. For example, during session 5 Petra handed her therapist a page of written material, describing her experience as a young girl while on holiday with her parents. She described an event when she was molested on the beach aged 13. She had kept this a secret for a long time and admitted she felt very ashamed about the experience. This was not she said, 'a serious assault' but she felt used and demeaned and was reticent in her expression of anger towards her parents for allowing her too much freedom during her early teenage years. She felt guilty about criticising her parents yet felt let down and ashamed of having put herself 'in such a stupid situation'. She found it difficult to discuss this verbally but was able to write about it, and her therapist then encouraged discussion of the writing in session and formulation of appropriate homework tasks. Treatment of the presenting panic had been initially unsuccessful and the presentation was rather atypical in that there were no catastrophic misinterpretations. Only after the trauma-focused work did addressing the panic become possible, using Clark's (1986) model, with graded exposure to her fear of being in the company of men and the associated arousal.

The Therapist's Shame

Therapists may need to be aware of what they bring to the therapeutic relationship. For example, therapist beliefs such as viewing one's self as 'expert and experienced' may lead to feelings of rejection or dismissal if a client does not share what is troubling them. It is worthwhile being cognisant of Richards and McDonald's (1990) expectations effect, which we expand on here:

1 clients are merely trying to cope with distressing circumstances in the best way they can;
2 they are responsive if we can form a collaborative enough therapeutic partnership;
3 they are honest and deserve therapist empathy, respect and compassion.

Important clues to therapists' own issues in therapy may include the experience of discomfort in the face of painful disclosure and, as a result, moving away from exploring or following through on a particular theme. Therapists may also experience fears around competence dealing with sensitive or distressing experiences. Disclosures may also trigger emotional reactions for the therapist, including their own shame and guilt, which may need to be attended to during supervision, reflective practice or personal therapy.

IN SUMMARY

Shame involves a complex interplay of interpersonal experience and a variety of emotional experience and reaction. It may therefore be a changing, moving thing that may emerge or never be revealed in therapy. Clients may feel anger, self-hate, disgust and discomfort. They may for very good reason choose to conceal and not address the source of their shame experience. They may at a cognitive level see themselves as useless, inferior, weak, rejectable, flawed or inadequate. These experiences can impede therapy, creating obstacles at different stages. Effective psychotherapists, both novice and expert, need to be able to identify and resolve shameful feelings constructively, both within themselves and their clients. Feelings of shame and guilt can emerge for both client and therapist and present an obstacle to therapy. Facilitated workshops by experts on shame and guilt experience are held regularly and attendance is encouraged to improve knowledge and skills of their management.

LEARNING ACTIVITY

Sarah engages in cutting behaviours, constantly berates herself and presents as angry and hostile towards her therapist. She suffered emotional abuse as a child due to a poor relationship with her mother who drank heavily, and criticised and beat her. She describes herself as 'abnormal and a psycho', and expects others to be intolerant and lack understanding of her behaviours. She is hostile but guarded in session and minimises the extent of the deliberate self-harm episodes, feeling ashamed that ordinary people would see the scars on her wrist and think badly of her.

- What factors might predispose Sarah to shame-related problems?
- What factors may be maintaining Sarah's shame?
- What are the challenges to engagement and treatment?
- What management strategies would be useful in this case?
- What are Sarah's long-term therapeutic needs?

FURTHER READING

Gilbert, P. (1986) *Overcoming Depression: A Self Help Guide Using Cognitive Behavioral Techniques.* New York: Oxford University Press.
Gilbert, P. (1998) 'Shame and humiliation in the treatment of complex cases', in N. Tarrier, G. Haddock and A. Wells (eds), *Treating Complex Cases: The Cognitive Behavioral Approach.* Chichester: John Wiley and Sons.
Tangney, J. and Dearing, R. (2002) *Shame and Guilt.* New York: Guilford Press.

REFERENCES

American Psychiatric Association (1994) *Diagnostic and Statistical Manual of Mental Disorders* (4th edn). Washington, D.C.: APA.
Andrews B. (1995) 'Bodily shame as a mediator between abusive experiences and depression', *Journal of Abnormal Psychology*, 104: 277–85.
Beck A.T., Rush, A.J., Shaw, B.F. and Emery, G. (1979) *Cognitive Therapy of Depression.* New York: Guilford Press.
Beck, A.T., Ward, C., Mendelson, M., Mock, J. and Erbaugh, J. (1961) 'An inventory for measuring depression', *Archives of General Psychiatry*, 4: 53–63.
Bennett-Levy, J., Butler, G., Fennell, M., Hackman, A., Mueller, M. and Westbrook, D. (eds) (2004) *Oxford Guide to Behavioural Experiments in Cognitive Therapy* Oxford: Oxford University Press.
Blackburn, I.M. and Twaddle, V. (1996) *Cognitive Therapy in Action: A Practitioner's Casebook.* London: Souvenir Press.
Blackburn, I.M., James, I.A., Milne, D.L. et al. (2001) 'The Revised Cognitive Therapy Scale (CTS-R) psychometric properties', *Behavioural and Cognitive Psychotherapy*, 29: 431–47.

Carr, A.T. (2002) 'Body shame: Issues of assessment and measurement', in P. Gilbert and J. Miles (eds), *Body Shame: Conceptualisation, Research and Treatment*. Hove: Brunner-Routledge. pp. 90–102.

Chemtob, C.M., Hamada, R.S., Bauer, G., Kinney, B. and Torigoe, M. (1998) 'Patients suicides: frequency and impact on psychiatrists', *American Journal of Psychiatry*, 145: 224–8.

Clark, D.M. (1986) 'A cognitive approach to panic', *Behaviour Research and Therapy*, 24 (4): 461–70.

Cook, D.R. (1989) *Internalised Shame Scale (ISS)*. Menomonie, WI: University of Wisconsin-Stout.

Gilbert, P. (1992) *Depression: The Evolution of Powerlessness*. Hove: Lawrence Erlbaum.

Gilbert, P. (1998) 'What is shame? Some core issues and controversies', in P. Gilbert and B. Andrews (eds), *Shame: Interpersonal Behaviour, Psychopathology and Culture*. New York. Oxford University Press. pp. 3–38.

Gilbert, P. (2000) 'The relationship of shame, social anxiety: the role of the evaluation of social rank', *Clinical Psychology and Psychotherapy*, 7: 174–89.

Gilbert, P. and Miles, J. (2002) *Body Shame: Conceptualisation, Research and Treatment*. Hove: Brunner-Routledge.

Gilbert, P. and Leahy, R. (2007) *The Therapeautic Relationship in the Cognitive Behavioural Psychotherapies*. London: Routledge.

Gilbert, P. (2007) 'Evolved minds and compassion in the therapeutic relationship', in P. Gilbert and R. Leahy (eds), *The Therapeutic Relationship in the Cognitive Behavioural Psychotherapies*. London: Routledge.

Gilbert, P. (2009) *The Compassionate Mind*. London: Constable Publications.

Grieve, G., Truba, N. and Bowers, S.D. (2009) 'Etiology Assessment and Treatment of Muscle Dysmorphia', *Journal of Cognitive Psychotherapy*, 23 (4): 306–14.

Grunert, B.K., Weis, J.M., Smucker, M.R. and Christianson, H.F. (2007) 'Imagery reprocessing and rescripting therapy after failed prolonged exposure in post-traumatic stress disorder following industrial injury', *Journal of Behaviour Therapy and Experimental Psychiatry*, 38 (4): 317–28.

Hastings, M., Northman, L. and Tangney, J. (2002) 'Shame, guilt and suicide', in T. Joiner and M.D. Rudd (eds), *Suicide Science: Expanding the Boundaries*. London. Kluwer Academic Publishers. pp. 67–79.

Hayes, S.C., Strosahl, K. and Wilson, K.G. (eds) (2004) *A Practical Guide to Acceptance and Commitment Therapy*. New York. Guilford Press.

Hill, C.E., Thompson, B.J., Cogar, M. and Denman, D.W. (1993) 'Beneath the surface of long term therapy: therapist and client report of their own and each others covert processes', *Journal of Counselling Psychology*, 40: 278–87.

Hook, A. and Andrews, B. (2005) 'The relationship of non- disclosure in therapy to shame and depression', *British Journal of Clinical Psychology*, 44: 425–38.

Kearns, C. (2010) 'A single case design: does adding imagery rescripting to CBT treatment as usual reduce distress and mages?', unpublished thesis, Oxford University.

Knox, S., Burkard, A., Hess, S., Jackson, J. and Schaack, A. (2006) 'Therapists in training who experience a client suicide: implications for supervision', *Professional Psychology; Research and Practice*, 37: 547–57.

Kugler, K. and Jones, W.H. (1992) 'On conceptualising and assessing guilt', *Journal of Personal and Social Psychology*, 62 (2): 318–27.

Lee, D., Scragg, P. and Turner, S. (2001) 'The role of shame and guilt in traumatic events: a clinical model of shame-based and guilt-based PTSD', *British Journal of Medical Psychology*, 74 (4): 451–66.

Lewis, H.B. (1971) *Shame and Guilt in Neurosis*. New York: International Universities Press.

Lewis, H.B. (1986) 'The role of shame in depression', in M. Rutter, C.E. Izard and P.B. Read (eds), *Depression in Young People: Developmental and Clinical Perspectives*. New York: Guilford Press.

Linehan, M.M. (1993) *Skills Training Manual for Treating Borderline Personality Disorder*. New York: Guilford Press.

Marks, I. (1987) *Fears Phobias and Rituals: Panic, Anxiety and Their Disorders*. New York: Oxford University Press.

Overmeier, J., Seligman, B. and Martin, E. (1967) 'Effects of inescabable shock upon subsequent escape and avoidance responding', *Journal of Comparative and Physiological Psychology*, 63 (1): 28–33.

Richards, D.A. and McDonald, B. (1990) *Behavioural Psychotherapy: A Handbook for Nurses*. Oxford: Heinemann Medical Books/Heinemann Professional Publishing.

Safran, J.D. and Segal Z.V. (1996) *Interpersonal Processes in Cognitive Therapy* (2nd edn). Northvale, NJ: Jason Avonson.

Salkovskis P.M. (1985) 'Obsessive compulsive problems: a cognitive behavioural analysis', *Behaviour Research and Therapy*, 23: 571–83.

Salkovskis P.M. (1996) 'The cognitive approach to anxiety: threat beliefs, safety-seeking behaviour, and the special case of health anxiety and obsessions', in P. Salkovskis (ed.), *Frontiers of Cognitive Therapy*. New York: Guilford Press.

Segal. Z.V., Willams, J.M.G. and Teasdale, J.D. (2002) *Mindfulness Based Cognitive Therapy for Depression: A New Approach for Preventing Relapse*. New York: Guilford Press.

Stekettee, G., Quay, S. and White, K. (1991) 'Religion and guilt in OCD patients', *Journal of Anxiety Disorders*, 5 (4): 359–67.

Tangney, J.P. and Dearing, R. (2002) *Shame and Guilt*. New York: Guilford Press.

Tangney, J.P., Millar, R.S., Flicker, L. and Barlow, H. (1996) 'Are shame guilt embarrassment distinct emotions?', *Journal of Personality and Social Psychology*, 70: 1256–69.

Tangney, J.P., Ferguson, T.J., Wagner, P.E., Crowley, S.L. and Gramzow, R. (1996) *The Test of Self Conscious Affect-2* (TOSCA-2). Fairfax, VA: George Mason University.

Teasdale, J.D. and Fogarty, S.J. (1979) 'Differential effects of induced mood on retrieval of pleasant and unpleasant events from episodic memory', *Journal of Abnormal Psychology*, 88: 248–57.

Thompson, R.J. and Berenbaum, H. (2006) 'Shame reactions to everyday dilemmas are associated with depressive disorder', *Cognitive Therapy and Research*, 30: 415–25.

Troop, N.A. and Connan, F. (2003) 'Shame social stress and eating disorders',in G. M. Ruggiero (ed.), *Eating Disorders in the Mediterranean Area*. New York: Nova Science.

Weiner, M.F. and Schuman, D.W. (1984) 'What patients don't tell their therapists', *Journal of Integrative Psychiatry*, 2: 28–32.

Wild, J., Hackman, A. and Clark, D.M. (2008) 'Rescripting early memories linked to negative images in social phobia: a pilot study', *Behaviour Therapy*, 39 (1): 47–56.

9

INTRUSIONS, RUMINATION AND AGITATION

MICHAEL MCDONOUGH AND CRAIG CHIGWEDERE

LEARNING OBJECTIVES

After reading this chapter the reader should:

- know how to identify and distinguish between the common kinds of (non-psychotic) distressing intrusive thoughts and repetitive (or perseverative) thinking (i.e. obsessions, worry, flashbacks/intrusive memories, negative automatic thoughts, racing thoughts and ruminative thinking);
- be able to recognise and assess the (non-psychotic) agitated patient;
- be aware of the common pitfalls when working with such presentations.

INTRODUCTION

When tackling problems involving intrusive thoughts and rumination therapists need to have a detailed understanding of the nature and characteristics of the various subtypes of these patterns of thinking. Clinicians need to be cognisant of similarities and differences, how they interact and overlap and how they connect to deeper cognitive themes such as meta-beliefs, core beliefs and underlying assumptions/rules.

An illustrative case (Kate) is presented first to highlight the importance of differentiating patterns of intrusive and preservative thinking. This is followed by a section defining and distinguishing the common forms of intrusive thinking, which in our experience are often not adequately taught on CBT courses. Then brief, illustrative discussions of real-life cases are presented with questions to guide reflection and problem solving. The reader should thus be able to test and apply their understanding of the concepts introduced earlier in the chapter.

LABELLING AND MISLABELLING THINKING

CASE OF KATE – AN AGITATED WORRIER

Kate, a 55-year-old woman, presents with intense, pervasive anxiety linked to repetitive thoughts about the financial problems facing her family's business. She says she has always been a 'worrier' and feels she will only get better if she can solve the problems and 'switch off her mind'. She is tormented with thoughts that the business will fail and that she will remain distressed. Her therapist collaboratively agrees to work on these worries using Wells's CBT model for generalised anxiety disorder – GAD (Wells, 1997: Chapter 9). After three sessions the therapy is making little progress. Kate has trouble concentrating in the sessions and what little progress is made socialising her to the model is quickly lost. At the end of the session Anne reverts to worrying and ruminating. She has not completed any homework tasks.

This is a common presentation in clinical practice. It illustrates the importance of careful exploration of the thinking patterns displayed in the distressed individual. Although at initial assessment Kate's account of her thoughts seemed to fit with the definition of worry as a chain of negatively affect-laden thoughts aimed at problem solving (Borkovec et al., 1983), closer examination reveals that much of her thinking is more akin to depressive rumination (Nolen-Hoeksema, 1991) mixed with frequent negative automatic thoughts (NATs) (Beck, 1967). The content of her thinking (e.g. 'Why can't I snap out of it? Why can't I get it together to do anything? Why won't my brain work?') is in keeping with Nolen-Hoeksema's definition of depressive rumination as a passive, repetitive brooding on the symptoms and consequences of depression. Mixed in are thoughts fitting Beck's description of Negative Automatic Thoughts (NATs) (e.g. 'I am a failure now. This is the end'). These thoughts were out of Kate's immediate awareness much of the time but were accessible through guided discovery. They were affect-laden and believable to her – in keeping with Beck's (1967) definition. In addition there were clear depressive symptoms of reduced motivation, withdrawal, agitation, early-morning wakening and weight loss. Not unusually, Kate herself did not view herself as depressed. Such so-called 'agitated' depression presentations (Benazzi, 2007) are often misunderstood and can be sometimes mismanaged as generalised anxiety.

Which CBT Intervention?

Working directly with cognitions in such presentations is difficult and may not be appropriate as focus and attention are severely affected. The therapeutic approach taken initially, involved behavioural activation (Jacobson et al., 1996) and practising detached mindfulness techniques (e.g. King in Davey and Wells, 2006: 347) which were well received by Kate as initial interventions. In consideration of the depressive symptomology, a course of SSRI antidepressant medication was also commenced.

As Kate's mental and physical agitation improved, she benefited from work on her tendency to worry excessively. In addition the cognitive aspects of her depression, such as negative automatic thoughts and thinking errors, were addressed in the usual way. Again not untypically, her tendency to worry was not nearly so apparent when her mood improved. This is in keeping with the mood-as-input view of worry, which theorises that negative mood is a key factor causing worry to persist (Davey in Davey and Wells, 2006: Chapter 13). However, addressing a worry tendency is an important part of relapse prevention in such cases, as exhaustion from worrying is often the gateway to agitated depression. For Kate much of the subsequent work focused on GAD and addressing negative core beliefs about failure and inadequacy. The associated rules to do with needing to be in control and striving to be successful, instrumental in her spiral into depression, were also attended to.

SUBTYPES AND PATTERNS OF THINKING

The case of Kate offers an illustration of one type of presentation; however, there are many ways in which intrusions into awareness present in therapy. Here some of the main forms of intrusions ruminations and agitation, which are likely to confront a therapist, will be outlined.

Worry

Worry has been defined as a chain of negatively affect-laden thoughts aimed at problem solving (Borkovec et al., 1983; Davey and Wells, 2006, for detailed review). It occurs in healthy individuals and in those with emotional disorders. Once triggered, the familiar 'What if ... ?' question begins the process. This is then supported by beliefs about the value of worry as a problem-solving method or as a way of being prepared for future negative events. What follows is a flow of thoughts and questions (predominately verbal, rather than images), which expand this theme often in a catastrophic way, resulting in an escalation of physical anxiety. For example, Kate might think, 'My husband hasn't phoned'; this could escalate to, 'What if he's in trouble? What if he has been in a crash? How will the business cope if he has to go on sick leave?' Complex factors interact to terminate worry such as mood, fatigue, intolerance of uncertainty, rules about problem solving, beliefs about the dangers of worry ('meta worry' or type 2 worry) and thought control/distraction and neutralising behaviours (e.g. reassurance seeking).

Worry is the central feature of GAD where it is more pervasive and perceived as less controllable. Worry themes in GAD vary across time. Worry linked to other disorders tends to focus on the theme of that disorder (e.g. anticipated social performance in social anxiety or planning a means of escape in panic-agoraphobia). GAD frequently underlies or co-exists with other anxiety and mood disorders. The leading therapeutic CBT models for GAD are Wells (1997), Dugas et al. (1998) and Borkovec and Costello (1993). These authors overlap somewhat theoretically but emphasise different elements of the cycle and are therapeutically distinct.

Obsessional Thinking

Obsessions are intrusive frightening thoughts, images or impulses that usually lead to the performance of a compulsion to neutralise the fear generated by the intrusion. The resultant compulsive acts can be completed either mentally or behaviourally (covert and overt compulsions). They differ from worries in that they are perceived as senseless and alien to the person's view of themselves (i.e. ego-dystonic), though they share the characteristic of worries relating to an imagined negative event or feared consequence (Wells, 1997: 5). Obsessions are more likely to present in the form of images or impulses. Obsessional thoughts are less realistic and more involuntary than worries and tend to result in an appraisal along the lines of, 'Where did that come from? Why did I think that?', whereas worries are accepted as part of the individual's natural flow of thought (ego-syntonic). Although the content of the obsessions may vary from person to person, they usually focus on a narrow repertoire of themes not tending to generalise. Like worries they are normal phenomena though, as illustrated by Salkovskis (1989), OCD sufferers have exaggerated responsibility beliefs, which make them more likely to appraise these intrusions as important, unacceptable and worthy of response. Typical examples include paedophilic thoughts (distinguished from true paedophilic thoughts in that they are not associated with pleasure or fantasy but rather horror and shame) or violent thoughts/ impulses or religious themes, such as images of the devil.

The pure obsessional subtype of OCD is of most relevance to this chapter, as the CBT models (e.g. Salkovskis, 1989), or exposure and response prevention (Meyer, 1966), are easier to apply when OCD is clearly associated with overt neutralising acts, such as checking or washing. In situations where much of the OCD cycle is going on covertly (e.g. mental rituals), exploration can be hampered by shame and cognitive avoidance, which can be challenging initially. Such cases demand an understanding of the meta-cognitive processes (see Wells, 1997: Chapter 9) at play such as thought–action–fusion (i.e. thinking something makes it likely to happen/have happened) (Rachman, 1993) and responsibility beliefs about thoughts (e.g. 'If I think something bad and don't fix it [neutralise] it's like I want it to happen') (Salkovskis, 1989). These processes can be subtle but powerful and can lead to frustration if not carefully conceptualised with the client.

Rumination

Obsessional Rumination

Confusion about the definition of obsessional rumination among theorists reflects the plight of therapists and sufferers in making sense of what is happening in OCD presentations. It is no wonder obstacles can occur when we meet such clients. Clients can engage in long periods of meditation on or analysis of obsessional themes such as good and evil, or safety and danger. The case of Sean illustrates this type of rumination.

THE CASE OF SEAN'S OBSESSION – A QUEST FOR THE IMPOSSIBLE?

Sean a 25-year-old philosophy graduate has always been proud of his ability to resolve mental conundrums. Lately, however, he has been plagued by thoughts related to the acts of a historical figure whom he has always admired, causing him great distress. After listening to a radio discussion, during which a well-known academic's views challenged his perception of his hero, he had the frightening thought, 'I have it all wrong, everything I have worked out is wrong'. Sean engaged in meditative effort to resolve the issue of the goodness or badness of his hero. He is now constantly preoccupied with this effort but can never seem to arrive at a lasting resolution. He spends countless hours trawling the internet and the media or meditating on the issues of right or wrong to the exclusion of other activities. His 'failure' to reach a resolution is associated with images of him being judged by his peers and a fear that he will never again be able to trust his own opinion.

Rachman (1971) initially referred to obsessional rumination as 'repetitive, intrusive and unacceptable thoughts', which made it impossible to distinguish rumination from obsessions and neutralising mental rituals. Thankfully De Silva has clarified things nicely: obsessional rumination is a process of wilful analysis of a theme arising out of an obsessional thought but in an open-ended, haphazard way with the aim of resolving matters or reaching a conclusion. Sean's philosophical analysis fits this definition with the triggering obsessional thought being 'I have it all wrong'. Although also aimed at easing distress, obsessional rumination is distinct from and much more protracted than mental compulsions, which are ritualistic and rigid in nature (e.g. saying a prayer in response to an obsessional image of evil) (Menzies and de Silva, 2003: Chapter 11).

Obsessional rumination is debilitating and, can be very prolonged and time consuming. Often new obsessions can intrude during an obsessional ruminative episode causing a surge in anxiety, sparking further rumination. It is somewhat akin to worry as it aims to solve a puzzle, is largely verbal but tends to be confined to specific, more esoteric, themes such as:

- 'What is the nature of right and wrong?'
- 'How can I know if evil exists?'
- 'How would I know if I was a pervert?'
- 'What drives people to paedophilia?'
- 'How likely am I to get cancer?'
- 'How much background radiation is there in the atmosphere?'

Similar to worry, positive beliefs are activated about the value of mental analysis and the value of working things out, that results in the selection of this mental activity. However, similar to the worry presentation, it leads to exhaustion and confusion rather than clarity. Also it might be argued, the central fear is never engaged with long enough for emotional processing to occur and for a new perspective to emerge.

This is of great clinical importance to therapists working with these more complex OCD presentations. Its therapeutic relevance is that patients need to be carefully socialised to the dangers of rumination and its place in the maintenance cycle of the presenting issue. It is important to avoid the pitfall of sessions being overtaken with discussion of obsessional themes in a ruminative, intellectualised way. This obstacle to the efficiency and focus of a therapy session needs to be attended to implicitly or as a separate goal of treatment. The best approach for treating this challenging subset of OCD characterised by covert neutralisation and rumination has yet to emerge. Menzies and De Silva (2003) advise exposure to frightening ideas/images until habituation occurs, which we suggest might be combined with metacognitive work on positive beliefs about rumination as per Wells (1997). Later, a review of the evidence supporting the obsessional fears can help, once perspective and anxiety have normalised somewhat. Salkovskis's model (1985) suggests working on underlying responsibility beliefs and challenging the meaning behind the intrusive thoughts rather than the intrusion itself. More recently, Rachman points to the importance of longitudinal case conceptualisation such as linking the feeling of 'mental contamination' with past betrayal experiences (Rachman, 2010).

Other Kinds of Rumination

Other kinds of rumination that can present in clinical practice involve themes of personal loss and failure (Papageorgiou in Davey and Wells, 2006: Chapter 2). In depression, as stated above, the sufferer broods on their depressive state with 'why?'-type questions (Nolen-Hoeksema, 1991). This differs from the obsessive rumination illustrated in the case of Sean and worry presentations, where the central questions are respectively 'what is … ?' or 'how … ?' and 'what if … ?'. Other disorders are associated with rumination on loss and failure but the content is specific to the problem and focused on the past (unlike worry), such as a social anxiety sufferer ruminating on a social encounter, where they felt humiliated or a post traumatic stress disorder (PTSD) client ruminating on why they were assaulted. As with OCD the extent of this rumination will determine its importance in the maintenance of the problem and the requirement for separate attention in therapy.

Negative Automatic Thoughts (NATs)

These are discussed here briefly to help distinguish them from the other forms of intrusive thinking. NATs occur rapidly and are outside of the focus of immediate awareness but are amenable to consciousness. They occur in verbal or image form and are believable at the time of occurrence (Wells, 1997: 5). They can be very distressing for clients, due to their believability. Their importance in the maintenance cycle of depression is well known to practitioners at all levels (Beck, 1967). Beck also uses this term in his schema theory of anxiety, where they are described as the surface cognitions when danger schemas are activated. They are again viewed as normal phenomena but tend to be more frequent and affect-laden in depression or anxiety states. Catastrophic thoughts in panic are a good example (Clark, 1986). NATs are an important focus of therapeutic work both as targets for verbal and experimental challenging and as clues to exploring underlying rules and beliefs.

Traumatic Memories and Post Traumatic Stress Disorder (PTSD)

When memories or flashbacks are clearly linked with an identifiable traumatic event therapeutic work in PTSD can be readily focused on the problem using, for example, the Ehlers and Clark model (Ehlers and Clark, 2000). However, in keeping with Brewin's dual representation model, much of the memories of traumatic events are laid down as *situationally accessible memories* which are disjointed, involuntarily triggered and associated with intense and wide ranging sensory information (Brewin et al., 1996). This means that fragments of the trauma experience can be reactivated in any sensory mode or in a wide range of cognitive or emotional events such as images, thoughts, nightmares and anger. The complexity of such a presentation merits discussion in its own right. The case of Max illustrates how PTSD may present.

THE CASE OF MAX'S SUPPRESSED TRAUMA

Max, a 50-year-old security guard, was stabbed while at work. He was responding to a request to move a group of young men who were drunk and disorderly in the shopping mall. He was talking in an apparently friendly way to one of the men, when he suddenly and unexpectedly stabbed him in the stomach. Physically, Max is healed but suffers nightmares of being attacked. He tries to avoid memories of the attack, which are easily triggered. Situational triggers which he tries to avoid include knives and media stories of knife attacks, the shopping mall, groups of men and the smell of alcohol. When triggered, the memories are 'very real', as though the event was happening again. Sometimes, he feels the pain in his wound. He is ashamed that he was caught unexpectedly, was unable to predict the attack and views himself as weak. When asked for the details of the attack by the therapist, he does not recall much of the event and describes feeling emotionally 'blocked'. He says his main problem is a grievance with his employers over pay and compensation and prefers to focus on this in session.

The case of Max, illustrating guilt, mistrust, anger and shame beliefs, combined with the various voluntary and involuntary attempts to suppress the memory (such as cognitive and behavioural avoidance, dissociative amnesia and emotional numbing), not uncommonly leads to a confused clinical picture. This is particularly evident in the early stages of a suppressed trauma coming to light. Hence in any case where intrusive thoughts or unexpected reactions are occurring without explanation, consideration should be given to an emerging PTSD. Exploring this possibility should be carried out delicately with much attention paid to establishing a secure, reliable therapeutic relationship and a sense of safety for the client. Working collaboratively with a client like Max, in a sensitive way, piecing things together slowly is important. It is wise to remember that many other disorders can have a traumatic onset or traumatic predisposing events. Thus, in apparently clear-cut cases of other disorders involving intrusive thoughts, trauma memories (not necessarily fulfilling PTSD criteria) can be mixed in, which often emanate from childhood experience, so that the individual does not readily link them to the current presentation. These frequently come to light later in therapy after the maintenance cycle of the presenting problem has subsided. Contracting further work on these traumas is generally indicated and can be fruitful. The nature of intrusive thoughts differ in PTSD compared with other disorders, as illustrated by the cases of Anne, John and Max outlined in Table 9.1. Failure to recognise and incorporate a traumatic memory into the conceptualisation and treatment can create an obstacle to the treatment of other disorders, so the impact of apparently well-constructed and implemented interventions is reduced. Therapists need good supervision and training in order to work with trauma presentations, particularly the more complex ones.

Mixed-mood States

The topic of mixed moods may appear out of place in this chapter but it is likely that every practising CBT therapist will encounter cases where subtle unrecognised mixed-mood states impact on therapeutic work. They may pose an insurmountable obstacle to productive therapeutic work particularly with very agitated clients. Clear euphoric mania or hypomanic cases are easily recognisable. However, more subtle states such as 'dysphoric' hypomania, mood cycling or mixed depression are more challenging to identify and can mimic agitated depression or GAD. Distinguishing mixed states from agitated depression (see above) can be most challenging. In true agitated depression the predominant emotion is anxiety (rather than frustration and irritability, which is seen in mixed states) and sleep tends to be disturbed with early wakening (rather than delayed onset in mixed states). Clients presenting with agitated

Table 9.1 Types of intrusive and repetitive thinking

Type	Content	Form	Emotion	'Meta' view	Typical response	Therapeutic approach
Worry	Concerning future negative events, aimed at problem solving	Mostly verbal, comes in bouts, starts with 'What if?'	Anxiety, apprehension	Engaged in willingly at least initially, seen as helpful	Continue until reassured or exhausted	Cost-benefit analysis Practise tolerating uncertainty Postponement and other experiments
Obsessions	Small number of themes, e.g. sexual, violent	Sudden, fleeting verbal, images or impulses (sometimes like 'pseudo'-hallucinations)	Fear Disgust Shame	Dystonic (seen as own thoughts but alien, not welcome) Appraised as dangerous and significant	Neutralise Distract Suppress Ruminate	Detached acceptance Imaginal exposure Thought action fusion experiments
Obsessional rumination	Mental analysis, dialogue	Verbal, triggered by obsession	Anxiety	Engaged in willingly Aimed at resolving a question	Continued until exhaustion or distraction	Cost-benefit analysis Detached acceptance of doubt Imaginal exposure to obsession
Depressive rumination	Mental analysis, dialogue Brooding (regarding past, present or future)	Verbal, may be triggered by negative automatic thought, starts with 'Why...?'	Sadness Shame Grief	Although painful engaged in willingly, i.e. mood congruent	Continued until exhaustion, complete demoralisation or distraction	Cost-benefit analysis Detached acceptance of feelings and thoughts without rumination (MBCT) Behavioural activation Work on underlying, stable depressive beliefs/assumptions and cognitive distortions
Flashback/ trauma memory	Relating to trauma often 'hotspot'	Intrusive image or sensation in any mode triggered by reminder of trauma	Terror (Shame)	Unwelcome Like reliving the trauma	Suppress Distract Escape	Challenge key cognitions, e.g. re shame reliving
Negative automatic thoughts	Any negative theme (self, world, future)	Usually verbal, may be vague, just outside consciousness	Sadness Anxiety Anger Shame	Seen as credible but not welcomed	Passes spontaneously or may lead to depressive rumination	Challenging verbally or through experimentation Explore for deeper formulation
Racing thoughts (mixed affective state)	Flitting between themes – often negative	Any but speeded, ill formed, incomplete	Sadness Tension Desperation Irritability	Seen as distressing and disordered	Search for relief, anger, escape, self-harm	Education Medication adjustments (NB sleep) Detached acceptance Reduce stimulation Postpone dealing with content until calmer

depression respond well to antidepressants, whereas mixed states can be made worse with antidepressants when used alone. Clinicians working with these client groups are well advised to be aware of these effects. The prevalence of mixed states in clinical populations is striking (30 per cent of major depressives and up to 70 per cent of symptomatic Bipolar I and II cases) (Benazzi, 2007). These mixed states represent variations on the bipolar spectrum of mood illness and, for the therapist, may or may not require separate therapeutic consideration. Engaging with these clients using the standard or individualised models for depression or bipolar disorder may not be effective in the acute phase.

Sufferers complain of *racing thoughts* (which they may report as worry but on closer scrutiny are more rapid, incomplete and crowded than worries), irritability, often intense suicidal impulses, which can make sessions difficult to manage. They can be agitated and energised yet withdraw from social contact and feel depressed. Their sleep cycle and mood can fluctuate wildly day-to-day, making linking sessions almost impossible.

Managing Mixed-mood-state Cases

The CBT therapist should work with the multidisciplinary team and appropriately qualified medical colleagues to establish appropriate pharmacological treatment (often mood-stabilising agents are required and a review of prescribed antidepressant medication). Clinically it may be necessary to either defer the CBT work until things are more stable or shift the focus of the work to stabilising daily rhythms and tracking moods and sleep. As with agitated depression attempting to work systematically on NATs, worry or underlying schemas during the acute phase is rarely productive (for a case example, see Chapter 3 – 'Jude's Sudden Recovery').

Psychosis

As Morrison and others have shown, psychotic experiences (such as auditory hallucinations, thought insertion, withdrawal and broadcast) are at least partially maintained by the meaning the individual attaches to these events and their subsequent responses, based on these appraisals. It is beyond the scope of this chapter to explore this category of intrusive experience in detail. In a case of intrusions from psychosis, the therapist is well advised to carefully and collaboratively explore these events with the client, drawing upon the existing therapeutic models for psychosis along with multidisciplinary input (see, for example, Morrison, 2002 and Morrison et al., 2004). These models emphasise careful engagement, trust building and normalisation early in therapy as a way of easing the often catastrophic interpretations that sufferers make of what is happening. It is not unusual for any disorder (but especially OCD) to evolve into psychosis particularly with clients in their late teens or early twenties (the peak age of onset of schizophrenia) or for clients with severe depression or co-morbid borderline personality disorder to suffer brief 'micro'-psychoses in the course of their recovery. As with trauma memories the clinician needs to be vigilant for tell-tale signs such as unexplained anger or hostility, disjointed thinking or breaks in thinking (thought disorder), loosening of the connection with reality, withdrawal and incongruity. Again, as with trauma, the clinical picture may take weeks or months to emerge. Such cases where the therapist senses something odd or different about the client should be brought up for discussion at supervision and at multi-disciplinary team meetings to clarify diagnosis and best management.

KEY SKILL: MINDFUL ACCEPTANCE OF THOUGHTS AND IMAGES

Approaches based on mindfulness meditation first trialled in clinical populations by Kabat-Zinn (Mindfulness-Based Stress Reduction – MBSR, Kabat-Zinn, 1982) have been applied to a host of emotional disorders and have been referred to as the third wave of CBT. Two mindfulness programmes of prominence have been developed and evaluated over recent times, Mindfulness-Based Stress Reduction (Kabat-Zinn, 1990) and Mindfulness-Based Cognitive Therapy (MBCT; Segal et al., 2002). Ost (2008) offers a note of caution and warns against assuming the efficacy of these approaches in the absence of well-conducted trials. Nonetheless, approaches and concepts adopted from mindfulness and integrated into CBT practice such as attention training (Wells, 1997: 273), detached acceptance and MBCT for depression (Teasdale et al., 2000) show great promise and are particularly useful for patients suffering intrusive and repetitive thinking. They teach the key skill of accepting mental events and negative emotions without judgement or response. Simply being with the experience is seen as positive and enlightening. According to Segal et al. (2002), mindfulness-based practice allows decentring and disengagement from repetitive, habitual ways of thinking – a crucial step in overcoming worry and rumination. As Borkevoc has proposed for worry (Borkovec et al., 1983) and as has been demonstrated for OCD, health anxiety (Salkovskis, 1989) and PTSD (Ehlers and Clark, 2000), attempts to dispel, fix or neutralise upsetting thoughts are counterproductive and maintain the problem. They prevent emotional engagement with the thought and disconfirmation or processing of the underlying fear.

For some clients, allowing these thoughts to remain in consciousness goes against the grain and may be intensely distressing. Max is consciously and unconsciously 'not going there'. In John's case, he makes efforts to reach an unachievable conclusion, which only serves to maintain his quest for certainty. For him to resist trying to resolve the issue of right and wrong is difficult and distressing. It is, however, a vital first step to breaking the cycle and to enabling the experiential work of CBT to commence. Depending on the model used, this skill can then be employed to facilitate and augment the various evidence-based CBT strategies such as cognitive exposure work and experiments testing metacognitive predictions (such as thinking something bad makes it real) in OCD, reliving in PTSD and building tolerance of uncertainty in GAD. Moving from responding and analysing to experiencing and exploring intrusions, is to covertly maintained disorders like obsessional rumination and PTSD, what behavioural experiments and graded exposure are to panic and phobias. Practitioners vary in how mindfulness approaches are utilised and integrated into their practice. Without an understanding of how to manage and manipulate distressing mental events CBT therapists will struggle to overcome the obstacles posed in the cases outlined in this chapter.

ILLUSTRATIVE CASES

This section contains case examples illustrating common obstacles along the therapeutic way. We suggest they are used as problem-based learning opportunities to test what has been learned through this chapter. We suggest the reader pause and reflect at key moments as we had to do repeatedly with the clients whose case material this section is based on.

Hidden Processes in Resistant Cases

THE CASE OF CAROL – WHAT'S THE PANIC?

Carol, aged 30, has suffered panics for two years and has become increasingly avoidant of crowded places and being far from home. She has been prescribed alprazolam by her GP and has been heavily reliant on this medication to cope with trips to work or when away from home. Her therapist agrees a treatment plan using Clark's panic model (Clark, 1986). Despite a thorough assessment the therapist has not identified any co-morbid disorders or additional schema-level problems. Catastrophic cognitions about collapse and losing control seem to fit the model but the work is inconsistent and slow. On occasions Carol can manage challenging trigger situations to her panic (e.g. trip on crowded tram) but on others she remains at home unable to face the journey to the therapy session. On such days she reports intense distress and physical discomfort in the form of nausea and abdominal cramps. In session, exploration and thought records don't reveal thoughts or images to explain these episodes other than a general sense of insecurity and threat.

Take a moment to reflect on this case:

- What needs to be considered here?
- Does the panic model fit the presentation?
- What co-morbidity may be emerging?
- What would reviewing her medication offer?
- What is behind the inconsistencies in her symptoms?

The multi-disciplinary team (MDT) discuss the case. It is suggested to put Carol on a longer-acting benzodiazepine – clonazepam – and attempt a gradual withdrawal, as there was a possibility that her physical dependency on benzodiazepines may have been contributing to the fluctuating pattern of her anxiety.

This medication change proceeds with Carol's agreement but as the dose is reduced Carol starts to recall segments of a sexual assault that occurred when she was 17. Initially she dismisses the importance of this and seems to be able to discuss it without distress but as the clonazepam is reduced, she develops flashbacks, nightmares and feels anxious and avoidant near men. She begins to make a connection between this trauma, her panic episodes, her physical symptoms (she vomited after the assault) and her fear of crowded places. A delayed PTSD reaction has emerged and she works with her CBT therapist on the trauma using the Ehlers and Clark (2000) model. She recalls elements of the trauma resurfacing around the time her panic started (possibly triggered by a new physical relationship) but felt she had successfully suppressed these memories with the help of alprazolam. She had not mentioned the assault to any of her family and wanted to 'keep it in the past' and seemed to genuinely not see its relevance to her emerging panic symptoms.

Comment on Carol's Case

This case illustrates the complex factors that can interplay and influence how clients present. As discussed in the section on PTSD, trauma can often be the underlying problem but often therapists and clients can knowingly or unknowingly not address the trauma. In Carol's case, she preferred to work on what she felt was the central issue, panic/agoraphobia. She was apparently well engaged and motivated in the sessions and didn't appear evasive. It is likely that her natural capacity to dissociate from the conscious memory and the emotion (though not the physical sensations) combined with the emotionally suppressing effect of alprazolam meant that the trauma memories were unconscious until the medication was reduced. Even when the memory was re-engaged consciously it took time for the link with PTSD symptoms to become evident. The therapist might have ignored the memory completely had her experience and the atypical nature of the presentation not primed her to be vigilant for hidden trauma.

Complex OCD Presentations: Dangers of Over-reliance on One Approach

CASE OF PATRICK: WHAT'S IN A NAME?

Patrick, 24, suffers with OCD since childhood but has become seriously hampered by it in the last year since commencing a physics degree. Previously his OCD was confined to checking his academic work for mistakes and sometimes re-doing it which was time consuming but not too disabling. However, after meeting a relative at college who remarked, 'So you are the next Paddy Keane. Your father and grandfather were great men. You are carrying on a great name!', he began to ruminate on the question of carrying on the family tradition. Both his father and grandfather were well-known sportsmen locally and renowned for being 'hard men'. He mulled the question over for hours. 'What does it mean to carry the family name? Am I as tough as them? How would I find out? If I am not is something wrong with me? Might I be gay?' These thoughts were associated with a nagging anxiety. He researched the internet and explored the fate of third-generation sons sharing the name of their fathers and grandfathers, such as Napoleon III. He applied himself to this question like a complex physics problem and thought that with enough analysis an answer would emerge that would somehow guide him in life. However, this relentless analysis wore him down and he became exhausted by his efforts. His studies suffered and he dropped out of college before his exams. Soon after returning home Patrick became increasingly depressed and developed thoughts of suicide. He began to suffer from intrusive obsessional thoughts that he was gay. He attempted to neutralise these thoughts by testing out if he became aroused by mental images of men or women. He felt a failure for dropping out of college. He had previously been proud of being a talented student but no longer felt capable or worthy.

Take a moment to reflect on this case:

- What needs to be considered here?
- How would you approach this case?
- What therapeutic model might be useful?
- Would imaginal exposure be helpful?

Patrick commenced CBT work with an experienced therapist who proceeded to a longitudinal case conceptualisation early in therapy to explore the origins of his core belief around inadequacy. This revealed bullying experiences in school (including taunts about being gay), limited ability in sports (much to his father's disappointment), a very protective mother, and positive experiences around excelling in science and chess. The therapist opted against imaginal exposure experiments to the obsessional thought that he was gay, as the thought was linked with sadness and loss as much as anxiety and fear. Also, there wasn't a strong thought–action–fusion meta-belief that 'thinking this makes it true', which might have been readily tested through exposure experiments.

The therapist agreed experiments with Patrick comparing the effect of detached acceptance of the gay thoughts and the thoughts about not matching up to his

(Continued)

(Continued)

father (carefully coached and practised in session) with the effect of rumination and 'testing' his sexuality by bringing on sexual images. This was linked with the case formulation and a collaboratively derived maintenance cycle of his OCD using the Salkovskis model (1985). Patrick discovered that by allowing the thoughts to come into and remain in his mind without engaging them, he was less distressed and less exhausted.

Further work focused on the positive metacognitive belief about rumination: 'analysing problems in my mind for long enough will eventually yield answers'. Patrick developed the revised belief that mental analysis and problem-solving works well for solvable problems like in maths and chess but is counterproductive for less clear-cut problems such as the themes of his obsessional rumination. Once the obsessional, ruminative cycle had been interrupted work was commenced on identifying and challenging negative core beliefs, as with depression. Childhood events were reviewed and rescripted in role play with 'adult' Patrick returning in imagination to scenes of bullying to protect 'child' Patrick as per schema therapy methodology (Young et al., 2003). The work was completed with a series of family therapy sessions co-facilitated with a systemic therapist aimed at establishing Patrick's place and value within the family.

Comment on Patrick's Case

Often, longitudinal conceptualisation is performed during middle or later sessions of therapy. A less experienced therapist working with Patrick might have stuck to this norm but recognising the nature of Patrick's rumination, his therapist opted for an early conceptualisation. This case illustrates the importance of early longitudinal case conceptualisation in certain cases where historical factors are important and where negative core beliefs are active. Exposure and response prevention work alone may well have overwhelmed Patrick and aggravated his negative beliefs about himself. This may have resulted in further deterioration and depression as the thoughts were associated with sadness rather than purely anxiety. Perusing exposure work to experiences associated with sadness can become an obstacle to therapy by aggravating and increasing depressive mood. Family difficulties are often a powerful component of the maintenance cycle and therapists need to consider the value of systemic work during or after CBT. Careful consideration needs to be given, however, to the question of whether the family has the capacity to manage this work and resolve their issues in a therapeutic way.

CASE OF JOEL – GETTING THE PICTURE

Joel has suffered with OCD since his twenties. He recently retired and his OCD problem is preventing him from enjoying this. He spends long days at home as he finds it hard to face walking the streets. When he was working his company would pay for taxis to the various work sites he visited as an architect. He can no longer afford taxis and when out walking imagines 'terrible things' in the shadows and must go back to check repeatedly that all is well. He presents for CBT. At assessment he reports a stable working life and stable upbringing. He is easy to engage and scores low on the depression scales. In the first session the therapist collaboratively draws out the 'vicious flower' maintenance cycle of Joel's OCD in line with the Salkovskis model. This goes quite well but Joel becomes anxious and vague when discussing what he imagines might be in the shadows – 'a body or something, someone hurt, maybe … who might need help'. They explore exaggerated responsibility beliefs and challenge them in session. The therapy proceeds to accompanied walks in the streets near the therapist's office. The therapist sets up an experiment with Joel to compare his anxiety when walking without visual checks (with his eyes straight ahead) with walking with exaggerated checking. Against the model's prediction there is little difference in his anxiety in each case. Undaunted they agree homework of walking to the local shop twice a day without checks and record his anxiety. After faithfully doing this for a week he remains just as fearful of going out and is reluctant to persist with therapy.

Take a moment to reflect on this case:

- How would you negotiate this obstacle in Joel's therapy?
- Any theories why he is not progressing?

The therapist decides to look in detail at what is happening cognitively when Joel is walking with his eyes 'straight ahead'. Joel discloses that he has regular fleeting images of parts of a body or a face as he walks along which he quickly distracts himself from by looking at the ground ahead or supplanting a 'nice' image. They theorise that these images and his neutralising of them is preventing Joel from processing and disconfirming his OCD fears. They agree they need to explore these images further and break the cycle of neutralisation. Joel bravely agrees to bring on the images in session. He closes his eyes and describes what he sees to the therapist and they rate his anxiety regularly. He describes it as like watching a terrible Polaroid picture developing. His anxiety peaks at 10/10 after a minute and he becomes tearful. The image is of a dead baby lying on a chair. He realises that the image is from his childhood where he encountered the body of a neighbour's child who had died. This deeply upset him at the time. With his therapist's encouragement he held onto the image for as long as he could. It became less and less vivid and frightening until after 20 minutes his anxiety had dropped to 5. He felt calmer after this exercise and a sense of release. Again they explored and challenged responsibility

(Continued)

(Continued)

and harm beliefs in relation to this memory and this time, this seemed to have a greater impact for Joel. He concluded that the image was simply an 'upsetting memory from the past and not a premonition of the future'. He came to see his OCD problem as more understandable and less out of control. This imagery work became a central part of the therapy and the 'developing the Polaroid' technique was used repeatedly with this and other images both in planned exposures and spontaneously using 'detached acceptance' during walking trips.

Comment on Joel's Case

Joel's case illustrates the importance of exploring imagery in OCD and other disorders as images are often involved in subtly maintaining the problem through covert neutralisation or avoidance. They can also contribute important clues towards a deeper formulation. Images are an exciting frontier of CBT research and the reader is advised to refer to the latest literature for up-to-date guidance (e.g. Holmes and Matthews, 2010).

SUMMARY

Disorders with intrusive thoughts and rumination are a complex and sometimes frustrating area for therapists and sufferers to grapple with. The challenges relate to understanding and distinguishing the various subtypes and patterns of these phenomena as well as measuring and capturing what is actually happening within the minds of the client. Breaking the cycle of semi-voluntary, ingrained patterns of thinking is never easy, particularly if that change comes with the heightened anxiety related to inviting frightening thoughts and images. Within this chapter, we have shown how meaningful progress can be made, even with complex cases when the right mix of knowledge, curiosity and persistence is utilised. We suggest creative use of the strategies described as many of the concepts covered are best understood through application rather than through a dry reading of the text. We have highlighted, based on our experience, when in-depth CBT may be better left for another day – such as with the severely agitated patient. We hope the reader finds this chapter a useful resource when dealing with difficult cases.

REFERENCES

Benazzi, F. (2007) 'Bipolar disorder-focus on bipolar II disorder and mixed depression', *Lancet*, 369: 935–45.

Beck, A.T. (1967) *Depression: Causes and Treatment.* Philadelphia, PA: University of Pennsylvania Press.

Borkovec, T.D. and Costello, E. (1993) 'Efficacy of applied relaxation and cognitive behavioural therapy in the treatment of generalised anxiety disorder', *Journal of Consulting and Clinical Psychology*, 51: 611–19.

Borkovec, T.D., Robinson, E., Puzinsky, T. and DePree, J.A. (1983) 'Preliminary exploration of worry: some characteristics and processes', *Behaviour Research and Therapy*, 21: 9–16.

Brewin, C.R., Dalgleish, T. and Joseph, S. (1996) 'A dual representation theory of post traumatic stress disorder',*Psychological Review*, 103: 670–86.

Clark, D.M. (1986) 'A cognitive approach to panic', *Behaviour, Research and Therapy*, 24: 461–70.

Davey, G.C.L. and Wells, A. (2006) *Worry and Its Psychological Disorders, Theory, Assessment and Treatment.* Chichester: Wiley.

Dugas, M.J., Gagnon, F., Ladouceur, R. and Freeston, M.H. (1998) 'Generalised Anxiety Disorder: a preliminary test of a conceptual model', *Behaviour Research and Therapy*, 36: 215–26.

Ehlers, A. and Clark, D.M. (2000) 'A cognitive model of post-traumatic stress disorder', *Behaviour Research and Therapy*, 38: 319–45.

Holmes, E.A. and Matthews, A. (2010) 'Mental imagery in emotion and emotional disorders', *Clinical Psychology Review*, 30 (3): 349–62.

Jacobson, N.S., Dobson, K.S., Traux, P.A., Addis, M.E., Koerner, K., Gollan, J.K., Gortner, E. and Prince, S.E. (1996) 'A component analysis of cognitive behavioural treatment for depression', *Journal of Consulting and Clinical Psychology*, 64: 295–04.

Kabat-Zinn, J. (1982) 'An outpatient programme in behavioural medicine for chronic pain patients based on the practice of mindfulness meditation: theoretical considerations and preliminary results', *General Hospital Psychiatry*, 4 (1): 33–47.

Kabat-Zinn, J. (1990) *Full Catastrophe Living.* New York: Bantum.

Mayer, V. (1966) 'Modification of expectations in cases with obsessional rituals', *Behaviour Research and Therapy*, 4: 273–80.

Menzies, R.G. and de Silva, P. (2003) *Obsessive Compulsive Disorder, Theory, Research and Treatment.* Chichester: Wiley.

Morrison, A.P. (2002) *A Casebook of Cognitive Therapy for Psychosis.* Hove: Brunner-Routledge.

Morrison, A.P., Renton, J.C., Dunn, H., Williams, S. and Bentall, R.P. (2004) *Cognitive Therapy for Psychosis: A Formulation Based Approach.* Hove: Routledge.

Nolen-Hoeksema, S. (1991) 'Responses to depression and their effects on the duration of depressive episodes', *Journal of Abnormal Psychology*, 100: 569–82.

Ost, L.G. (2008) 'Efficacy of third wave of behavioural therapies: a systematic review and meta-analysis', *Behavioural Research and Therapy*, 46 (3): 296–31.

Rachman, S. (1971) 'Obsessional ruminations', *Behaviour Research and Therapy*, 9: 229–35.

Rachman, S.J. (1993) 'Obsessions, responsibility and guilt', *Behaviour Research and Therapy*, 31: 149–54.

Rachman, S. (2010) 'Betrayal a psychological analysis', *Behaviour Research and Therapy*, 48: 304–11.

Salkovskis, P.M (1985) 'Obsessional compulsive problems: a cognitive behavioural analysis', *Behaviour Research and Therapy*, 23: 571–4.

Salkovskis, P.M. (1989) 'Cognitive behavioural factors and the persistence of intrusive thoughts in obsessional problems', *Behaviour Research and Therapy*, 27: 677–82.

Segal, Z,V., Williams, J.M.G. and Teasdale, J.D. (2002) *Mindfulness Based Cognitive Therapy for Depression: A New Approach to Preventing Relapse.* New York: Guilford Press.

Teasdale, J.D., Segal, Z.V., Williams, J.M.G., Ridgeway, V.A., Soulsby, J.M. and Lau, M.A. (2000) 'Prevention of relapse/recurrence in major depression by mindfulness-based cognitive therapy', *Journal of Consulting and Clinical Psychology*, 68: 615–23.

Wells, A. (1997) *Cognitive Therapy of Anxiety Disorders: A Practice Manual and Conceptual Guide.* Chichester: Wiley.

Young, J.E., Klosko, J.S. and Weishaar, M.E. (2003) *Schema Therapy: A Practitioner's Guide.* New York: Guilford Press.

10

WORKING WITH PHYSICAL SYMPTOMS

CRAIG CHIGWEDERE

LEARNING OBJECTIVES

After reading this chapter, the reader should:

- recognise physical symptoms as obstacles to therapy;
- be able to formulate a CBT-based bio-psychosocial understanding of physical symptoms as obstacles to progress in therapy;
- understand a hypothesis-based approach to the targeting of obstacles associated with physical symptoms.

INTRODUCTION

Physical symptoms, with or without a medical explanation, can distress clients and those around them. It can be difficult for clinicians to distinguish the 'real' from the 'imagined' and the symptoms themselves can become an obstacle in therapy. The case of Pat illustrates a client presenting with physical symptoms.

THE CASE OF PAT – 'IT'S MY BODY NOT MY BRAIN!'

Pat has been referred by her GP, suffering with pain in her limbs. She complains of swollen legs, particularly her ankles. She's finds it increasingly difficult to walk.

(Continued)

(Continued)

She lies in bed for prolonged periods, avoids standing and sits in a chair while performing most household tasks. She attributes her symptoms to an unknown medical condition. She has given up work, no longer plays tennis and restricts activities unless accompanied by her husband. She fears she will get worse and not cope. She is increasingly fatigued, depressed and anxious. Pat remembers her aunt dying of an incurable genetic disorder. Though investigations for this disorder have been negative, Pat still worries she has it, especially when anxious or stressed. Pat was always anxious about becoming ill. Her mother constantly worried about illness and monitored Pat and her siblings even when the illnesses were minor. She became very stressed when her son got into trouble with the law. She began to worry about unusual sensations, such as tightness in her chest, difficulty breathing and headaches. These symptoms were accompanied by images of her aunt looking frail in a wheelchair. She sought medical investigations, which did not reassure her.

Pat's experience of physical symptoms might well suggest the presence of an organic illness. An understandable and acceptable explanation for the interaction of psychological and physical symptoms is important for clients. Without such an explanation, engagement and treatment become very challenging. There is an emerging body of research on CBT interventions for physical symptoms, both with and without a medically explained cause. Various studies have supported the efficacy of CBT in the treatment of lower-back pain (Turner and Clancy, 1988; Lamb et al., 2010), distress associated with cancer (Syrjala et al., 1995; Hopko et al., 2005) and rheumatoid arthritis (Bradley et al., 1987). CBT-based interventions have been shown to increase functioning in epilepsy (Goldstein et al., 2003), psychogenic non-epileptic seizures (Goldstein et al., 2010) and chronic fatigue syndrome (Chalder et al., 2002; Price et al., 2008). Cognitive components of treatment include verbal thought challenging, behavioural experiments and surveys. Behavioural components include graded pacing of activity with prescribed rest periods, exposure, relaxation and distraction (Goldstein et al., 2003). The negative effects of activities such as bed-rest and reduced exercise have been demonstrated in research (e.g. Kortobein et al., 2007; van Duijnhoven et al., 2008). Through our work with medically unexplained symptoms, we have identified some obstacles to treatment, which can occur as a result of physical symptoms.

It is not within the scope of this chapter to offer an in-depth exploration of the breadth of physical presentations that can confront clinicians. There are basic principles, however, which can guide a therapist in formulating such problems. The first part of this chapter will introduce the reader to a helpful generic bio-psychosocial way of understanding clients presenting with physical symptoms. Some possible obstacles will then be illustrated with the help of case examples.

EXPLAINING PHYSICAL SYMPTOMS: A GENERIC CBT MODEL

Physical experiences (e.g. pain and fatigue) are influenced not only by the physio-logical experience (e.g. damage to the body) but also by subjective experience (i.e. thoughts, feelings and behaviours) (e.g. Turk et al., 1983). These subjective experi-ences also exert an influence on how the client interacts with their environment and vice versa. Viewing the individual as a system of reciprocal parts makes it possible to focus treatment on a part of that system (e.g. behaviours employed in response to symptoms) within the control of the client. This can be reassuring and empowering for clients, who can be demoralised by their experience.

The main objective in the CBT management of physical symptoms, such as those associated with epilepsy, cancer or fatigue is not *cure* but rather, to relieve distress and improve functioning. A model that explains all physical symptoms has yet to be developed. There are, however, common factors, which can not only help clinicians derive a useful formulation of the client's experience but can be the source of obsta-cles in therapy. As illustrated in Figure 10.1, these include:

- *Attribution*: this relates to how one explains causality (Kelley, 1971). Patients may therefore attribute physical symptoms to various causes, including physical illness. The attributions may not only have understandable origins but may also affect how one responds to the symptoms. In Pat's case, though she is mistaken in attrib-uting her symptoms to a serious and terminal genetic illness, she has an under-standable cause for that attribution (i.e. her aunt's illness and early experiences of her mother's worry).

- *Perception of threat*: the attribution of symptoms to a physical cause becomes associ-ated with a sense of danger. A strong belief in the dangerousness of symptoms will naturally result in apprehension, distress and further symptoms. In Pat's case, she became concerned that she was in danger of death in similar circumstances to her aunt. She thus experienced increased distress and images of the adverse conse-quences (i.e. her aunt in a wheelchair) and further symptoms (e.g. increased pain, fatigue and swollen limbs).

- *Behaviours*: if one feels at risk, it is reasonable to take measures to minimise that risk. This may include overt behaviours, such as Pat's reduced activity, taking to the bed and changes in her routine. Clients may also engage in covert behaviours, such as tensing or favouring limbs and paying particular attention to the affected area.

- *Physiological changes*: physical changes may occur as a response to reduction or increases in behaviours and activities. Pat, for example, experienced increased fatigue and swelling of the ankles and wrists. Over time, these effects may include reduced stamina, reduced blood flow and muscular de-conditioning due to con-tinuous episodes of reduced activity.

- *Affective changes*: these symptoms exert an influence on functioning, resulting in motivational and mood changes, such as frustration, demoralisation and diminished self-confidence. There is reduced reinforcement of non–illness related behaviours, so that depression is experienced (Lejuez et al., 2001). These physiological and

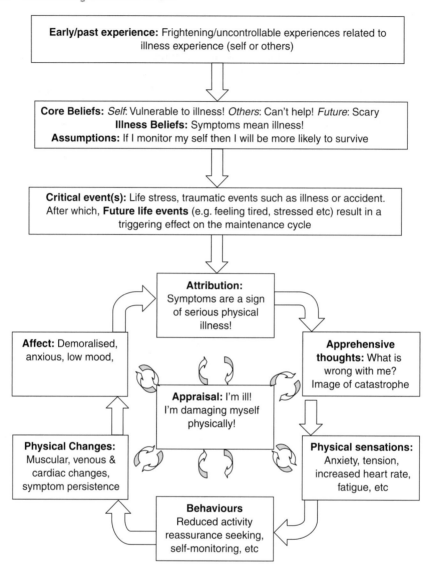

Figure 10.1   A problem-focused formulation

emotional changes may result in the development of new symptoms, which are further interpreted as evidence of 'illness or damage'.

Alternatively the client may, following a period of illness-related reduced activity, return to engaging in high levels of activity before their body is fully recovered or ready. The consequent fatigue or other physical symptoms and inability to function at previous high levels may be interpreted as evidence of something being wrong. There may be frustration, demoralisation and unhappiness, leading to further increases in activity, which impedes recovery and perpetuates the cycle. This can become an obstacle to the application of CBT interventions. In a thematic way, the next section considers some ways in which these obstacles can present in therapy.

THEMES OF OBSTACLES

Due to the wide range of problems that could be addressed in this chapter, offering a 'laundry list' of specific interventions will be resisted. Alternatively, we will offer a series of broad hypotheses for understanding symptom maintenance and planning treatment. Engagement issues are particularly important with this client group; therefore we will start with some engagement-related obstacles before discussing treatment-related obstacles.

OBSTACLES IN ENGAGEMENT

Confusing Explanations

Clients come to therapy seeking an explanation for their symptoms, reduction of distress and improvement of functioning. They often come after consultations with several medical specialists, with a variety of explanations, which can result in confusion. Clients can often be:

- sceptical about the effectiveness and credibility of therapy;
- ready to defend the physical origin of their symptoms;
- in doubt about the extent of any psychological cause or have a strong organic attribution (i.e. belief that symptoms are due to a physical cause).

In their quest for an organic explanation, clients may seek further medical investigations. The credibility of a psychologically based explanation is likely to be reduced if the client is still undergoing medical investigations. Therefore, it is best to:

- support the client in completing *recommended* investigations before commencing psychological interventions. This also reduces the likelihood of giving conflicting messages to the client, increasing anxiety and scepticism. Pat, for example, was awaiting an appointment for investigations, which she believed would confirm her genetic condition. The CBT therapist agreed with her that she would conclude these and then attend the CBT assessment if necessary;
- have regular communication amongst all the clinicians involved in the client's care. This prevents obstacles around engagement and treatment credibility;
- avoid any further investigations once there is agreement to commence therapy.

The Causality Conundrum

Therapists can get caught in the causality conundrum, in which they attempt to prove that the problem is a psychological and not a physical one. Consequently, clients can think their problem is not being taken seriously. They may think they are being accused of being 'mad' or that the problem is 'all in the mind'. It is imperative that therapists:

- *Resist getting drawn into an intellectual battle or engaging in arguments*: In Pat's case, she wanted to convince the therapist that she had a hereditary problem, which had been missed in investigations. Attempting to argue with her was quickly recognised as unhelpful. In fact, the therapist thought it was reinforcing the sense that she was not being believed, hence the above-mentioned agreement to suspend therapy until the conclusions of medical investigations.
- *Offer to liaise with other involved professionals*: Agreement that the therapist could have regular contact with Pat's neurologist validated her concerns, which helped her engage more openly in exploring a psychological model.
- *Engage the services of other professionals*: Pat's therapist discussed the involvement of a physiotherapist, thus reinforcing the bio-psychosocial perspective.

Treatment can be focused on causation or maintenance. Causation is more difficult to explain than maintenance and is harder to test (unless one is somehow blessed with the gift of time travel, so that they can return to the exact moment of onset!). It can be helpful to say to the clients something along the lines of:

> 'We are both uncertain about what the exact cause of the problem is, as it may well be a combination of things. It may be useful to look at how we can work together to alleviate some of the symptoms.'

Testing hypotheses about attribution and catastrophic predictions would then become the main aim of treatment. The maintenance cycle (Figure 10.1) introduces the reader to a hypothesis, which the therapist and client attempt to clarify, prove or disprove through different interventions during treatment. Focusing on the maintenance issues makes it easier to avoid mind–body duality. This bio-psychosocial maintenance rationale allows for a holistic focus of attention and explanation for the client. The fact that it includes physical, psychological and behavioural factors to help the client understand their experience is helpful. Thus, the therapist should collaborate with and socialise the client to the model, based on a clear understanding of 'what therapy can change' and 'how change can be achieved'.

Motivations for Engaging with the Approach

When clients have strong organic attributions, they may attend therapy for reasons other than engagement with treatment. Pat, for example, initially attended with an intention 'to prove to my doctor and my husband that I tried it and it doesn't work!' This may require:

- The ability to motivate the client to simply complete the assessment, without which it is difficult to formulate the problem or commence treatment. With Pat, an agreement was reached to simply complete the assessment by saying, 'Now that we're here, what harm will it do to go through the assessment?' She then agreed to attend five treatment sessions followed by a review.
- Motivational interviewing, including teasing out the pros and cons of engaging with the psychological approach or maintaining the search for a cause. Pat, for

example, agreed to engage with CBT after the therapist's motivational interviewing, based on the Miller and Rollnick (2002) approach, helped her to recognise the unhelpfulness of her continuing search for an organic cause. She realised that her functionality was continuing to deteriorate and no end was in sight, potentially for many years into the future unless she sought a different route. Questions like 'How do you see things being in two, five or ten years if you are still unsuccessfully seeking a cause?' were helpful.

- A period of extended socialisation to the model
- Provision of space to express frustrations, anger and doubts about their illness and unpredictable recovery process, with the therapist listening, accepting and acknowledging the client's experience and feelings.

Though Pat completed a course of therapy, it may at times be necessary to accept that the CBT approach may not be appropriate for the patient or that the time is not right as per Prochaska and DiClemente's (1986) cycle of change. Pat, for example, could easily have chosen not to return to therapy after completing her investigations. Some broad areas of consideration in engagement include:

1 *Get a shared understanding of the problem*: this includes avoiding mind–body duality and, as much as possible, making certain that investigations to rule out the extent of any organic causes have been performed.
2 *Motivations for engagement*: this includes providing space for clients to express their frustration and anger concerning confusion in diagnosis and treatment and clarifying the pros and cons of engaging and not engaging.
3 *Socialising the client to the approach*: includes performing a thorough functional assessment to formulate a problem of focus and explanation of its maintenance and how treatment might help.

THERAPIST CAUTION

Resist 'the guru trap': Therapists should guard against presenting themselves as an expert or guru, putting forward clever explanations in an attempt to impress the client. In our experience, most clients are respectful of the therapist who is not 'a guru who knows it all'. Admitting uncertainty at times fosters trust, because the client will be more likely to trust a therapist who is open and honest regarding difficult therapeutic issues. The CBT model, through the collaborative empiricism built into interventions (e.g. behavioural experiments), allows for the therapist not to know it all. This enables the client and therapist to journey together, making personal 'guided discoveries'.

OBSTACLES TO TREATMENT

Effective CBT involves a series of hypotheses or formulations, followed by efforts to prove or disprove those hypotheses. A therapist is more likely to be effective with their client if they can construct testable hypotheses that will be proven correct by an improvement in the client's condition or identified problem. Interventions are likely to be more effective if they are able to support these hypotheses and are based on empirical research and theory. In our experience, this hypothesis-led treatment approach is the best way of working with this client group to prevent obstacles occurring along the way. Here we will discuss four broad themes of how physical symptoms may present as obstacles, including:

- belief in symptoms as signifying serious illness,
- safety behaviours and their related consequences,
- relationships between thoughts and mood,
- learnt responses.

Client Belief in Symptoms as Signifying Serious Illness

THE CASE OF BOB – 'THE DOCTORS ARE ALL WRONG!'

41-year-old Bob, a keen sportsman, has no history of serious physical illness. He recalls watching a medical documentary, during which a man his own age was diagnosed with prostate cancer. An expert on the documentary mentioned the possibility of death. Afterwards, he became aware of a pain in his own groin. He visited his local hospital and saw a junior doctor, who mentioned the possibility of an enflamed prostate but urged Bob to seek the advice of a genito-urinary specialist. Bob became fixated on the enflamed prostate diagnosis and sought confirmatory opinions from several other physicians, with no evidence of its presence. Bob now avoids sports, being intimate with his wife and any other activity that focuses attention on his groin. His mood is low and he no longer goes to work. He is aware of the pain in his groin all the time and becomes anxious, as soon as he notices any change in sensations. He avoids TV programmes or magazines containing medical information about his perceived problem. He believes very strongly that he has a misdiagnosed prostate problem, which has been missed by all the specialists, except the junior doctor.

While Bob strongly believes that his symptoms signify serious illness, any interventions will be doomed to failure. His prior knowledge (i.e. fate of the man in the TV documentary) suggests possible death from his symptoms. If the perceived likelihood of surviving an event is low, compared to the related perceived dangerousness or risk, the associated anxiety will be high (Salkovskis, 1996: Chapter 5). In Bob's case, without reducing his belief in the risk associated with his symptoms, he will continue to be anxious and respond accordingly, thus maintaining his problem as in the formulation (Figure 10.1). The challenge for the therapist is therefore to help to reduce the strength of Bob's belief in his symptom attribution. This may involve the following.

Sharing an Explanatory Rationale

It is necessary to share the rationale outlined in Figure 10.1 with Bob in a way that has a personal meaning to him. The preliminary maintenance and treatment hypothesis (rationale) is best shared with the client immediately after initial assessment, thus allowing the therapist to use the client's own language and experience to illustrate the maintenance cycle. This means the rationale should conform to CBT principles in that it should:

a   Be idiosyncratic, fitting the model to the client not the client to the model. For example, Bob's therapist identified his avoidances, and using these, the negative results of investigations and the inconsistencies in his presentation (e.g. intermittent nature of his pain) was able to illustrate his personal maintenance cycle.

b   Emphasise areas of the cycle that are specific to the client, minimising or omitting others that are not. For example, Bob had reduced a lot of activities but this is not always the case and not all patients believe they have an incurable disease, which will kill them. Some may merely be intolerant of the feelings (see Chapter 7).

c   Enable the client to see the personal applicability of such a rationale. Bob's therapist for example, emphasised collaboration by resisting lecturing him but instead encouraging him to fill in the different parts of the cycle himself.

d   Foster hope and improve engagement. Bob's therapist resisted stopping at an explanation of the cycle but instead suggested what CBT could do to 'break the cycle' and try to create change.

Many novice therapists expect the client's understanding and acceptance of the rationale not only to be automatic but to result in an immediate change. This rarely happens and it is necessary to return to it idiosyncratically with each new challenge throughout treatment. Clients with physical symptoms can be tentative and cautious, so working at their pace is important.

Using Behavioural Experiments

In certain cases, symptom improvement can occur from a good explanation of the problem. For example, in non-epileptic seizures, patients have been known to improve significantly following diagnostic neuro-imaging and the provision of an explanatory bio-psychosocial rationale (Farias et al., 2003). Explaining the rationale alone is however, usually insufficient to 'shake' strongly held symptom attributions. Behavioural experiments provide a way of illustrating and testing the effects of specific perspectives and behaviours. They can be therapist assisted (i.e. in session) or planned as homework. Examples can include the illustration of the effects of attention and catastrophic misinterpretation. For example, Bob's therapist encouraged him to focus on specific parts of the body (his finger tips) and noting sensations that were previously out of awareness prior to the experiment (see Chapter 7). This type of intervention can greatly strengthen the believability of the rationale. Behavioural experiments with Socratic questioning are helpful in that they reduce lecturing of the client, which:

- can affect acceptability of information given;
- can affect recall (i.e. experience is easier to recall than didactic lecture);
- can require repeated reiteration;
- encourages guided personal discovery and experience of alternatives.

Bob, for example, was encouraged to experiment with his attribution of symptoms to an enflamed prostate. He predicted that if he continued to exercise when his symptoms were present, he would become seriously ill and need hospitalisation, due to dangerously raised temperature, persistent sweating and other objective symptoms. First, his therapist agreed to model partaking in Bob's avoided exercise in the gym, describing the subjective effects. Bob then performed the exercise with very similar effects. He concluded that attribution to catastrophic causes may be the main difference between his and the therapist's experience. He, however, feared that continued activity might still result in the feared consequences of an organic illness. They then agreed that he would suspend his safety behaviours for a week and to test his catastrophic predictions. When these were not realised, Bob's belief in his attribution reduced further. Behavioural experiments can therefore be a powerful method for bringing about change with this client group (Bennett-Levy et al., 2004).

Safety Behaviours and Related Physiological Changes

THE CASE OF JESSICA – 'PAIN MEANS I'M DOING DAMAGE!'

Jessica has pain in her lower back, shoulders, chest area and neck, depression and anxiety. Neuro-imaging has revealed some degeneration in her back due to the natural effects of ageing. This is considered insufficiently severe to explain Jessica's reduced level of disability. Pharmacological interventions, including pain-relieving morphine injections, have been stopped for fear of dependency. Her activity levels are greatly reduced. She will sit in a chair for most of the day, with occasional spells on the bed. She was previously a very active person, who 'never stopped' and was unable to relax. At the onset of the problem, she would work through the pain 'but would be in agony by the end of the day'. The pain intensity is unpredictable and unrelated to activity levels. She attributes her problem to the degeneration, wants more medical treatment and is frustrated. Jessica believes that her safety behaviours are preventing further damage, which is signified by her increased pain and fatigue. She has agreed to the admission to 'tick off another thing that did not work' and to prove that a psychological approach is useless.

Client reliance on, and belief in, the helpfulness of safety behaviours can strongly affect therapeutic progress and become obstacles. Where the obstacle discussed above is primarily about the attribution, that attribution alone may not be enough to maintain the problem, without the use of safety behaviours. Safety behaviours create a 'near-miss' outcome (i.e. the impression that the feared consequence has *just* been prevented by the use of the safety behaviours). Though Jessica wrongly thinks her physical symptoms are due to dangerous causes, she does have a medically diagnosed degeneration in her back. Where there is the experience of pain or other distress as in Jessica's case, there is often the mistaken belief that pain or discomfort means one is doing irreparable damage. Safety behaviours then become perceived as necessary but unfortunately have important exacerbating effects on mood, motivation and pain tolerance (Hopko et al., 2005). Safety behaviours thus present a significant obstacle to CBT treatment.

In the case of Jessica, her therapist hypothesised that, whatever the cause of her problem, she was suffering the effects of increased rest/reduced activity, which explained her increased fatigue and increased inability to tolerate small amounts of activity. He hypothesised that working with her on dropping some of her safety behaviours might affect her symptom experience. After giving a maintenance rationale based on a comprehensive assessment, therapists may need to consider:

1 *Behavioural experiments*: behavioural experiments to reinforce alternative explanations and attributions, as illustrated in the case of Bob, are a useful way of increasing success in dropping safety-behaviours. While belief and fear are high, safety behaviours are likely to be maintained.

2 *Personal safety behaviours*: patients will need to reduce their safety behaviours but they may initially experience significant discomfort. Jessica, for example, found it distressing and uncomfortable to increase her activities (e.g. to reduce the length of time she spent sitting). This needs to be explained.

3 *Illness behaviour gains*: when clients become ill, significant others in their lives will often respond differently to them (see Chapter 5). The client themselves may gain materially, emotionally and practically from the use safety behaviours, so that it is difficult to resist them. Safety behaviours are therefore not only those that the individual practises but also things that others may do. Without changing these and the possible gains for the patient and significant others, treatment can be significantly negatively affected.

4 *Reducing negative mood states*: the use of safety behaviours often means that patients reduce contact with reinforcers of the perception of self as healthy (Lewinsohn, 1974). Unfortunately, the impact of negative mood states, such as depression and anxiety, can make it difficult for patients to recognise or respond to positive life events, thus increasing the likelihood of using safety behaviours. Therapists may need to increase the use of:

   a *exposure tasks*: where anxiety is high, the use of exposure could help to increase habituation and tolerance of the distress, thus making it more likely that safety behaviours will be successfully resisted;

   b *behavioural activation*: the behavioural activation model indicates that systematically increasing activities affects mood (Jacobson et al., 1996; Ekers et al., 2008); this includes cases where there is a strong physical cause (Hopko et al., 2005);

   c *graded exercise*: where exposure increases tolerance of subjective arousal, graded exercise can increase physical fitness and stamina, including neurological capacities (e.g. blood volume) (e.g. Kortobein, et al., 2007; van Duijnhoven et al., 2008).

For example, in Jessica's case, tolerance of pain and fatigue increased with graded exercise and behavioural activation.

Clients' Values and Expectations: Relationship Between Thoughts and Mood

THE CASE OF OZZIE – 'I AM A LAZY AND WEAK MAN FOR NOT COPING WITH PAIN'

Since developing an infection while working abroad two years ago, Ozzie has been complaining of feelings of tiredness, aches and pains in his limbs and joints, and headaches. He works very long days as a carpenter. He drives for long periods daily due to the distance from his home to his work. He returns home late each evening, when he then wants to play with his young children and spend time with his wife. He has very strong values about work and feels that he should work hard and be a good father and husband. He values hard work and fears being perceived as lazy at work. He therefore makes sure that he works very hard and meets all his deadlines. His pain and fatigue are better in the mornings and worse as the day proceeds. By the time he gets home from work, his hands are painful and his muscles ache. He takes pain medication and has a hot shower to ease his discomfort. Ozzie is becoming demoralised and believes that he is 'not pulling his weight' at work, as he has had to leave early on a number of occasions. He no longer engages in hobbies or meets with his friends. At work he tries to work fast to get all his work done in the morning, when his pain is more manageable. By the time he gets home, he feels too tired and in pain to spend time with his family, meet with friends or engage in enjoyable hobbies like playing his drums. He has been referred with depression, because he is now regularly tearful, poorly motivated and hopeless. He thinks of himself as lazy and a weak man.

Clients' expectations of themselves and their personal values affect how they respond to illness. Such responses can affect the experience and progress of the illness. For example, behavioural theory of depression holds that the depressed mood persists, as a result of lack of reinforcement of healthy or non-depressed behaviour and negative reinforcement and positive reinforcement (or both) of depressed behaviour (Lewinsohn, 1974). The cognitive model holds that reinforcement of depressive or anxiogenic thinking styles maintains negative affect (e.g. Beck et al., 1979; Wells, 1997). Research and literature suggest that increased contact with reinforcing environmental contingencies leads to corresponding improvements in thoughts, mood and overall quality of life (Jacobson et al., 1996; Hopko et al., 2003; Ekers et al., 2008). Likewise experimentation and challenging of thinking styles will change mood (Beck et al., 1979). Thus, Ozzie, for example, values hard work and mental and physical strength. He needs to pace his activities but is unlikely to do so, because this is associated with being weak or lazy. Interventions to increase pacing or to increase management of his problem are likely to fail, if they are at odds with his values. The therapist would need to help the patient to identify and strengthen alternatives. This may include:

- *Identification of schemas*: patients may respond to their environment as they do, due to the influence of their schema (Beck et al., 1979). The values they hold may be associated with personal and family schemas (see Chapter 5), so that without challenging these, the patient is unlikely to be open to alternatives. Ozzie, for example, found the possibility of pacing activities (e.g. his work) or meeting his friends without engaging in accepted and valued group behaviours (e.g. heavy alcohol use) extremely threatening. The therapist needed to help him to identify the source of such thinking (i.e. early experiences and related schemas), its consequences and then alternative perspectives. For successful identification and challenging of cognitions a good and acceptable formulation will be vital.
- *Reducing belief-strength*: if we consider individual values as being the expression of schemas, then identifying the schema and finding a range of alternatives creates a broader range of acceptable values. Thus, the usual cognitive approaches to the identification of alternatives to cognitions will need to be employed. This might include:

   a identifying and challenging negative automatic thoughts;
   b identifying and challenging conditional assumptions;
   c identifying and challenging core beliefs;
   d identifying and reinterpreting early experiences.

Ozzie, for example, identified his negative automatic thoughts (NATs) through the maintenance of a cognitive diary. From work based on the NAT 'They think I'm lazy for leaving early', when he was leaving work early after a heavy morning and increasing pain and fatigue, his core beliefs were identified and challenged. It became evident that he was only paying attention to information supporting his core beliefs, identified as 'I am weak' and 'others are critical and rejecting'. Different cognitive methods were used including the gathering of evidence to support and dispute the beliefs. Once the supporting evidence has been challenged, an alternative and more helpful statement needed to be formulated. An example of this is offered below:

EXAMPLE OF FORMULATING AN ALTERNATIVE STATEMENT

Therapist: Looking at these two lists, there seems to be evidence supporting and going against your belief that you are a weak man. You somehow seem to believe very strongly that you are weak. What sense do you make of this?

Ozzie: Yes, there is a lot of evidence there to say that my workmates don't think I'm lazy, isn't there?

(Continued)

(Continued)

Therapist:	I agree. I wonder how this fits with your belief that your friends think you are lazy, which then results in you working so hard and fast and being in pain?
Ozzie:	Well it doesn't completely fit. I don't think it does. There is a lot of evidence there that they don't but I don't usually focus on it.
Therapist:	With this evidence, after this exercise, what would be a more balanced or fact-based statement?
Ozzie:	I'd say that it's more that I am afraid of my friends thinking that I am lazy but really they don't. I always do that ... focus on the negative!
Therapist:	How does it feel to think of it that way, Ozzie?
Ozzie:	Well, it certainly doesn't feel as depressing as the way I was thinking of it before. My usual way seems to make it a reality.
Therapist:	How much would you say you believe that new statement?
Ozzie:	Oh quite strongly actually, about 75 per cent I'd say. It makes a lot of sense to me.
Therapist:	That's great, Ozzie. What do you think you might need to do to really reinforce that new way of thinking?

Reinforcing New Cognitions

The last question by Ozzie's therapist encourages the client to consider the application and reinforcement of the new learning. Without reinforcement, thinking can easily return to its 'default mode'. For example, when his pain is present and he is working, Ozzie could easily return to thinking the perspective that friends think he is lazy. The therapist thus used the results of the in-session verbal challenging to identify a way of reinforcing the new thinking as homework. For example, as an experiment, he practised working slowly and monitoring his colleagues' responses for evidence that they thought he was weak. Coping methods (see Chapter 5) were also practised for those occasions when the responses of others were likely to trigger his schema. For example, he feared being ridiculed by his friends when he met with them and resisted drinking heavily.

Themes of Thoughts

Clients with physical symptoms may develop errors in thinking, so that certain themes recur. The thought diary is not only helpful for identifying negative automatic thoughts but also for identifying themes in thinking. These themes of thinking (cognitive) errors are helpful to identify because they can be easier to recognise or challenge on a day to day basis. Negative automatic thoughts can be so varied and frequent that they can be exhausting for the client to monitor. Themes are easier to work with because, once identified, the client can easily learn to recognise a 'type of thought', and to practise specific challenges for it. Clients with physical symptoms can be prone to specific cognitive errors, some of which are listed below.

1   *Comparing self unfavourably with others*: clients may compare themselves unfavourably with others, who may be perceived as somehow better or blessed. This can result in low mood, demoralisation and frustration. They may then not attempt things.
2   *All or nothing or perfectionistic thinking*: clients may think in black and white ways, so that they develop unrealistically high expectations where nothing but a very high and often unachievable standard will do.
3   *Negative abstraction*: identifying the negatives and ignoring the positives in any situation.
4   *Glorifying the past*: seeing the past (i.e. prior to the illness/symptoms) as having been wonderful and perfect, when in fact there were difficulties and life was not perfect. Clients can then focus very much on the deficits in the present and magnify the positives in the past. Current achievements can often seem insignificant because they may not reach a glorified standard from the past.
5   *Identifying self with the illness/symptoms*: thinking that one is 'nothing but the symptoms' or is viewed by others as such, as opposed to a whole person with an illness or symptom.
6   *Fortune telling*: when the client behaves like a fortune teller, who knows what the future will hold.

Learned Responses

There are occasions when clients appear to experience symptoms that are not easily explained by thoughts or behaviours. Clients can experience physical symptoms such as pain, which may appear very real or may continue after a trauma or injury has healed. Such symptoms can be difficult for the therapist and client to explain. Due to the baffling nature of such symptoms, clients can often seek and undergo intrusive surgical interventions, often with negative consequences. The apparent inexplicability of such symptoms can become an obstacle to therapy.

Learning theories may help to explain the occurrence of such symptoms. A possible simple hypothesis is based on conditioning theories. In brief, the two-process model (Mowrer, 1947, 1960) posits that the client might develop their distress in response to specific stimuli, through classical conditioning. Due to reinforcement effects of covert (e.g. psychological) and overt (e.g. behavioural) responses, physical symptoms associated with a problem may be worse than the original cause. Thus, Jessica's pain might be worse than would be expected from the degeneration in her back. Victims of accidents may experience worse pain from an injury that has objectively healed than from the original injury. It is not uncommon for clients to describe an increase in pain and distress, simply from thinking about the symptoms. Bob's groin pain, for example, can be triggered by memories, thinking or attention. Specific thoughts, sensations and situational stimuli may trigger the symptoms in a classically conditioned association. Subjective experiences may become conditioned stimuli, so that their presence triggers conditioned physiological responses. Therapists and their patients can struggle if they focus on:

- trying to find an explanation;
- symptom cure.

Instead they could:

- *Reduce illness behaviours*: as discussed under the case of Jessica, illness behaviours are varied but have a negative impact on symptoms and general functioning. Their reduction increases a sense of control over symptoms.
- *Increase functioning*: patients, as was the case with Jessica, can wish to resist activity, until the symptoms are gone or are better. This is unhelpful, as it increases attention upon the negative effects of the presenting problem. Instead, therapists can encourage patients to increase engagement with normal behaviours, thus increasing their sense of control and management of the symptoms.
- *Increase acceptance*: such approaches as mindfulness (Segal et al., 2002), Acceptance and Commitment Therapy (ACT) (Hayes et al., 1999) offer useful interventions that can be applied with a goal other than symptom change.

CONCLUSION

With the use of existing literature and research, it is possible to derive a hypothesis-driven approach for this potentially challenging area of CBT practice. Clinicians grappling with the presence of physical symptoms can resolve some of the presenting obstacles by referring to available research and theory. To work psychologically with clients presenting with physical symptoms, the therapist is called upon to be highly creative. It is not possible to write a 'dictionary list' of techniques for every eventuality. The best approach is the use of empirical, evidence-based hypotheses, allowing the therapist to become the scientist, who experiments and explores problems and solutions creatively and collaboratively with the client.

LEARNING EXERCISE

1 Reflect back on patients you have worked with and identify any physical symptoms that may have interfered with treatment.
2 Based on the suggestions in this chapter or your own theory-driven hypotheses, how would you formulate how the symptoms became obstacles?

REFERENCES

Beck, A.T., Rush, J.A., Shaw, B.F. and Emery, G. (1979). *Cognitive Therapy of Depression*. New York: Guilford Press.
Bennett-Levy, J., Butler, G., Fennell, M., Hackman, A., Meuller, M. and Westbbrook, D. (2004) *Oxford Guide to Behavioural Experiments in Cognitive Therapy*. Oxford: Oxford University Press.
Bradley, L.A., Young, L.D, Anderson, J.O., Turner, R.A., Agudelo, C.A., McDaniel, L.K., Pisko, E.J., Semble, E.J. and Morgan, T.M. (1987) 'Effects of psychological therapy on

pain behaviour of rheumatoid arthritis patients: treatment outcome and six-month follow-up', *Arthristis and Rheumatism*, 30: 1105–14.

Chalder, T., Tong, J. and Deary, V. (2002) 'Family cognitive behavioural therapy for chronic fatigue syndrome: an uncontrolled study', *Archives of Disease in Childhood*, 86: 95–97.

Ekers, D., Richards, D. and Gilbody, S. (2008) 'A meta-analysis of behavioural activation therapy for depression', *Psychological Medicine*, 38 (5): 611–23.

Farias, S.T., Thieman, C. and Alsaadi, T.M. (2003) 'Psychogenic non-epileptic seizures: acute change in event frequency after presentation of the diagnosis', *Epilepsy and Behaviour*, 4: 424–9.

Goldstein, L.H., McAlpine, M., Deale, A., Toone, B.K. and Mellers, J.D.C. (2003) 'Cognitive behaviour therapy with adults with intractable epilepsy and psychiatric co-morbidity: preliminary observations on changes in psychological state and seizure frequency', *Behaviour Research and Therapy*, 41 (4): 447–60.

Goldstein, L.H., Chalder, T., Chigwedere, C., Moriarty, J., Toone, B.K., Mellers, J.D.C. and Khondoker, M.R. (2010) 'Cognitive behavioral therapy for psychogenic non-epileptic seizures: a pilot rct', *Neurology*, 74: 1986–94.

Hayes, S.C., Strosahl, K. and Wilson, K.G. (1999) *Acceptance and Commitment Therapy*. New York: Guilford Press.

Hopko, D.R., Bell, J.L., Armento, M.E.A., Hunt, M.K. and Lejuez, C.W. (2005) 'Behavior therapy for depressed cancer patients in primary care', *Psychotherapy: Theory, Research, Practice, Training*, 42 (2): 236–43.

Hopko, D.R., Lejuez, C.W., LePage, J., Hopko, S.D. and McNiel, D.W. (2003) 'A brief behavioural activation treatment for depression: a randomised trial within an inpatient psychiatric hospital', *Behavioural Modification*, 27: 458–69.

Jacobson, N.S., Dobson, K.S., Traux, P.A., Addis, M.E., Koerner, K., Gollan, J.K., Gortner, E. and Prince, S.E. (1996) 'A component analysis of cognitive behavioural treatment for depression', *Journal of Consulting and Clinical Psychology*, 64: 295–304.

Kelley, H.H. (1971) *Attribution in Social Interaction*. Morristown, NJ: General Learning Press.

Kortobein, P., Ferrando, A., Lombeida, J., Wolfe, R. and Evans, J.W. (2007) 'Effects of ten days of bed rest on skeletal muscle I healthy older adults', *Journal of the American Medical Association*, 297 (16): 1772–4.

Lamb, A.E., Hansen, Z., Lall, R., Castelnuovo, E., Withers, E.J., Nichols, V., Potter, R. and Underwood, M.R. (2010) 'Group cognitive behavioural treatment for low-back pain in primary care: a randomised controlled trial and cost effectiveness analysis', www.thelancet.com.

Lejuez, C.W., Hopko, D.R. and Hopko, S,D. (2001) 'A behavioural activation treatment for depression: treatment manual', *Behavior Modification*, 25 (2), April: 255–86.

Lewinsohn, P.M. (1974) 'A behavioural approach to depression', in R.M. Friedman, and M.M. Katz (eds), *The Psychology of Depression: Contemporary Theory and Research*. New York: Wiley.

Miller, W.R. and Rollnick, S. (2002) *Motivational Interviewing: Preparing People for Change*. New York: Guilford Press.

Mowrer, O.H. (1947) 'On the dual nature of learning – a reinterpretation of "conditioning" and "problem solving"', *Harvard Educational Review*, 17: 102–48.

Mowrer, O.H. (1960) *Learning Theory and Behaviour*. New York: Wiley.

Price, J.R., Mitchell, E., Tidy, E. and Hunot, V. (2008) 'Cognitive behaviour therapy for chronic fatigue syndrome in adults', *Cochrane Database of Systematic Reviews*, 3. Art. No.: CD001027. DOI: 10.1002/14651858.CD001027.pub2.

Prochaska, J.O. and DiClemente, C.C. (1986) 'Transtheoretical psychotherapy: towards a more integrative model of change', *Psychotherapy: Theory Research and Practice*, 19: 276–88.

Salkovskis, P.M. (1996) 'The cognitive approach to anxiety: threat beliefs, safety-seeking behavior, and the special case of health anxiety and obsessions', in P.M. Salkovskis (ed.), *Frontiers of Cognitive Therapy*. New York: Guilford Press.

Segal, Z.V., Williams, J.M.G. and Teasdale, J.D. (2002) *Mindfulness-based Cognitive Therapy for Depression: A New Approach to Preventing Relapse*. London: Guilford Press.

Syrjala, K.L., Donaldson, G.W., Davies, M.W., Kippes, M.E. and Carr, J.E. (1995) 'Relaxation and imagery and cognitive-behavioural training reduce pain in cancer treatment: a controlled trial', *Pain*, 63: 189–98.

Turk, D.C., Meichenbaum, D., and Genest, M. (1983) *Pain and Behavioral Medicine: A Cognitive-behavioral Perspective*. New York: Guilford Press.

Turner, J.A. and Clancy, S. (1998) 'Comparison of operant-behavioral and cognitive-behavioural group treatment for chronic low back pain', *Journal of Consulting and Clinical Psychology*, 58: 573–9.

van Duijnhoven, N.T.L., Bleeker, M.W.P., de Groot, P.C.E., Thijssen, D.H.J., Felsenberg, D., Rittweger, J. and Hoopman, M.T.E (2008) 'The effect of bedrest and exercise countermeasure on venous function', *European Journal of Applied Physiology*, 104: 991–8.

Wells, A. (1997) *Cognitive Therapy of Anxiety Disorders: A Practice Manual and Conceptual Guide*. Chichester: Wiley.

Part 3
THERAPEUTIC CONTEXT

11

SUPERVISION: OBSTACLES IN NURTURING THE SKILLS OF NEW THERAPISTS

BRIAN FITZMAURICE

LEARNING OBJECTIVES

After reading this chapter the reader should be able to:

- recognise the challenges of establishing and maintaining regular CBT supervision;
- explore and evaluate how supervision informs professional development as a CBT therapist;
- recognise how supervision and professional development requirements evolve over time.

INTRODUCTION

In recent years there has been a strong drive to increase the availability of CBT, partly by structured and well-defined national programmes, such as Improving Access to Psychological Therapies (IAPT) in England, which train graduates *de novo* and re-train and re-deploy existing health professionals into CBT practice. The growth of CBT prior to IAPT was, however, more a haphazard and 'organic' process of self-selection, determined by who sought and completed what CBT training was available. The lack of clear selection processes and clearly defined career pathways for CBT therapists at the outset of training is very different from most professional training. Fundamental issues, such as defining who is suitable for CBT training and how the criteria for suitability is agreed, is rarely addressed in a comprehensive way. Academic courses often set their own criteria and become the gatekeepers of who enters the 'CBT profession'. There may be great variability in the entry criteria applied and the level and standard of training provided, even in closely neighbouring areas or regions. The other significant factor that determines if potential entrants into CBT training can proceed is the availability of appropriate supervision. Often there is a relative lack of supervisors to meet the needs of aspirant trainees. If there is a high demand for CBT and an overall shortage of CBT therapists, then it is logical that trained therapists will have limited time within their posts to provide supervision. Consequently, it is difficult for aspiring therapists to tap into a supervision network that allows them to use the cognitive behavioural model within their existing roles under supervision. This results in significant levels of 'underground' CBT, or cognitive behavioural approaches (CBA) (i.e. influenced by, but not meeting criteria for definition as CBT) by enthusiastic but unsupervised individuals. There is a danger that the effectiveness of CBT becomes heavily diluted and that its reputation will be slowly eroded.

Supervision promotes reflective learning and provides support for CBT practitioners. The reflective component of acquiring knowledge has been defined as the engine of lifelong learning (Bennett-Levy et al., 2009), and supervision may be a key method of fostering it. It aims to improve the clinical skills of therapists, thus delivering better quality therapy for patients. It is beyond this chapter to address all aspects of supervision and the supervisory relationship. Instead the focus will be on the different contexts in which supervision occurs. The main objective is to explore the contextual obstacles, which can often challenge effective supervision.

Although fundamentally, supervisor and supervisee generate the direction and focus of supervision, a wide range of contextual factors shape and influence the culture of supervision – the organisations in which we work, our professions, the character of our training, accreditation processes and defined roles. More basic elements, such as the physical environment in which it takes place, the time available and the medium through which it is provided (e.g. face-to-face, by telephone or webcam), may also influence outcomes. The scenarios described explore common contextual obstacles, which may occur through the different stages of a therapist's career.

THE CASE OF ANDREW – A NEW CONVERT TO CBT

Andrew has worked as a social worker in a mental-health service for 15 years and has to date had a limited counselling role in a community mental-health team. He views CBT as a good opportunity for career development. He sees clear benefits from the approach, many of his patients specifically request CBT, and there is some line-management pressure to demonstrate that social workers are capable of broadening their professional roles. He has attended a range of weekend workshops on CBT. He is unable to find a CBT therapist working in his service who can provide supervision but he has started to put into practice some of the skills demonstrated in workshops. He decides to subscribe to an online supervision service provided by a reputable CBT training provider. He is able to access 'face-to-face' supervision using a webcam, approximately once a month. He is, however, not able to do this in his workplace, as the internet service is blocked for video content/communications. He instead schedules supervision in the evenings when he is at home. His employer is not prepared to fund this supervision and he brings home casenotes, which is contrary to his work's rules on storage of confidential material. Andrew is unsure how long he will be able to sustain the expense of supervision and the inconvenience of this being detached from his core professional role.

Andrew has clearly found it difficult to tap into a local supervision network. This may be due to the relative lack of available CBT-trained supervisors. However, it may also reflect that potential supervisors locally, have difficulty justifying the time commitment needed to provide supervision for Andrew. Andrew's attempt to circumvent this difficulty has risks of establishing a practice, unlikely to be sustainable. In the short term, the supervision by web-camera may be a reasonable compromise that is educationally sound. Both he and his supervisor must however, take care to establish:

- An extremely clear written supervision contract (particularly important, as a supervisor from a different and potentially distant organisation may struggle to have a real understanding of Andrew's working context).
- Clear lines of responsibility and contingencies, if problems arise.
- Direct observation of CBT practice, established through his supervisor, assessing recorded sessions and providing feedback in supervision sessions.

As Andrew seeks to develop and implement CBT skills with the help of his online supervisor, his CBT practice is still difficult to define within his service. Whilst a potentially valuable extension of his professional roles, several hazards still need to be addressed:

- He is not afforded opportunities to present CBT cases to colleagues or meaningfully discuss emerging case conceptualisations within his team.
- He has limited access to peer supports that can often normalise the challenges of implementing 'standard' CBT approaches in the muddle of normal clinical settings. This can be important in generalising and validating what is learnt from supervision and also is important in developing a clinician's emerging identity as a therapist.
- He has joined the 'underground' culture of CBT provision. Potential fear of disapproval may further stifle discussion about his emerging practice with colleagues, limiting opportunities to develop his use of CBT.

In this instance, Andrew started to question the sustainability of online supervision and he enlisted a local psychologist to help him find more sustainable supervision and ultimately, an organisational acknowledgement of his further training needs in

CBT. The psychologist, although not CBT trained, was willing to provide some interim supervision, until a more enduring solution could be found. A key issue in arranging supervision at Andrew's level is who is competent to provide CBT supervision. Ideally, it should be an accredited CBT therapist, who has undertaken a supervisor-training programme. However, without the ideal being available, can a supervisor from a non-CBT background provide effective supervision for Andrew?

Roth and Pilling (2008) have devised a supervision-competence framework that allows us to examine what supervisory skills might be required to support Andrew. They identify four main categories of supervisory competences:

- generic supervision competences;
- specific supervision competences;
- application of supervision to specific models/contexts;
- meta-competences, which are essentially the supervisor's ability to adapt supervision to maximise the supervisee's ability to learn.

The first three clusters of competences are summarised in Table 11.1.

Starting off with supervision provided by a CBT therapist seems logical, as it is easier for a supervisee to learn one clear model, rather than being distracted by other models being used. Whilst a supervisor from a different modality can helpfully focus on generic therapeutic skills, they are unlikely to incorporate the necessary disorder-specific CBT models into their supervision. They are also less likely to focus on key generic elements of CBT, such as agenda setting, homework and feedback, thus limiting a supervisee's capacity to learn. It is only as therapists become more experienced in the practice of CBT that they will be better able to tolerate and productively use supervisory insights from other modalities of psychotherapy. However, competence in supervision of CBT is only one aspect of the overall supervisory competences and it should not be overly weighted, particularly when the options for supervision are limited. Better that Andrew's learning experience is rich and encouraging with a supervisor who accurately identifies their own limitations with CBT, than a potentially negative experience with a CBT therapist, lacking generic and specific supervision competences.

There is very limited research available detailing what makes for effective supervision at any stage of a therapist's development or which competences are critical within the supervisor. Milne and James (2000), in a review of CBT supervision, identified some successful activities, including close monitoring of the supervisee in order to provide contingent feedback, modelling of specific competences, providing specific instructions and goal setting. Shanfield et al. (1993, 2001) suggest that 'good' supervisors tended to allow the supervisee's story to develop, track the most immediate concerns/queries of the supervise and make comments that were specific to the material being presented. Ladany (2004) emphasises the role of a sound 'supervisory alliance' as the basic building block for successful supervision that can reduce unhelpful supervisee behaviours, especially non-disclosure of important clinical information. Ladany et al. (1996) identified the following supervisor behaviours which make non-disclosure more likely – being unaffirming, unsupportive, unstructured and less interpersonally sensitive. The evidence hints that the supportive psychologist

Table 11.1 Supervisory competence framework

Generic supervision competences	Specific supervision competences	Applications of supervision to specific models/contexts
Ability to employ educational principles which enhance learning	Ability to help the supervisee practice specific clinical skills	
Ability to enable ethical practice		Supervision of clinical case management
Ability to foster competence in working with difference	Ability to incorporate direct observation into supervision	
Ability to adapt supervision to the organisational and governance context		Supervision of low-intensity interventions
Ability to structure supervision session	Ability to conduct supervision in group formats	
Ability to help supervisee to present information about clinical work		Supervision of CBT
Ability to help supervisee's ability to reflect on their work and the usefulness of supervision	Ability to apply standards	
Ability to use a range of methods to give accurate and constructive feedback		Supervision of psychoanalytic/ psychodynamic therapy
Ability to gauge supervisee's level of competence		Supervision of systemic therapy
Ability of supervisor to reflect (and act) on limitations in own knowledge and experience		Supervision of humanistic/ person-centred/experiential therapy

Source: adapted from Roth and Pilling (2008) 'Supervision competence framework'. www.ucl.ac.uk/clinical-psychology/CORE/supervision_framework.htm.

who Andrew has approached with an implicit sense of trust and who understands their own limitations in CBT might adequately supervise him at this juncture. Ideally supervision would be structured, enable clear goals for supervision to be set and would incorporate both role-play of specific skills and some direct observation of Andrew's CBT sessions.

Roth and Pilling (2008) also highlight that supervisors of therapists providing 'low intensity interventions' often supervise in a context of high caseloads, briefer, less structured contacts and sometimes relentless focus on outcomes. Even very experienced 'high intensity' CBT supervisors must then adapt their supervision to needs that differ from therapists offering 'traditional' one-hour sessions of CBT. Similarly, there are often specialist contexts such as eating disorders, somatoform disorders or forensic settings, where a supervisor also needs to understand specific illness contexts of patients and the organisational contexts of service provision, if they are to optimise supervision. In Andrew's case, he has taken on two 'CBT cases' and provides one-hour sessions in his own office, which is suitable for one-to-one work. The interim supervision with the psychologist proves appropriate and very welcome.

Although for Andrew, accreditation processes are at an early stage, ultimately he will be required to develop a written summary of his clinical experience and of supervision he has received. At the outset, he should be encouraged to keep a logbook of cases seen, educational events attended and supervision received. It is likely that with sufficient structure and guidance, Andrew can avoid the pitfalls of remaining 'underground' and can openly survey some of the challenges that lie ahead, should he proceed to further training in CBT.

POST-TRAINING STRESS DISORDER

Completion of any CBT training presents new obstacles. Organisations have motivations for supporting therapy training, which may be different to those of the individual seeking to complete the training. These differing objectives may therefore present obstacles to the development of a therapist and their practice with patients. The case of Susan illustrates some of these obstacles.

CASE OF SUSAN – THE 'YOU OWE US' DILEMMA

Susan is a nurse who has just completed a Diploma in CBT and has returned to her normal role in a community team. She has little time to see patients for CBT because of an excessive existing caseload and lack of supervision. She is disappointed that her line manager thinks she should be grateful for having been given the time and funding to attend the course. Her manager had supported her request to do the course, as it fitted with organisational strategy, and he is surprised that she cannot just provide CBT for patients within her normal caseload. She feels quite isolated, because her colleagues have had to carry some of her cases whilst she was attending the course. She doesn't wish to be seen to complain or to seek their support to free up more time to see patients for individual CBT. It is hard for her to ignore all the hard work just undertaken to achieve her qualification. She feels she is now in a professional cul-de-sac.

Negotiating for a Future as a CBT Therapist

Within organisations, decisions are made through a set of socially driven negotiations. The prospective trainee may seek training to fulfil their own personal and professional needs. Within the negotiation, the trainee usually engages in a reciprocal undertaking to provide greater use of psychotherapeutic skills within a service. In Susan's case, this led to the negotiated agreement to complete the Diploma course.

A typical professional training in healthcare, such as nursing or social work, involves students entering training with the expectation of study, development, progression and, ultimately, completion over a specific number of years. CBT training rarely has the same predictable pattern. In organisational terms, the CBT trainee who has completed a course needs to view themselves as being at the start of a new negotiation process. They should be prepared once again to create and strengthen their argument for further development. In Susan's case, whilst the initial negotiation process had a very clear focus and objective, trainees' post-training needs may not be clear. Without a clarity of purpose, trainees like Susan are likely to be thwarted in their ability to negotiate the necessary time, supports and supervision needed to further develop CBT skills.

Returning to the Fold

Far from being unique, Susan typifies common dilemmas for those completing CBT courses. Although her training was linked to her service's aspirations, there was no clear plan for how best to utilise and enhance her new skills. Susan might be rightly surprised at the lack of follow-on organisational support or strategic planning on how best to integrate her new skills. Organisations often do not fully understand, at a practical level, the importance of ongoing supervision and continuing professional development. Like Susan, many trainees in CBT find themselves adrift, with little time to consolidate and build their CBT skills after completing academic courses. As a consequence it is not uncommon to feel deflated and annoyed when this arises. Practitioners may then find themselves unable to practise, losing skills or being expected to work beyond their competence.

A Way Forward

Grant et al. (2004) suggest six principles for advancing CBT development within an organisation:

1 Follow the path of least organisational resistance – think about ways most likely to mobilise support from members of the organisation.
2 Don't focus on lost causes – don't try to persuade those who are antagonistic to the approach or change.
3 Identify allies – start with those in the organisation most likely to welcome your ideas.
4 Work in teams or small groups – benefits include moral support, solidarity, shared problem solving.

Then collectively:

1 Check out authority – who will have influence, either because of their position or interpersonal style, recruit support of people with clout to support your cause.
2 Proceed on a realistic timescale – process of change is lengthy in organisations and results can sometimes take years rather than months.

These strategies may help to guide a budding CBT therapist to orientate themselves within their organisational culture.

It proved most helpful for Susan to seek out the advice and support of colleagues with some experience of CBT training. Finding a sympathetic mentor helped to tackle the stress and isolation that can be a normal part of the CBT training process. Key aspects of this dialogue were validation of the complex challenges faced and both articulating and writing down a set of desirable strategic goals. These included prioritising arrangements for ongoing CBT supervision and specifically identifying what CBT activity is likely to be attractive to those with whom negotiations must begin (e.g. managers and colleagues). A strategic plan specifically included individual CBT and group work aimed at consolidating prior learning, and also ideas for ongoing development and mentorship.

In Susan's case, when she spoke with a senior colleague it was arranged for her to meet just twice with a CBT supervisor in a local service. This 'interim supervision' resulted in the identification of appropriate opportunities in the organisation and a proposed secondment nine months later. Her supervisor's early awareness of Susan's contextual factors meant that the supervision sessions focused on both a worrying clinical dilemma and the organisational issues. This enabled Susan to understand how much her personal context was impacting on her therapeutic work. She realised that her insecurities about how to progress as a therapist drove a compensatory perfectionism in her work with patients, which was becoming a therapeutic obstacle. She appreciated that supervision can meaningfully have a much broader focus than simply dialogue about cases.

KEEPING ON TRACK: ONGOING SUPERVISION AND MAINTENANCE OF STANDARDS

The Important Role of Supervision

CASE OF JOHN – PROFESSIONAL ISOLATION

John is a therapist in a mental-health service. His long-term supervisor, who worked in a neighbouring service, has gone on extended sick leave with a severe illness. John now needs a new supervisor, which will require payment and managerial acknowledgement of the cost of supervision necessary for CBT practitioners. There have been additional concerns that his CBT work has not developed much in recent years and that he appears to apply the same approach to most of his patients, even when it does not appear to be benefiting some of his patients. Some members of the MDT are reluctant to make referrals to him.

Like John, many CBT therapists find themselves working somewhat isolated from other CBT colleagues. Supervision arrangements can often be informal. John and his supervisor enjoyed a strong personal relationship. A 'high support–low challenge' approach inhibited his supervisor's ability to challenge the stagnation of John's practice. John needed to:

- find and fund a competent supervisor;
- ensure the optimal development of his skills and practice.

His supervisory relationship had hitherto failed to reach its full potential, thus becoming an obstacle to his practice and development. The organisation had failed to support his professional development, thus creating an obstacle to John's career progression.

Maintaining Standards – Direct Observation

Whilst a key strength of CBT training is direct observation of therapy, through the use of recording and competence scales (e.g. the CTS-R), once qualified or accredited, the role of direct observation in supervision becomes less explicit. An explicit role for observation increases the likelihood of therapists and supervisors regularly listening to and accurately appraising practice, thus developing therapists' 'internal supervisor' skills. Additionally, supervisors will more accurately understand their supervisees' strengths and weaknesses. Such supervision is more likely to address areas around personal development and therapeutic skill.

It can be particularly difficult to incorporate direct observation into peer supervision groups, one of the commonest forms of CBT supervision. The time allowed for each of the peers' cases often makes it difficult to routinely include direct observation. Even in individual supervision, direct observation is very often avoided (Townend, 2002). A potential key strength of supervision is typically a missed learning opportunity. Accreditation bodies (e.g. BABCP) have highlighted the importance of listening to live recorded sessions in peer supervision and now require this to be recorded on supervision logs, which should encourage this practice.

Meeting the Aims of Supervision

CBT supervision aims to promote supervisee learning and provide support, thus enhancing the quality of patient treatment. Good CBT supervision will be characterised by a predominant focus on therapeutic tasks and process, clearly distinguishing it from personal therapy/mentorship. Therefore, supervision must move dynamically between different functions, including:

- normative function (i.e. articulating necessary standards, best practice);
- restorative function (i.e. providing support when working with complexity, resistances, challenging cases);
- formative function (i.e. highlighting areas of knowledge and skill that the supervisee needs to further develop) (Armstrong, 2006).

In John's case, these aims were not met, so that both he and his patients were disadvantaged. With a wide range of roles for both supervisor and supervisee, the flexibility which both demonstrate in moving between these roles is likely to influence the success or failure of the supervisory relationship. Although partially determined by specific situations (e.g. therapeutic or supervisory crisis), the focus of supervision is best evolved through an active and collaborative process. This allows a good balance between the ongoing learning needs of the supervisee and focus on therapeutic practice with patients.

Responsibility for the Objectives of Supervision

Clinicians, as collaborative supervision partners, need to articulate and monitor the achievement of their supervisory goals. Thus, the failure in John's case was not only an organisational one but also a supervisee's failure to recognise and articulate personal goals. Therapists need to take responsibility for their own development in order to safeguard their skills. A supervision contract with clear goals and responsibilities is one way to provide a therapist with a reference point for the adequacy of their supervision. The expectations and responsibilities within supervision are unlikely to be met, unless fully articulated at the outset with some effort to write down a supervision contract. This agreed structure of supervision, as it emerges, will directly impact on the focus of supervision. The explicit structure of supervision contracts should nearly always include:

1   identification of learning needs;
2   agenda setting and prioritisation of time;
3   two-way feedback;
4   record keeping by both parties;
5   role-play/experiential work;
6   periodic review of its success/failure;
7   process issues;
8   crisis management and procedures.

What is brought to supervision, and the form that it is brought in (e.g. tape, verbal report), needs to be reviewed periodically. This ensures the focus is meaningful and the benefits and objectives of supervision remain clearly understood by both parties. The objective is a 'high support–high challenge' supervisory relationship.

The Supervision Contract and Funding

John was fortunate that when he found a new supervisor, the majority of the first four sessions involved carefully developing a written supervision contract. During this phase, his supervisor asked him at the outset to bring a recording of a recent CBT session and a CBT formulation on a patient with whom he was working. This enabled both John and his supervisor to quickly define agreed learning needs. His supervisor also made explicit the cost of supervision and that he and his employer would be invoiced every six months for the hours of supervision.

Initially, John had a lingering worry about how he would obtain funding for his supervision. Additionally, he felt slightly intimidated by having to bring recordings to supervision once again. The initial formality and structure were different to what he had become accustomed. He, however, felt more confident that this more structured supervision would help him develop his CBT practice and skill. This enabled him to more clearly articulate the purpose and benefits of supervision for his professional development, his patients, his multidisciplinary team and the organisation to which he belonged. Such clarity makes it easier to negotiate with budget-holding managers. Grant et al. (2004) suggest that if CBT therapists are to protect their needs and those of their patients, they need to be conversant with the political language of organisations and be clear about the benefits of what they do. John's case illustrates how easy it can be for therapists to lose their way. Newly qualified therapists can be especially vulnerable, especially when working in isolation or in a system where the accountability for the standards of therapeutic work becomes blurred or ignored.

Monitoring Own Practice

Had his original supervisor not become ill and forced a change in direction, John himself might have identified signs that he was not working optimally. Listening to recordings of his work, and continuing to write out and share case formulations with others might have been important ongoing ways of maintaining good practice and identifying deficits. The capacity to reflect on one's own practice as a therapist is vital (Bennett-Levy, 2006). Self-reflection might have enabled John to recognise shortcomings in his practice and bring them to supervision. The authors would recommend the self-practice and self-reflection model (Bennett-Levy, 2006; Bennett-Levy and Thwaites, 2007) as an integral part of any CBT training. This not only increases awareness of issues that might negatively impact on therapy but also helps therapists to develop greater self-awareness, thereby gaining a deeper and better understanding of the intra- and inter-personal issues that affect the therapist and the patient. Whilst John might have reflected on intrapersonal contributions to the problems with supervision, supervisors also need to competently identify and highlight areas where their supervisees may need to undertake some self-focused, personal development work or personal therapy.

Linking Supervision and the Organisation

Within healthcare organisations, CBT supervision is sometimes allowed to continue without the capacity to identify and report on underperformance of therapists. Without direct observation of therapy at some point, a lot of assumptions must be made by the supervisor if they are to either vindicate or question the therapist's standard of practice. Supervisors often have little or no role in reporting back to any management structure that is accountable to the patient. Supervision can often operate outside or parallel to governance structures, particularly when provided externally to the therapist's service team. It is therefore important for supervisors to consider and articulate how they will address therapist failings or inadequate professional standards in the process of negotiating the supervision contract. With the ongoing development of accreditation standards the supervisor will inevitably have to provide a supervisor's report to a professional body (e.g. the BABCP in the UK), which will provide accreditation or re-validation of the therapist's competencies and standards of practice.

As the supervision contract affects the patient, the team, and the organisation to whom both therapist and supervisor should be accountable, there is a case for a copy of the supervision contract to be shared with a head of a department or line manager. Clearly stating its value to the organisation and role in clinical practice provides clear justification for funding or allocation of resources to supervision.

A further strengthening of organisational standards for CBT can be achieved through regular clinical audit and external evaluation of CBT teams or departments every three–five years. This can ensure that the culture, practice and outputs of CBT practitioners and their supervisors are in line with current standards. John's difficulties, however, could have been addressed earlier by his former supervisor or by John himself, through much less elaborate means.

SUPERVISING ORGANISATIONAL DEMANDS

THE CASE OF CHRIS – SQUEEZING BLOOD FROM A STONE?

Chris is working in a specialist mood disorder service, which was launched a year ago. The number of referrals now exceeds the capacity of therapists in the service. Management have proposed that, rather than allowing a waiting list to build up, each therapist should increase their caseload by 10–15 per cent temporarily, to match the delivery of therapy to available resources. It was proposed that this could be achieved by increasing number of cases seen per therapist from 18 per week to 20–21 per week. Some of Chris's initial patients have failed to recover with CBT but have wanted to continue working with him. They feel the work has instilled a sense of hope and enabled some limited progress. Chris feels overwhelmed, as he thinks he is working beyond his personal capacity and at times the evidence base of CBT for depression. He is reluctant to raise these issues in supervision, as he feels they are 'managerial' and 'personal' difficulties.

The Victim of Expectations Dilemma

Specialist services can be a double-edged sword for therapists. They allow the opportunity to apply a model of CBT in a focused way, which also allows evaluation of work in meaningful audit or research. They promote teaching and training roles and novel ways of working that are appealing to many clinicians. At their inception, however, a first wave of difficult patients may have been stored up in primary and secondary care, awaiting a new service to carry the burden of their challenging cases. Expectations can therefore be high, not least from the therapists themselves, and resources don't always match demand for CBT.

The Victim of Success Dilemma

While new specialist services can fall victim to expectations, individual therapists and established services can fall victim to success. Often, as a service's reputation grows, so do referral volumes, along with referrer and patient expectations. In many ways, this has been the case for CBT as a therapeutic modality. As in Chris's case, he is challenged by his current caseload and, if it grows further, this may become an obstacle to his practice. He may no longer have the time to learn and apply appropriate techniques for working with challenging patients. This will undermine his confidence and the vital sense of hope he has managed to instil in many challenging cases. His primary responsibility is to the cases he has already taken on and it is the problems he encounters with them that have historically formed much of the agenda in his supervision. Chris's supervisor, however, noticed and commented on the deflation that was increasingly evident when discussing cases, about which he had previously been enthusiastic.

His supervisor was alert to the 'nihilistic cycle' that emerges, when the therapist under pressure can quite easily view his patient's situation as 'unresolvable', that 'nothing more can be done'. Alternatively, the patient is seen as 'not sufficiently psychologically minded' or 'is poorly motivated'. Both patient and therapist begin to share a belief that there is no longer a point in attempting change, thus presenting an obstacle to effective therapy. When discussion of this issue was facilitated in supervision, it allowed Chris to discuss and more clearly understand the dilemmas in his work context and the personal challenges it was creating. These quickly became a priority in the agenda for supervision sessions and he was encouraged to reflect upon his options, to improve his evolving work context.

Chris and his supervisor considered a range of options before tackling management proposals to see yet more patients. Complex cases such as chronic depression, borderline personality-disorder or bi-polar disorder create very specific challenges. In light of his high caseload, a 'chronic disease management model' with more modest expectations, rather than CBT aimed at cure or complete recovery, was a more productive and realistic objective. They discussed 'categorisation' of problems, which can be a helpful means of defining the focus and goals of therapy in such cases. It was agreed that one approach might be to facilitate his clients in breaking problems down into the following categories:

1 Day-to-day problems – practical problems interfering with function (e.g. symptoms, limited range of activities).
2 Interpersonal problems – relationships with others.
3 Intrapersonal problems – internal world/sense of self.

Seeking progress in one domain may be less overwhelming than trying to tackle the whole range of problems that often arise with chronic disorders. It breaks progress and change into more manageable chunks for both patient and therapist. It also allows patient-centred prioritisation of a domain to which they would choose to orientate their time and energies.

In Chris's case, this categorisation approach also facilitated setting clear contracts with his patients for blocks of therapy of specific duration with a specific purpose. Explicit treatment plans were then able to incorporate a pre-planned break from therapy to consolidate any gains achieved in one domain. This approach allowed Chris to contract with some patients, for example, an initial 12 sessions with a specific focus followed by a three–four month break, which eased some of the caseload pressures he was experiencing. As a general principle, it is helpful to regularly and explicitly review progress at least after every six sessions with a patient, with the possibility of pausing or terminating treatment that is 'stuck' or not achieving its objectives. Such approaches can reduce the hazards of having many open-ended contracts for CBT with difficult-to-treat presentations. A process of reviewing progress is also necessary for supervision arrangements, and should probably occur after each block of ten supervision sessions or at least annually. To facilitate such reviews, supervisors might consider numbering supervision sessions or highlighting review dates in their supervision notes.

Ignored Professional Guidelines

Once Chris had addressed the difficulties with his existing caseload, he needed to reflect upon the proposal to provide more face-to-face therapy-hours per week. To do so, he needed knowledge of the professional guidelines on the number of cases seen by CBT therapists in a normal working week. Most CBT literature and organisations remain silent on this issue. Job descriptions for CBT therapist posts, though they define the scope of practice and range of responsibilities, frequently do not specify the recommended number of face-to-face hours of therapy expected of therapists. In their desire to increase patient turnover and reduce waiting lists and perhaps – particularly for private organisations – meeting financial pressures, organisations may make demands on practitioners to carry increasingly large caseloads. This will affect therapist energy, effectiveness and empathic skills with patients, creating therapeutic obstacles. This is a real challenge with the shift in investment in CBT to 'lower intensity interventions'.

Historically, guidelines for the employment of counsellors suggest a full-time counsellor should schedule about 15 sessions per week and have a maximum of 20 hours face-to-face contact with patients per week. This would equate to a CBT therapist seeing no more than four or possibly five patients in a working day. Sufficient time must be allowed to ensure adequate note-keeping, communication with the source of referrals, development of case formulations, photocopying of patient reading materials and scales, supervision, mentorship, teaching and management issues. CBT, with a tradition of recording sessions, must also allow time to review these recordings of clinical sessions, facilitating reflection on work in progress and decisions around casework and practice, which will benefit from discussion at supervision. Managers will naturally argue for higher levels of 'productivity', but they need to be reminded that a decline in therapy standards, possible patient dissatisfaction and 'predictable stress' for employees will ultimately be far more problematic and costly for the organisation. In this instance, Chris and his colleagues needed to assert that their current ceiling of 18 sessions a week was already working beyond established guidelines and this needed to be acknowledged and addressed by management over time. Chris agreed with his supervisor that dialogue with peers and collective decision-making about this issue were likely to be extremely important components of his self-management of the 'personal' stress that arose from organisational demands.

SUPERVISION ON THE RUN – PROVIDING INFORMAL SUPPORTS FOR CBT

Brian is a senior clinician who is eager to see the growth of CBT practice in the mental-health service where he works. He has arranged many workshops in his service run by both himself and CBT colleagues from other services. At each of these, he invites members of staff with an interest in CBT training to come and speak with him and has successfully persuaded managers to support staff training, financially and with flexibility around clinicians' workloads whilst training. Brian often agrees to provide a small amount of supervision to staff prior to them enrolling on any formal training programme. This seems to be popular and valued by staff but because of time pressures within Brian's roles and its relatively short-term nature, no supervision contracts or formal review of supervision occur. Although he keeps written supervision notes and facilitates the setting of learning objectives, he can only occasionally participate in direct observation of the efforts of the 'new enthusiasts' to implement some CBT skills in their existing roles. Brian's dilemma is that everything he reads about supervision in CBT suggests this 'supervisory practice' is inadequately structured, yet it seems to provide an important forum in his organisation to encourage the necessary growth of CBT provision.

Whilst there are limitations in the literature about formal CBT supervision, there appears to be almost nothing written about 'informal' supervision. This can often be the crossroads, where an interested clinician is encouraged to turn from aspirations of developing new skills to the commitment of undertaking some CBT training. In Roth and Pilling's (2008) supervision competence framework, Brian is providing more than supervision of clinical case management but probably less than the formality required for supervision of low-intensity interventions. This type of supervision is often well contained within an organisation's governance structure, where there are clear lines of accountability for all clinical practice. However, Brian should probably invest some time at the outset of such supervision, to set a brief written contract clarifying the relative responsibilities alongside the process of setting learning objectives. Without the safety net of clinical governance structures, 'informal' supervision is much more difficult to justify and more likely to bring Brian and CBT into disrepute.

In the absence of a literature that allows us to use theoretical models/constructs or research evidence it is difficult to guide Brian much further. It seems logical that he should be encouraging work with good 'training cases'. These Cognitive Behavioural Approaches (CBA) undertaken should perhaps also be circumscribed to just one clear goal. Such training cases are characterised by:

- a clear, well-circumscribed presenting problem;
- a likelihood of responding favourably to a standard, well-established CBT model;
- absence of significant co-morbidity or personality disorder.

Such training cases are hard to find in secondary care mental-health settings, such as Brian's service. If cases are identified, the goals set should be realistic and the limited expectations on both client and therapist should be made explicit. Well-established, user-friendly models such as behavioural activation, activity scheduling, graded desensitisation, and exposure and response prevention might be prioritised at the outset with appropriate cases. An agreement at the outset to redirect the case to an experienced therapist should greater complexity evolve is also advisable.

It is likely that guidelines or standards that address this area will emerge with time. It is helpful, however, to reflect that definition of standards generally begins at the top to describe the attributes of the 'super-qualified', when operating in 'ideal' environments. Often there is a competitive edge between different psychotherapeutic modalities to demonstrate who sets the higher bar at the top of the pyramid. It takes time to achieve the key task of determining the absolute minimum standards at the broader base of the pyramid and on its fringes. In general, CBT has been commendably pragmatic and realistic in its approach to such guidelines. The BABCP, for example, in setting standards for 'Psychological Wellbeing Practitioners', have engaged with what historically would have been considered the fringes of CBT by starting to define who is competent to undertake some of the basic building blocks of CBT. This bottom-up approach has successfully widened the availability of interventions based on Cognitive Behavioural Approaches (CBA – see Table 12.1). It provides real options for practitioners that want to start to work in this area, whilst preventing the use of CBA from going underground. It also broadens opportunities for the teaching and development of supervisory skills. Brian, whilst wishing to support those showing curiosity and interest in CBT, needs to avert the risk of becoming a 'CBT missionary'. Propagating the CBT 'message' can become something of a 'faith' for some practitioners, somewhat blind to the challenging contexts in which clinicians often practice and the limitations of CBT/CBA's evidence base, when it is not carried out by trained and qualified therapists. Those enthusiastic about training and education are perhaps most susceptible to William Butler Yeats's idea that 'education is not the filling of a pail, but the lighting of a fire'. In professional training, caution must somewhat temper excessive enthusiasm and, at its heart, CBT must retain its empiricism and provide evidence to justify CBT approaches being used with lower levels of training. Ensuring that this work is adequately supervised is a pivotal step. At the very least, Brian should audit or survey the benefits, outcomes and costs arising from this informal supervision process, rather than simply believing it to be helpful. This would helpfully contribute to a literature addressing this dilemma. Ultimately, findings from the low intensity arm of the large-scale IAPT studies should provide us with some guidance on what works best when providing different forms and levels of supervision across the full spectrum of CBT practice.

LEARNING EXERCISE

- Examine your current supervision contract. When was it established? Are there issues which now need to be included, addressed or reviewed?
- Ask your supervisor to review your supervision contract and identify issues which ought to be addressed in the next year.

REFERENCES

Armstrong, P. and Freeston, M. (2006) 'Conceptualising and formulating cognitive therapy supervision', in N. Tarrier (ed.), *Case Formulation in Cognitive Behavioural Therapy*. London: Routledge.

Bennett-Levy, J. (2006) 'Therapist skills: a conitive model of their acquisition and refinement', *Behavioural and Cognitive Psychotherapy*, 34: 57–78.

Bennett-Levy, J., Thwaites, R., Chaddock, A. and Davis, M. (2009) 'Reflective practice in cognitive therapy: the engine of lifelong learning', in R. Dallos and J. Stedmon (eds), *Reflection in Psychotherapy and Counselling*. London: Open University Press. pp. 115–35.

Bennett-Levy, J. and Thwaties, R. (2007) 'Self practice and self reflection in the therapeutic relationship: a conceptual map and practical strategies for the training, supervision and self-supervison of interpersonal skills', in P. Gilbert and R.L. Leahy (eds), *The Therapuetic Relationship in Cognitive Behavioural Psychotherapies*. London: Routledge.

Grant, A., Townend, M., Mulhearn, R. and Short, N. (2004) *Cognitive Behavioural Therapy in Mental Health Care* (1st edn). London: SAGE.

Ladany, N. (2004) 'Psychotherapy supervision: what lies beneath?', *Psychotherapy Research*, 14: 1–19.

Ladany, N., Hill, C.E., Corbett, M, and Nutt, L. (1996) 'Nature, extent and importance of what therapy trainees do not disclose to their supervisors', *Journal of Counselling Psychology*, 43: 10–24

Milne, D.L. and James, I. (2000) 'A systematic review of effective cognitive behavioural supervision', *British Journal of Clinical Psychology*, 39: 111–27.

Roth, A.D. and Pilling, S. (2008) 'Supervision competence framework'. www.ucl.ac.uk/clinical-psychology/CORE/supervision_framework.htm.

Shanfield, S.B., Mathews, K.L. and Hetherly, V.V. (1993) 'What do excellent psychotherapy supervisors do?', *American Journal of Psychiatry*, 150: 1081–4.

Shanfield, S.B., Hetherly, V.V. and Mathews, K.L. (2001) 'Excellent supervision: the resident's perspective', *Journal of Psychotherapy Practice and Research*, 10: 23–27.

Townend, M., Iannetta, L. and Freeston, M. (2002) 'Clinical supervision in practice: a survey of UK cognitive behavioural psychotherapists accredited by the BABCP', *Behavioural and Cognitive Psychotherapy*, 30: 485–500.

12

ORGANISATIONAL EXPECTATIONS AND RESOURCES FOR CBT

BRIAN FITZMAURICE AND CRAIG CHIGWEDERE

LEARNING OBJECTIVES

After reading this chapter the reader should be able to:

- recognise the challenges and opportunities encountered by different disciplines in developing CBT services within organisations;
- explore and evaluate the role of CBT within organisations;
- recognise ways in which organisations may create an obstacle to the therapeutic process.

INTRODUCTION

CBT has evolved from being delivered initially by a small number of health professionals working within mental-health services to a whole host of organisational settings. This includes primary and secondary care and physical health settings. It has also become a preferred mode of treating employees in occupational-health services or employee-assistance programmes. Public awareness is growing and there is a high level of demand for CBT services offered through private practice. Practitioners may work as single-handed professionals within organisations or as a conglomerate of therapists, perhaps sharing a building or a common referral system.

CBT practice, with its open, collaborative and non-judgemental culture, has not restricted those who practise to one professional grouping. In most instances, CBT involves incorporating a new skillset for existing healthcare professionals (e.g. a psychologist, nurse, social worker or doctor). This has sidestepped the need for establishing its own profession or discipline. The increasing diversity of settings makes it difficult to generalise about CBT within all organisations. Often, however, CBT is embedded in a psychological therapies division, comprising different disciplines and schools/modes of psychotherapy. Whilst CBT can flourish and grow in such settings, its expansion and growth is more likely when a number of CBT therapists operate as an autonomous department or unit within a service. This facilitates a clearly defined referral, assessment and treatment planning system, which may be part of a multidisciplinary team (e.g. within a mental-health service). Not only does this enable clients to have access to CBT therapy but also fosters peer support and clinical supervision opportunities. This chapter will illustrate, using case vignettes, a range of common organisational dilemmas that a CBT therapist may expect to encounter during the course of their careers. Because each organisation has very different contexts the chapter cannot be comprehensive but it is hoped the reader can generalise principles from the different themes in the scenarios. How organisations can present obstacles to the therapist–patient relationship will also be explored.

CBT IN ORGANISATIONS

The diverse skill mix and pluralist culture in healthcare systems has traditionally allowed professionals considerable autonomy. Historically a CBT therapist might have completed limited CBT training and been able to practise with little scrutiny. However, clear divergences in measurable standards of healthcare, have resulted in a requirement for greater accountability in health systems. Events such as the Bristol Royal Infirmary Inquiry (Department of Health, 2001) have established the need for clinical governance, which articulates standards, audits outcomes and ensures minimum standards of staff training. A CBT therapist within a health service must now have the following:

1 minimum standards of training and accreditation;
2 CBT therapists' management and accountability issues within healthcare organisations;
3 advocacy for the development of CBT within organisations;
4 ongoing supervision;
5 continuing professional development.

TRAINING AND ACCREDITATION

At present there is no internationally agreed minimum standard for training in CBT. Standards often differ across organisations in the same country. In an effort to redress this issue some European countries have taken positive steps to safeguard the public. Governments have encouraged professional bodies representing psychotherapists to assist in setting national or European standards across a range of modes of counselling and psychotherapy, including CBT. There has understandably been a desire that all counsellors and psychotherapists would have a recognisable and broadly similar standard of training and competency. Accreditation bodies to appraise standards related to this process are being established in most European countries and in future will become the main arbiters of who can practise CBT. Different measures have been taken by different jurisdictions. Within the UK, for example, developments in this area have culminated in the proposed Health Professions Council registration guideline on the restricted titles of counsellor and psychotherapist. Similarly a set of National Occupational Standards has been proposed for psychological therapies, that clarifies the competences required from CBT training. They are used by employers and others in developing roles and in commissioning education and training programmes but have not been used to regulate individual professionals.

CBT has similarities with and distinct differences compared to the other psychotherapy modalities. As further efforts are made to harmonise and create similar levels of training across the counselling and psychotherapy professions, differences of emphasis in training requirements will further challenge CBT trainees, practitioners and organisations. For example, the statutory regulation guidelines in Ireland maintain a requirement for all psychological therapists to incorporate 250 hours of personal therapy or its equivalence into training. This is very sympathetic to the tradition and needs of psychoanalytic trainees whilst being somewhat out of step with the CBT tradition which does not emphasise a requirement for personal therapy. CBT training organisations consequently often have to adapt to their local circumstances. Differences in national training requirements for CBT, however, risks ultimately restricting the movement of therapists and their skills across national boundaries.

DELIVERING CBT SKILLS IN DIFFERENT HEALTH SETTINGS

The challenge for healthcare providers is to meet the directives of those who commission the development of psychological services. In the UK, the development of the Improving Access to Psychological Therapies (IAPT) programme (Department of Health, 2007) has implications for increasing the skill sets of mental-health workers to enable service users to access therapy. The IAPT programme is based on a stepped-care model of service delivery ranging from 'low intensity' interventions (e.g. guided self-help, computer-based CBT support work) to 'high intensity' interventions (e.g. delivering formal psychotherapy to particular client groups based on a treatment manual/protocol). In organisations this stepped care model needs to be nurtured and managed, supporting training programmes and supervision needs. The publication of guidelines that cite CBT as a treatment of choice for many disorders also exerts its influence on training and therapist development. A new group of staff called Graduate Mental Health Workers (GMHWs) was established within 'The NHS Plan' (Department of Health, 2000) to provide brief evidence-based therapeutic interventions and self-help in primary care settings. The key challenge is to develop shorter models of training and increasing competency, while also being cognisant of treatment outcome and care to clients. It is worth examining the challenges, implications and obstacles to such developments within organisations.

THE CHALLENGE OF LEADERSHIP

The lack of clarity around the roles of CBT practitioners professionally can be a source of uncertainty and tension. One such area of uncertainty relates to the responsibility for management and leadership in organising the delivery of CBT services. Due to the competitive environment for funding in healthcare, this can mean that different professional disciplines vie with each other for the governance of CBT. This lack of clarity in role definition is more likely to become an obstacle to the development of CBT, rather than maximising its availability. Professional identity is important, especially when working within a multi-modality team. Without it, an individual therapist can find themselves over-ruled by others with a stronger identity. As an example, it is not unusual to hear clinicians using the term 'psychotherapy' to describe psychodynamic or other modalities. When they discuss CBT, however, they are unsure what to call it or indeed what it has to offer clinically. This can create unrealistic expectations of the CBT therapist either to be a 'miracle worker' if expectations are based on media reports of CBT or a sense of being tolerated by colleagues with stronger identities if one is not seen as a 'proper psychotherapist'. Too often there are organisational obstacles to patients accessing CBT for their difficulties. Grant et al. (2004) describe their collective experiences of CBT within organisational structures. They acknowledge the need for CBT therapists to understand how organisations function and that the nature of healthcare organisations is highly complex. This complexity has resulted in a variety of models of CBT services.

USING THE COGNITIVE BEHAVIOURAL APPROACHES (CBA) IN NORMAL CLINICAL PRACTICE

CBT principles form a part of the interventions of many mental-health practitioners. There is a real danger that if all such work is called CBT then it can cause a serious 'devaluation' of CBT with respect to other therapy models. It is, however, often difficult for patients and therapists themselves to decide if what they are doing is CBT or something else. The case of Alex illustrates this dilemma.

CASE OF ALEX – IS THIS CBT?

Alex is an accredited counsellor who has read a great deal about CBT as part of his ongoing professional development. He is always struck by the simplicity and practicality of the model and can see how he can apply this to patients in his normal clinical practice. He has integrated some CBT skills, such as activity scheduling, drawing maintenance cycles and setting homework into his routine practice, but is not sure how to describe this approach or how to further develop CBT skills.

Counsellors and other mental-health workers like Alex may be in an excellent position to use Cognitive Behavioural Approaches (CBA) as they may already have established generic skills in building therapeutic relationships, providing explanatory models for psychological symptoms/problems, and supporting patients to manage difficult emotions and life events. Core elements of CBT (e.g. agenda setting, collaboration, guided discovery, seeking feedback from patients and making links between thoughts, actions and emotions) can enhance the skillset of many practitioners. Their integration with some cognitive or behavioural change strategies will have undoubted benefits to almost any therapeutic process. After mastering these skills two questions are worthy of reflection:

1   Can mental-health workers like Alex's use of CBA be described as CBT?
2   How can we distinguish between use of CBA from CBT itself?

Table 12.1 attempts to delineate the major differences between use of a CBA and CBT, though the boundaries between them will sometimes remain blurred.

Table 12.1   Identifying differences between CBT and CBA

Criteria	CBT	CBA
Conducted by	Accredited CBT therapist (or trainee CBT therapist)	Healthcare worker with CBA supervision
Competences	Specific range of competences defined by accrediting body	Limited range of defined competences in specific disorders and settings
Scope of practice	Autonomous practice possible with ongoing supervision	Closely supervised practice with significant supports necessary
Session length	Typically 50–60 mins	Variable often < 30 mins
Session content	Must include agenda setting, review of homework, CBT case conceptualisation, linking thoughts/ behaviours to emotions, generation of homework, change methodology	Will only include some elements of typical CBT session
Duration of treatment	Usually occurs on a weekly basis for 6–20 sessions. Expectation of complete termination of work at end of contracted sessions	Variable, usually less frequent than weekly and may be incorporated into long-term care with patients
Location	Usually office based	Variable
Medium used	Face to face primarily	Face to face, telephone, email, computer based
Focus	Change or management of psychological/medical problems or symptoms. Goals and outcomes usually clearly specified and measured. Model & formulation driven	Better understanding of problems in a Cognitive Behavioural framework, supportive, psycho-education, prompts for behavioural change (e.g. exposure, behavioural. activation, response prevention)

REQUIRED COMPETENCIES

CBT therapists should have a sufficient range of knowledge, skills and attitudes to treat patients with specific disorders and to adapt the CBT model to the challenges of co-morbidity or cases presenting with additional complexity. Roth and Pilling (2007) describe a 'map' of competencies against which a practitioner might judge whether they have sufficient training and experience to describe the work they conduct as CBT. They describe the skills required for a therapist to deliver effective CBT, including:

- use of a structured clinical interview to elicit relevant cognitions and target problems;
- selection of assessment tools to guide formulation (e.g. self-rating scales, questionnaires);
- formulation of most patients, highlighting key cognitions, beliefs and maintaining factors, and explicitly sharing the formulation with the patient;
- development, maintenance and repair of a collaborative therapeutic alliance that enables active, problem-focused therapy to take place;
- adherence to the structure of CBT sessions, e.g. agenda setting, using guided discovery, setting appropriate homework, eliciting feedback;
- targeting key cognitions for change through cognitive restructuring and behavioural experiments;
- adherence to a contracted number of sessions and developing a relapse prevention 'blueprint' by treatment end;
- knowledge of generic cognitive models of emotional disorder as well as specific CT models, e.g. of panic, GAD, PTSD, substance misuse.

Roth and Pilling helpfully subdivide CBT competences into five domains:

1 generic competences for psychological therapies;
2 basic cognitive and behavioural competences (used in most CBT interventions);
3 specific CBT techniques;
4 problem-specific CBT skills/techniques – for specific problem/presentations;
5 meta-competences – that allow therapists to work with the above skills and adapt CBT to each individual patient.

The Second-grade Practitioner Effect

The significant overlap between CBA and CBT can lead to understandable confusion about required levels of training. To reduce confusion some will argue that only those with full competence to deliver CBT interventions should be enabled to incorporate CBA work into their practice. Obstacles and restrictions on CBA practice are often proposed as a legitimate means to manage risk and ensure appropriate clinical governance of psychological therapies. This might be justifiable if there were already sufficient numbers of trained CBT therapists to meet demand, or evidence that well-supervised CBA work caused significant harm or hazard to patients.

However, the failure to provide timely psychological treatments at different levels of intensity seems more likely to cause damage and increase the risks of chronicity and treatment resistance in patients. Accrediting bodies need to articulate standards for both CBA and CBT practice, or risk limiting the capacity of practitioners within an organisation to use CBA/CBT. A significant therapeutic obstacle might also present if therapists perceive the CBA practitioner as a 'second grade' practitioner within a team. CBA practitioners themselves could feel ashamed to seek support from senior colleagues when problems arise in therapy. They may feel that they 'should know' or experience the 'omnipotence error' and resist passing on a complex client, so that with good intentions, they persist.

Problem–competency Matching

Referring to the case of Alex, it is clear that he probably has the generic competences (e.g. ability to engage client and work with emotional content) and only some of the basic competences of CBT (e.g. agenda setting, homework tasks). Indeed, patients may appreciate the more active therapeutic stance within CBA sessions compared to a client-centred counselling approach and may as a result feel they are progressing. However, Alex's lack of problem-specific skills and meta-competencies is likely to limit the scope and effectiveness of his CBA work with patients who present with more severe disorders. Patient selection is therefore a key issue (see Chapter 3).

Many patients with milder disorders do not require the intensity of work proposed within a CBT treatment protocol. A clinician like Alex might provide very valuable 'low-intensity' work using the CBA. Conversely, it is vital that Alex is not pushed to see cases for which he is under-skilled or has not been trained to take on using CBA. The competency of the therapist should be matched with the presenting needs of the patient to ensure the comfort of both parties. Mental-health workers with some CBA skills, who are competent to work clinically with low-intensity clients, can come under pressure within organisations to treat clients whose needs are beyond their competency level. Organisational pressures to clear waiting lists or increase numbers of patients seen for CBT are a particular danger for practitioners like Alex, who may not feel in a position to decline such expectations. Supervisors have a key role in enabling therapists, both in training and beyond accreditation, to manage organisational expectations and ensure that therapists select suitable patients. Along with therapist level of competency, considerations of patient selection should include hours available, access to rooms, and appropriate supervision and case management support. This issue of competency and problem mismatching may lead to patients and therapists becoming frustrated and stressed.

CBA Training and Competency

Clearly defining what practitioner training is required and necessary to successfully implement 'low-intensity'/CBA work is a challenge. A reasonable approach would be to expect that CBA practitioners should be able to demonstrate all of the generic therapeutic, basic CBT competencies and the majority of the specific CBT techniques outlined in Roth and Pillings's (2007) framework. Practitioners should demonstrate:

- capacity to form therapeutic alliances with patients;
- a good theoretical understanding of clinical diagnoses;
- familiarity with the specific CBT models/strategies appropriate to patient needs.

This will incorporate both the generic CBT model and disorder-specific components of CBT. Familiarity with and availability of suitable worksheets, self-help material and rating scales for patients are further important requirements. This initial declarative knowledge may be learnt from books, lectures and a range of other sources, such as the IAPT Low Intensity Student Manual, which focuses on depression and anxiety disorders.

Application of the declarative knowledge and materials will require further skills-based training, including directly observed supervised role-play and clinical practice. As CBA practice emerges, it should be supported by regular supervision and assessment of training needs. Even with good organisational supports and regular supervision, it can be difficult for practitioners without a specific CBA/CBT training programme to maintain a structured approach that incorporates the essential components of CBA for a specific problem. In Alex's case, he needs to be encouraged to engage in a structured training programme that will ensure adequate skills development to further develop effective CBT/CBA skills. Westbrook et al. (2008) evaluated a ten-day CBT course and concluded that the training not only impacted on practitioner skills but also on patient outcomes. Likewise, Williams et al., (1991) concluded that prior knowledge of basic behavioural skills improved trainees' understanding of more complex cognitive concepts. While accepting the limitations of these evaluations, the results support the importance of foundation-level training for CBA level practitioners like Alex. Access to supervision for such practitioners must also be provided.

Role of the Collaborative Therapeutic Alliance

Although the therapeutic alliance remains a critical determinant of outcome in CBT/CBA (see Chapter 2), Beck et al., (1979) viewed it as 'necessary but not sufficient' to effect real change for patients. In CBA work, the brevity of patient contact might make even higher demands on the therapeutic alliance. Brief therapy models of working require more rapid engagement and imply earlier termination of therapeutic work. The therapist must therefore be skilled in early and accurate problem definition, use of accessible psycho-educational material, and have a capacity to motivate patients to complete tasks independently of face-to-face therapy sessions. CBA workers often work flexibly and engage patients through a range of media including emails, telephone calls, computerised CBT, as well as face-to-face sessions. A good example of the recognition of the need for CBA worker competencies can be found within the UK IAPT programme. 'Low-intensity' workers or 'Psychological

Wellbeing Practitioners', as is now the preferred term in IAPT, are expected to be specifically competent in:

- behavioural activation;
- cognitive restructuring;
- medication support;
- exposure therapy;
- problem solving;
- managing panic;
- sleep hygiene.

These are clearly baseline competencies for a practitioner wishing to develop CBT skills in anxiety and depression. Practitioners working with other problems or disorders will require specific additional skills. They will, most of all, need to learn to manage difficulties which arise in establishing, maintaining and successfully dissolving the collaborative therapeutic alliance in the particular clinical setting.

'ORGANISATIONAL LIMITATION' OBSTACLES

Organisations are bound by the limitations of the personalities within them. This includes their ability to understand and engage with the needs and objectives of clinicians. Such limitations can create obstacles for therapists. The case of Anne illustrates how such an obstacle can present.

CASE OF ANNE – A PROBLEM OF OVERCROWDING

Anne is a chartered psychologist who has accredited her CBT practice through a national body accrediting behavioural and cognitive psychotherapies, and has been involved in CBT teaching and training for many years. As the demand for CBT has grown she was successful in persuading her local managers to appoint a number of colleagues in CBT. At the time of appointment it was hoped that a new building might be available for the expanded number of therapists. None of the therapists have their own office and have to use a diary system for the available therapy rooms to book appointments. They must all do any administrative work in a small common room to maintain the availability of rooms for patient therapy sessions.

HABITUATION TO INADEQUACY

CBT therapists appear to be eternal optimists. There is a subcultural belief (recurrent cognitive distortion) that once there are enough therapists available to deliver therapy, somehow all other practical issues can be resolved. This schema includes a belief that the popularity of CBT and positive patient feedback will be enough to persuade managers to provide adequate facilities to practice CBT effectively. There is an expectation that the rationality of therapy, where the evidence may point to need, will be translated into an appropriate behavioural response from the organisation. It ignores the perception that organisations often react more readily to emotions than logic. Often the most intense or uncomfortable emotions have most power.

Overcrowding, as in Anne's case, has a very significant impact on patients and the therapy process. The lack of adequate office space predicts that office doors will be knocked on or opened during sessions, therapists will get distracted by the need to be out of an office by a set time and the patient might conclude that the therapist cannot offer them a safe, secure, contained environment to reflect on emotionally troubling aspects of their life – clear obstacles to the therapeutic process. This can have implications for the therapist's ability to be fully present to the needs of the client and may impede the development of a strong therapeutic alliance (see Chapter 3).

The therapist in these instances often feels the necessity to persevere without complaint. Cultural values of healthcare workers tend to put the needs of the patient first. Therapists can believe that regular apology for intrusions is sufficient to correct the damage being caused to the therapeutic relationship. After a period of time therapists often become desensitised to the shortcomings of inadequate or inappropriate therapy space, so that they *habituate to the inadequacy* of their circumstances.

THE ORGANISATIONAL OPAQUENESS PROBLEM

Organisations have rules and language, which one must learn in order to be heard or satisfied. Without an understanding of these rules and language, organisational decision-making processes may seem opaque, illogical and impenetrable, leading to frustration. For example, one of the repeated frustrations in Anne's case is that the allocation of office space does not appear to be a transparent process. Despite her numerous efforts, she finds herself despairing when others who do not appear to her to be providing any additional patient care benefits, leapfrog over her CBT practitioners and are offered new office space.

RECOGNISING ORGANISATIONAL NEED – 'PLAYING THE GAME'

Anne did well to reflect on the advice of Grant et al. (2004) on strategies to influence change within organisational cultures (see p. 216). In general, organisations may not welcome the identification of problems. Although problems can sometimes act as an impetus for change, organisations tend to prefer developments or solutions. Linkage of accommodation to a service development/enhancement seemed more likely to appeal to the decision makers. Anne's solution involved linking the need for accommodation to the establishment of a sub-specialist CBT for psychosis service, which some of her colleagues had already started to work on in an informal way. She sought out strategic alliances to facilitate both service development and better accommodation in an interlinked way. Though unclear to her who was the key person with authority to grant accommodation, it was possible for her staff to get allocated new accommodation in the run-up to the launch of the new psychosis service. There was reward and recognition for innovation and providing organisational solutions.

SERVICE DEVELOPMENT AND LEADERSHIP OBSTACLES

Rationed Therapy – Stretching the Rubber Band

The motivation to use CBT resources most effectively in a healthcare organisation is legitimate. Traditional autonomous CBT practice is difficult to advocate for if patients are not receiving assessment and treatment in a timely way. Some CBT therapists can be slow to discharge patients and typically might see patients for more sessions than suggested in research trials. Adherence to specific models for different disorders can be sometimes *ad hoc* with an over-reliance on generic CBT principles or trans-diagnostic approaches. The following vignette describes John's experience, illustrating the possible consequences of organisations seeking to police therapy delivery.

THE CASE OF JOHN – DECIDING HOW MUCH CBT PATIENTS GET

John has been working in CBT for the last decade and has practised CBT with considerable autonomy. His work has been valued by patients and this has been acknowledged within the organisation, who often ask his advice on psychotherapy service development and general patient care. He was recently asked to help with a waiting-list initiative, which would enable patients to be taken on more quickly by putting a limit on the number of individual sessions any one patient might receive in a calendar year. He has been asked to draw up a protocol for five disorders, which would set a cap on the number of individual sessions to be provided in each disorder based on evidence from trials using effective manualised approaches. If he implements this protocol, he has been promised an increase in staffing levels to enable his service to meet a proposed target that all patients should have access to a CBT therapist within two months of referral.

The Rationing Solution

In John's case, the proposal to set a cap on sessions at an organisational level makes sense and it is understandable that further investment in services might come with conditions. It is important to understand that planning requires a numerical approach to quantify and project the resources required to deliver a service into the future. Where general levels of morbidity are modest and clients are able to function reasonably well, such as in primary care, employee assistance programmes or student counselling services,

Stepped Care

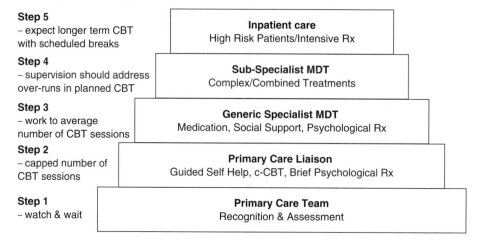

Step 5
– expect longer term CBT
with scheduled breaks

Inpatient care
High Risk Patients/Intensive Rx

Step 4
– supervision should address
over-runs in planned CBT

Sub-Specialist MDT
Complex/Combined Treatments

Step 3
– work to average
number of CBT sessions

Generic Specialist MDT
Medication, Social Support, Psychological Rx

Step 2
– capped number of
CBT sessions

Primary Care Liaison
Guided Self Help, c-CBT, Brief Psychological Rx

Step 1
– watch & wait

Primary Care Team
Recognition & Assessment

The right principles for the right setting

Figure 12.1   Different settings and different parameters for CBT provision

caps on the number of treatment sessions may be pragmatic. In these instances, there is usually the capacity to refer on to a specialist mental-health service in a position to provide a more open-ended response. In this instance, capping the number of sessions may be an important mechanism identifying patients who have higher levels of need at an earlier point, so that they can quickly step up to a more robust care package. This is one of the principles of stepped-care (see Figure 12.1 below).

A Stepped-care Model

Roth and Fonaghy (2004) warn that the stepped-care model has risks as well as benefits, principally if it is implemented without regard for individual need. Overall they argue that with clear criteria for determining when an intervention is ineffective, it provides a good model for organising therapy services, allowing evidence-based principles to be combined with good clinical judgement.

Rationing CBT in line with research trials needs to be considered more carefully in mental health services at or beyond Step 3, where co-morbidity and severe disorders may be the norm. In the treatment of single disorders without co-morbidity, valid comparisons can be made with research studies. Recruitment methods for research trials can include advertisement for patients, who may not have the same level of morbidity as patients who are referred into healthcare organisations. These patients might be expected to improve more quickly. Very few research trials place a ceiling on the number of contact hours a patient receives, although they will report outcomes at the end of a specific amount of the manualised CBT intervention. Review by research workers/back-up professionals can provide additional support, which is more open-ended and available for both the CBT treatment group and controls. Setting a rigid cap on sessions in this context, whilst in theory may be potentially helpful by setting deadlines for the patient, is often not based on comparable clinical practice settings (see case vignettes throughout this book, e.g. see Chapters 2 and 3).

Rationing as an Obstacle to Therapy

Placing a cap on the number of CBT sessions is unfortunately likely to have significant effects on the process of individual therapy sessions. Pacing of therapy is a critical issue in the development of a good therapeutic relationship and the timing and number of sessions should be informed by patient needs. Introducing a timeline right from the outset of therapy is likely to be distracting for the therapist and corrupts the collaborative set-up of therapy as the therapist already has an imposed agenda, insensitive to the needs of the patient. Similar effects occur when a therapist is moving jobs, going on prolonged leave or makes a decision for other reasons to limit the number of sessions offered to an individual. The option of referring cases to another therapist if work has not been completed is an important principle which safeguards the best interests of the patient. Rationing can disrupt further work being undertaken and can profoundly affect the morale of the therapist, compromising their ongoing capacity to engage, engender real hope and give encouragement to patients.

Using the Evidence

Engaging managers in a dialogue about the average numbers of CBT sessions required for specific disorders at Step 3 would be a useful strategy. Averages take advantage of reasonably high drop-out rates from all psychological therapies (nearly always >25 per cent and often as high as 50 per cent). They provide commissioners of services with the numerical data to plan, resource and compare services. This also encourages a process of clinical audit where outcomes, duration of treatment and patient turnover/drop-outs can be examined in an objective manner. Differences in therapists' preferences, practices and outcomes can be more readily explored with this data. Assessment and documentation of the presence of co-morbidities such as personality disorder or substance misuse may also justify or explain the need for longer treatments. In more specialist services, this type of data is also valuable. Exploration of over-runs in therapy might form an important focus of CBT supervision. As cases have higher levels of severity within Steps 4 and 5, the issue of supporting therapists engaged in longer-term CBT becomes the priority, as there is often more explicit understanding that such work creates savings in the wider health system. This has been the strong economic argument for dialectical behavioural therapy, which proposes intensive weekly individual CBT in addition to weekly skills groups for patients with borderline personality. Though an expensive provision, this can be offset by savings in inpatient admissions, presentations to accident and emergency departments and reductions in prescribing.

SERVICE DEVELOPMENT

AN ESTABLISHMENT PROBLEM – PROPOSAL FOR A NEW CBT THERAPIST

A rural community mental-health service has just reviewed its patient activity. On average patients referred to two part-time clinical psychologists wait over six months to be offered therapy. Patient advocacy groups have repeatedly indicated availability of CBT is a high priority for service users. Management also believe considerable savings will accrue from reduced prescribing costs. There is, however, little confidence that this aspiration will be realised. The management of psychological therapies rests with a senior psychotherapist in a neighbouring service. He provides supervision and line management for the two part-time psychologists. He does not believe that CBT is suitable for most patients and thinks that it would be much better to appoint a further clinical psychologist who could offer a more eclectic range of psychological approaches. The community mental-health team leader is frustrated that the psychologists are not managed like the other disciplines within the team-management structure and is adamant that a new CBT therapist should be an integral part of a team structure rather than operating independently.

The Advocacy Dilemma

The dilemma of who owns and advocates for provision of CBT/psychological services is central here. Any proposal to provide CBT has a financial implication. Managers may have to weigh up CBT ambitions against the suppression of another activity or a delay in a planned expansion elsewhere. Negotiations and decisions about which staff grouping or activity that must first be reduced will quickly demonstrate how difficult it can be to incorporate and expand CBT services within existing services/budgets. Squeezing out or overtaking existing psychotherapy prompts considerable anxieties and insecurities, while attempts at pulling resources from nursing/medical activity can also be resisted by powerful and well-established lobbies within healthcare services.

There are a range of possible solutions to this dilemma. The most obvious and perhaps the easiest is to do nothing, thereby neglecting the need to advocate for provision of psychological therapies for patients. This requires no negotiation or expenditure and would be by far the easiest option for any manager. An ideal, global solution would be to simultaneously promote all psychotherapies by appointing a new clinical psychologist to this service in addition to, or contingent upon recruitment of a CBT therapist. This is an expensive option and the price of such a decision could be the alienation of other disciplines within the service, making it more difficult to articulate the argument for CBT and the development of other psychotherapies in the future.

A Training Solution

Training existing healthcare staff in CBT, counselling and other psychotherapies has a proven track record. It is often economical, particularly if there are significant staff pools seeking or needing redeployment. It is a slow-burn solution and the time taken to re-train staff is considerable, delaying the day when patient needs are adequately met. This can be partially offset by the number of training cases taken on by a trainee providing CBT work. In the above vignette, the CMHT manager could lobby the senior psychotherapist for supervision hours for identified clinicians, who can take training cases, thus helping to reduce the psychotherapy waiting list.

The proposition of training even a small number of existing staff in CBT is not immune from tensions. It can be perceived in some organisations as the appointment of untrained therapists 'by the back door', causing disquiet and concern. It is vital in this instance to ensure that adequate training and accountability/governance structures are in place to oversee and manage the therapy practice of the emerging CBT therapist. The responsible healthcare organisation will try to anticipate its own training needs in CBT and should provide the necessary supports, including adequate availability of therapy rooms and access to supervision for trainees, in a timely way, to maximise the organisational gain from such training.

A Pooling Solution

A service could also consider outsourcing the provision of CBT sessions. This could be facilitated through a cross charging mechanism/cost-sharing within a health service or through the merging of different CBT practitioners across a broader region to provide a specialist CBT service. This can be a particularly coherent option when there is strong evidence base for CBT in a particular disorder (e.g. OCD, depression, bulimia nervosa, psychosis). This has the advantage of improving the quality of services not only by making CBT available but also having a group of therapists who can become sub-specialists in the treatment of specific disorders and contribute to research and training. This type of option requires like minded services in close proximity to each other and a flexible approach to such proposals from clinicians and managers and needs to be supported by a refined and accurate assessment process to facilitate the appropriate allocation of cases.

The Pilot Project Solution

An alternative to establishing posts or teams is to run a pilot project or programme, which may be constructed in the form of a research or quality initiative that exists more independently. Returning to the 'Establishment Problem' vignette, setting up a pilot CBT service could help to resolve the obstacle presented by the psychotherapist's negative perception of CBT. Setting up a pilot CBT service requires the case for its development to be made in writing. The proposal should articulate and quantify potential savings or definable health gains, which may require like-minded advocates as discussed earlier. Whilst not requiring a purist health economics analysis it will require the production of a document that lays out some cost–benefit analysis and makes a coherent argument for this pilot compared to other initiatives. Successful CBT proposals are likely to incorporate lower-level training of significant numbers of existing staff and early delivery of low-intensity options for a wide pool of patients. They should clearly articulate the enhanced benefits or potential improvements in quality of care. Service-user perspectives also legitimise the value to end users. Any likely savings as a result of the initiative must also be incorporated. This bottom-up approach is most likely to influence commissioners of services and gain the necessary momentum to establish CBT within a service.

KEY OBSTACLES

Based on evidence from the IAPT initiative in the UK, there is now precedent and a strong argument to develop CBA and CBT in tandem. Ultimately the more practitioners that are engaged in CBA work, the more likely there will be an increase in demand for further training in CBT and this 'tide' will lift both the availability and profile of CBT still further. However, even when the strategy of provision of CBT/CBA is decided, some key issues/obstacles still have to be resolved (e.g. line management and remuneration rates for therapists), as illustrated in the 'Establishment Problem' vignette. Remuneration can present a considerable obstacle, especially where therapists have different professional backgrounds. There is a tension when prioritising between demanding higher reimbursement for therapists and seeking an expanding number of therapists. Advocating for both doubles up the cost of CBT service provision and may erode the compelling argument for development of CBT/CBA services. There must also be care not to set unrealistic expectations as failure to deliver on promised outcomes can damage credibility.

SUMMARY

Whilst setting training standards is a cumbersome task, taking years to implement, there are many important practical issues within organisations that can be resolved in a shorter timeframe. These include securing adequate accommodation, working with sensible caseloads, implementing supervision contracts, supporting peers who are completing training, and developing a network of mentors for novice and more senior therapists. These tasks relate to how CBT organises itself within and across organisations and not always only dependent on funding. Continuous examination of the governance and accountability structures within which CBT therapists and supervisors operate is crucial throughout this process.

CBT therapists must seek a lead role in organisations to advocate for appropriate structures, supports and resources to develop CBT/CBA practice. Healthcare managers cannot be expected to understand the complex and changing context of how CBT services and training evolve. The numbers of CBT therapists and CBA workers continues to increase in healthcare organisations. This strengthens the case for an independent CBT profession, that can take on the role of articulating how organisations can optimise their CBT services in the future. The future challenge for CBT therapists is not just to provide further evidence-based practice, but also to share their experiences of success and failure in training and development negotiations. George Bernard Shaw once called professions 'a conspiracy against the laity'. For CBT to retain its value to those most in need of interventions, a new CBT 'profession' must partly conspire to ensure it can flourish but its continued development will be best maintained by keeping the client central to how it evolves.

LEARNING ACTIVITIES

Read:

- Grant, A., Townend, M., Mulhearn, R. and Short, N. (2004) *Cognitive Behavioural Therapy in Mental Health Care* (1st edn). London: SAGE:

    - Chapter 5 'Establishing Cognitive Behavioural Work Cultures'
    - Chapter 16 'Organisational Factors Impacting on Cognitive Behavioural Practice'

- Roth, A. and Fonaghy, P. (2004) What Works and for Whom – A Critical Review of Psychotherapy Research (2nd edn). London: Guilford Press:

    - Chapter 16 'The Contributions of Therapists and Patients to Outcome'
    - Chapter 17 'Conclusions and Implications'

Draw diagrams of:

1 where CBT/CBA practitioners currently fit within your own organisation (include structures for line management of therapists, supervisors, indemnity, accountability, access to decision makers/resources);
2 ideal structures to manage and promote CBT/CBA within your organisation.

REFERENCES

Beck, A.T., Rush, A.J., Shaw, B. and Emery, G. (1979) *Cognitive Therapy of Depression*. New York: Guilford Press.
Beck, J.S. (1995) *Cognitive Therapy: Basics and Beyond*. New York: Guilford Press.
Department of Health (2001) *Bristol Royal Infirmary Enquiry*. London: Crown Publications.
Department of Health (2000) *The NHS Plan: A Plan for Investment, a Plan for Reform*. London: The Stationery Office.
Department of Health (2007) *Improving Access to Psychological Therapies (IAPT) Programme*. London: The Stationery Office.
Grant, A., Townend, M., Mulhearn, R. and Short, N. (2004) *Cognitive Behavioural Therapy in Mental Health Care* (1st edn). London: SAGE.

Roth, A. and Fonaghy, P. (2004) *What Works and for Whom – A Critical Review of Psychotherapy Research* (2nd edn). London: Guilford Press.

Roth, A. and Pilling, S. (2007) *Department of Health: The Competences Required to Deliver Effective Cognitive and Behavioural Therapy for People with Depression and with Anxiety Disorders*. London: The Stationery Office

Westbrook, D., Sedgwick Taylor, A., Bennett Levy, J., Butler, G. and McManus, F. (2008) 'A pilot evaluation of a brief CBT training course: impact on trainees' satisfaction, clinical skills and patient outcomes', *Behavioural and Cognitive Psychotherapy*, 36: 569–79.

Williams, R., Moorey, S. and Cobb, J. (1991) 'Training in cognitive-behavioural therapy: pilot evaluation using the cognitive therapy scale', *Behavioural Psychotherapy*, 14 (4): 373–6.

INDEX

Note: page numbers in *italic* refer to figures and tables.